Jesus Ascended

For Jacob

Heart of the Lion
Loyal to the Death
Heart for the Lion of Judah

For Catherine+Charles
May the ascended Jesus
even continue his ministry
in you and through you!
Gerrit Dawson
July 2013

Jesus Ascended

The Meaning of Christ's Continuing Incarnation

GERRIT SCOTT DAWSON

P U B L I S H I N G
P.O. BOX 817 • PHILLIPSBURG • NEW JERSEY 08865-0817

T & T CLARK INTERNATIONAL
A Continuum imprint
LONDON • NEW YORK

First published in Great Britain in 2004 by
T&T CLARK International / Handsel Press
Continuum International Publishing Group Ltd
The Tower Building
11 York Road
London SE1 7NX, UK

www.tandtclark.com

First published in the United States in 2004 by
P&R Publishing Company
P. O. Box 817
1102 Marble Hill Road
Phillipsburg, NJ 08865
USA

www.prpbooks.com

British Library Cataloguing-in-Publication Data
A catalogue record for this book is available from the British Library

Library of Congress Cataloging-in-Publication Data
Dawson, Gerrit Scott.
Jesus ascended: the meaning of Christ's continuing incarnation/Gerrit Scott Dawson.
p. cm.
Includes bibliographical references and index.
ISBN 0–87552–849–X (alk. paper)
1. Jesus Christ–Ascension. 2. Incarnation. I. Title.

BT500.D33 2004
232.9'7–dc22   2003064787

ISBN 0 567 082210 (T&T Clark)
ISBN 0 87552 849 X (P&R Publishing)

Typeset by BookEns Ltd. Royston, Herts.
Printed and bound in Great Britain by Antony Rowe, Chippenham, Wiltshire

Contents

Acknowledgements viii
Permissions ix
Foreword *by Dr Douglas Kelly* x

PART I Why Recover the Ascension? 1

 Introduction 3
  The Story 4
  A Continuing Incarnation 5
  How to Use This Book 10

1. The World Is Too Much With Us 13
  A Letter to the Angel 14
  As the Pastor Sees His Flock 18
  Voices From a Comparable Age 21
  A Current Study 23
  The Antidote 25

PART II Toward a Concise Theology of the Ascension 29

2. The Ascension as Public Truth 31
  Public Truth 35
  When Did Jesus Ascend? 36
  How Did Jesus Go? 37
  Where Did He Go? 39
  What Kind of Body? 42
  If Jesus is in Heaven, How Can He Be With Us? 44

What Kind of Space?   46
How Does the Ascension Cause Us to Regard Jesus
Now?   50

3. The Triumph of Jesus   53
    Jesus Glorified in Scripture   57
    The Ascension as Enthronement   60
    The Victor's Procession in the Fathers   61
    The Stronger Strong Man   63
    The Glorious Entrance   65
    Who Was Set Free?   69
    Reason For Celebration   70

4. The Ascension and the Person of Christ   73
    Urgent Challenges   74
    Biblical and Patristic Texts Relating the Ascension
    to the Person of Jesus   77
    Simultaneous Presence   82
    The Ascension and the Pledge   87
    The Glory Secured   89

5. Union with Christ: The Head and Firstfruits   93
    Gregory of Nyssa and the Exaltation of Humanity   97
    Our Ascended Head   101
    Augustine and the Whole Christ   104
    Firstfruits   108
    Chrysostom and the Celebration of the Firstfruits 110

PART III   The Present Implications of Jesus Ascended 115
6. The Priesthood of Christ in the Power of the
    Holy Spirit   117
    The High Priest in Israel   119
    Jesus the High Priest   122
    The Offering and the Intercession   125
    Worship and the Priesthood of Christ   134
    The Priesthood and Our Prayers   138

7. Citizens of a Far Country   143
    Three Errors to Avoid   146

Withdrawal from the World 147
Creating the Kingdom Here on Earth 148
Conformity to the World 150
The Place of Tension 151
Citizens of Heaven 153
Yet Citizens of Earth 155
Augustine's Vision 157

8. Spiritual Ascension 163
Deification or Humanization? 166
What Prevents Us? 169
The Quest to Ascend Spiritually 172
Renunciation 174
Clothing According to Our Station 177
Means of Grace: The Lord's Supper 179
Whatever? No, What of It! 181
Summary 182

9. Models for Recovering the Ascension in the Life
of the Church 185
Model One: Use of Core Research 186
Model Two: Teaching Series 191
Model Three: Thirty-Day Prayer Guides 195
Model Four: Christ in the Marketplace 198
Model Five: Retreat for Mission Planning 200

10. Three Concluding Images 205
Staying in the Ship and Staying the Course 207
Investing Against All Odds 209

Notes 211
Appendix: Prayer Guides 227
Morning Prayer I: Ascending into Heaven 229
Evening Prayer I: Ascending into Heaven 232
Morning Prayer II: Citizenship 234
Evening Prayer II: The Living Way of Hebrews 237
Select Bibliography 241
Index 251

Acknowledgements

The congregation of the First Presbyterian Church of Lenoir, North Carolina has graciously and willingly participated in this quest to recover the doctrine of the ascension as a vital agent in transforming the church. They have come to Bible studies, listened to sermons, experimented with prayer forms, and allowed me to take them into the deep waters of this exploration. I am grateful for their trust, their patience and their willingness to take risks in thought and life.

Thanks to Dr Douglas Kelly for encouraging me, inspiring me, and shaping me over the last six years. Theology always leads him to worship, and he passes that on to his students and friends.

I am grateful, too, for my colleague in ministry, Robert Austell, and his help in everything from theological debate to formatting the text. My secretary, Evelyn Creason, enabled me to find time for this work while still tending the church. The Lorraine and Harper Beall Evangelical Study Center in Lenoir offered a lovely week of peaceful space. And, of course, my wife, Rhonda, is the very backbone of my life, my constant inspiration, my true theological partner and the reason I can ever move forward in ministry.

I am eager to hear from readers as you begin to recover the ascension in the life of your local church and particular ministry. Please feel free to contact me.

Gerrit Dawson
gerritdawson@juno.com
Glen Lorien
Pentecost 2003

Permissions

Foreword

Having taught Systematic Theology for some twenty years, I have often longed for a current volume on the ascension that would be thoroughly biblical, patristic, catholic, reformed and contemporary. Now I rejoice in having found it! Dr Gerrit Dawson's splendid work, *Jesus Ascended* as of this year will be a required text in my classes, and – I suspect – as it becomes more widely known, it will be set reading in many divinity faculties and seminaries. And beyond that, it could be the channel for a stream of new life in local churches of scores of denominations (for it is specifically written with the life and mission of the local congregation in mind; that is one of its strengths).

For whatever reason, the ascent of the glorified body of Christ bearing our new humanity to the Father's Throne has been generally neglected for centuries in most theological and ecclesiastical traditions. This perhaps 'benign' neglect (even where it is confessionally affirmed) is strange because, as Gerrit Dawson demonstrates, the ascension of our Lord is one of the mainsprings of joy, power and love in Christian life and mission in a most demanding world.

Then again, this neglect may be rather less benign than at first glance we would have thought. Dr Dawson appositely raises a penetrating question: could many churchmen (and 'worldly' persons as well, who are still vaguely influenced by the remnants of western Christendom) have an aversion to this doctrine, which willy-nilly pits the continuing and total Lordship of the 'Man in the glory' against the self-sufficient attempts at 'the good life' of multitudes of modern consumerists, not to mention the pretensions of 'sovereign' political orders, who fear any transcendent limitations to their authority?

That may be at least part of the reason why much of the church is far more comfortable reducing the 'public truth' of Christ's bodily ascension to the Father to a 'private truth' (as Dr Dawson paraphrases the insightful Lesslie Newbigin), for private truth cannot make ultimate loyalty claims (which our pluralistic culture fiercely resents). As Gerrit Dawson has stated (drawing on Douglas Farrow): '. . . if we spiritualize the ascension, and get Jesus safely diffused and dissolved into the heavens, then he no longer seems a threat to the rulers of the world. Rather, we can neatly divide the regions of authority between the spiritual and the worldly.'

And yet, I believe this desire to push the at-times-uncomfortable Christ out of our daily lives and loyalties cannot be the whole reason for failing to appropriate a tithe of what his ascension could mean for us. From early times there have been many theological and cultural challenges to a soundly biblical and credal view of the Person of Christ, including in particular, to his genuine bodily ascension. Ancient dualism between God and the created order, between the 'spiritual' and the 'physical', keeps reasserting itself in ever new forms. For instance, the way 'Higher Critical' methods have for over two centuries 'deconstructed' the integral testimony of the Holy Scriptures to who Christ is has left us with a de-supernaturalized Christ, who was never truly Incarnate God (whether in the womb of the Virgin or back on the Throne of his Father). Hence, Ascension to the Highest Heavens would be unthinkable for the kind of Jesus acceptable to reductionistic Naturalism.

And there is yet, I think, another reason for the relative neglect of much-needed ascension teaching in our churches. It is not surprising that varied forms of Deism and Naturalism preclude much of the public from any serious thinking about Christ's bodily lifting up to his heavenly Father. But why has there been so much neglect of this doctrine among multitudes of truest believers?

I am uncertain, but I suspect it is because long generations of even the best preaching tradition in the majority of churches have tended to treat Christ's ascension as a sort of footnote or addendum to his central work of dying for our sins and rising to give us new life. Yes, all orthodox denominations have always confessed the ascension, but how many of them have preached it one hundredth as frequently as his atonement, his resurrection and (especially during the last century) his second coming? Have we preachers missed the gripping relevance of Christ's ascension? If so, help is at hand.

In failing to give anything like the same emphasis to the ascension of Christ that the scriptures (and indeed, the patristic tradition) do, much light, strength and joyous service have been lost to millions of Christians in the midst of the battle. But enough of the negative (for this book is massively positive!).

Reading Gerrit's book inspires me with hope that many a pulpit once again will hold forth in a fresh and vital way the gloriously applicable truth of the going up of the Risen Christ to the bosom of the Father, thence to send down every needed blessing; most of all, his own personal presence in the Holy Spirit! I believe that this clearly written, theologically astute book is marked by pastoral insight and a warm-hearted humility that will commend its potentially transforming truths to students, preachers, and even to seekers who may wonder what the ascension is all about and whether there is anything in it for such as them.

Gerrit's accurate and careful survey of biblical teaching on this doctrine is complemented by a competent, and indeed thrilling, look at the rich patristic treatment of the Lord's ascension. He rejoices with Clement of Alexandria on how the risen Jesus 'Clad now in a priestly garment of glorified flesh, humanity in its fullest, restored unto eternal life' ascended into the Most Holy Place. And in company with John Calvin (especially in his Commentary on Hebrews), Gerrit sets forth the absolute necessity and the absolute sufficiency of the continuing priesthood of Jesus Christ, still in our flesh, in the presence of the Father above.

This book is especially helpful in thinking through and applying what Christ's continuing priesthood really means for prayer, for mission, for the right way to deal with the world around us and for helping the poor. Dr Dawson has been enabled to handle profound theological truth in a way that sparkles with loveliness and light.

Douglas F. Kelly
Jordan Professor of Systematic Theology
Reformed Theological Seminary
Charlotte, NC

PART I

Why Recover the Ascension?

Introduction

'Listen,' says the voice of my friend on the other end of the phone. 'This is the sound of my head falling to the desk.' I hear a thump. 'That's how long you have to tell me about the ascension before I'm asleep.' No, the ascension does not seem to be a scintillating doctrine. Though part of what the church has called *the rule of faith* from the beginning, the ascension of Jesus into heaven does not occupy the foremost part of our usual conversations about Christ. We may profess it on Sundays, yet forget it the rest of the week. The ascension is even left out of recent confessional documents such as the 1983 *Brief Statement of Faith* as well as the *Confession of 1967* of the Presbyterian Church (USA). We have such difficulty conceiving how, or even believing that, the body of Jesus went to heaven that we may want the doctrine to remain in obscurity.

Yet, in a time when the western church is fiercely debating the uniqueness of Jesus and our people are drowning in the flood of busy, demanding lifestyles, the ascension is an absolutely crucial part of the gospel story to recover. Through the ascension we discover that the incarnation continues. Jesus remains united to our human nature. Thus he cannot be spiritualized into some kind of Christ principle, or collapsed into one manifestation of a God who is known in many ways. Moreover, the presence of our brother Jesus in heaven dramatically affects how we see our lives and place in the world today.

The Story

The second article of the Apostles' Creed reads like a narrative. In a highly condensed form, the creed moves from the incarnation through the sojourn of Jesus Christ among us on earth to the anticipation of his return in judgement at the consummation of all things. Of the twelve verbs which follow the opening affirmation, nine are past tense, one is present and two are future. We affirm that we believe in Jesus Christ his only Son our Lord, who was

- **conceived** by the Holy Ghost
- **born** of the Virgin Mary
- **suffered** under Pontius Pilate
- **was crucified**
- **dead** (died)
- and **buried**.
- He **descended** into hell.
- On the third day he **rose** again from the dead.
- He **ascended** into heaven
- and **sitteth** on the right hand of God the Father Almighty.
- From thence he **shall come**
- To **judge** the quick and the dead.

We can see how important the final past-tense verb is to the entire story. Dramatically speaking, the narrative would be stuck in the past without the ascension. 'The third day he rose again from the dead' and ... what? If there had been no ascension, what would have happened to Jesus? If Jesus' new life does not continue, then he could have died again. In that case, however, death, not life, would have had the last word. The resurrection requires an ascension to be completed. There is no triumph over death if it is only of a temporary, Lazarus-like quality. Moreover, if Jesus continued to live but never left us, the sending of the Spirit would not have happened and the church would not have begun. We would still be looking for him in the flesh, and that, obviously, is not the case.

But what kind of ascension occurred? Though we seldom think of it at all, we may have a vague notion that while Jesus rose up into the clouds before his disciples' eyes, as recorded in Acts 1, when he got beyond their sight he slipped from the body, dissolving, as it were, into the spiritual realm. C. S. Lewis observes:

> We also, in our heart of hearts, tend to slur over the risen *manhood* of Jesus, to conceive Him, after death, simply returning into Deity, so that the Resurrection would be no more than the reversal or undoing of the Incarnation.[1]

In this way, we may believe that he went up, but suspect that as soon as the audio-visual demonstration of his departure was completed, he dropped the body of flesh and went back to being the eternal Son of God. This spiritualizing is a more appealing idea than some sort of space travel to a distant heaven that is nonetheless part of the known universe.

Yet, enormous theological problems are raised by disembodying Christ's ascension. For instance, if it is the case that the Lord slipped out of the body, who, then, is sitting at the right hand of God? Is it Jesus, whose voice the disciples heard, whose touch they felt, with whom they sailed on the Sea of Galilee and shared the cup in the Upper Room? Or is it the eternal Son of God, who once knew what it was like to be a man but is no longer bone of our bone and flesh of our flesh? If the latter, what effect would a bodiless Christ have on the future work affirmed in the Creed, his coming again and his judgement of the living and dead?

To put it bluntly, if Jesus did not go up as a man, he cannot come again as a man. The Judge would not be our Brother, not the one tempted in all ways as we are, not the man with the nail-scarred hands and the 'rich wounds yet visible above'. He might be God in that case, but he would not be human. And we would be lost.

A Continuing Incarnation

Our redemption depends on the reality that the eternal Son of God came to us as a man. If he did not come fully down, then we are not fully saved. But the incarnation is the news that Jesus became what we are, fully entering our lost and forsaken condition, taking up into himself our very humanity. God crossed the gap between us and himself. He leapt both the breach in our communion created by sin, and the fissure gaping with our mortal frailty and decaying form. He came to get us. He came to live on our behalf the life of faithful response to the Father required of us but beyond our capacity. Such obedience led Jesus, in our name and in our flesh, even to endure the cross, the full consequence and penalty for human sin. Even in the moment of utter dereliction, he yet committed his spirit to the Father whose love he trusted though he could not feel it. Thus, Jesus our faithful Saviour is the new Adam, the new beginning of the entire human race. His obedience in life and in death founded our salvation. Because he united himself to us, we may, through the power of the Holy Spirit, be united to him.

Moreover, our salvation depends on his *continuing union* with us. If the Son of God came to us where we are, but then left us, if he went away and did not take us with him, we would still be lost. In fact, we could then begin a whole new series of books entitled *Left Behind*, though with a decidedly gloomier slant! For any view of the ascension as Jesus slipping off his humanity is a sentence of condemnation. We cannot be united to him in the Holy Spirit if he is no longer flesh of our flesh and bone of our bone. If the one who sits at the right hand of God is not still fully human as well as fully God, then we will never enter within the veil. If he dropped the hypostatic union with humanity, then he dropped us, and we are left forsaken on this side of the great divide, unable to fulfil our purpose, find forgiveness and restored communion, or enact our mission.

Thankfully, a Nicene, historically orthodox view of the ascension safeguards our understanding of Christ's continuing incarnation. Further reflection on this reality can release a flood of joy in the church. For example, Frederick Farrar, in examining paintings depicting scenes from the life of Christ, first suggests that the ascension would be better left unpainted. But pondering why artistic renderings of the ascension fail adequately to represent the event leads Farrar to the heart of the matter. He concludes that the main thought in the ascension 'is that Christ has forever taken into the Godhead the form of the Manhood'.

This thought so thrills Farrar that he appends to his commentary this enigmatic but triumphant fragment of a poem:

'Tis the weakness in strength that I cry for! my flesh that I seek
In the Godhead! I seek and I find it! Oh Saul, it shall be
A Face like my face that receives thee; a Man like to me
Thou shalt love, and be loved by for ever; a Hand like this hand
Shall throw open the gate of new Life to thee! See the Christ stand![2]

'A Hand like this hand shall throw open the gate of new Life to thee!' A human hand will grasp us as we make our way into heaven. We shall be greeted by a face — the face of Jesus — that has a form we recognize. The incarnation continues, and so we are included in the life of God. That is the essential meaning of the ascension. We are not left alone. Jesus has gone before us in a way we may follow through the Holy Spirit whom he has sent, because the way is in his flesh, in his humanity. Jesus is himself that new and living way. The fully human one has gone within the veil in our name and even in our skin. United to him by the Spirit, to the one who remains united to us, we may follow where he has gone.

Now we follow spiritually, but at our deaths we will follow in soul. Then, on the day of his return, soul will be reunited with body. Thus we will be with him always, in his Father's house, in the place prepared for us since before the foundation of the earth, prepared in his sacrificial work, and still being prepared in his priestly work among us now. So, as Paul declares to the Philippians, 'Our citizenship is in heaven, from which we eagerly await a Saviour, even Jesus Christ who by the power that enables him to bring all things under his control shall transform our lowly bodies to be like his glorious body' (Philippians 3:20–1).[3] The ascension of the glorified body of Jesus has established the very identity of the Lord's pilgrim people on earth. We are on our way to a place and a condition like his. By Jesus' ascension, we may, in the power of the Holy Spirit, ascend to God as well.

To summarize, the Son of God did not come down in order to stay. Nor did he come to us in order to slum for thirty-three years before shedding our skin and returning to the splendour of heaven. The Lord Jesus Christ descended to us in order to gather us up and bring us with him to his Father in heaven. He went back still wearing our flesh – 'the selff samyn body', declares Knox in the *Scots Confession* – in which he had been born, lived, died and rose.⁴ In fact, the Son of God maintains our humanity, writes Karl Barth, 'to all eternity . . . It is a clothing which He does not put off. It is His temple which He does not leave. It is the form which He does not lose.'⁵ In no way, then, did the ascension signal simply a return to business as usual between God and humanity. Rather, the ascension of Christ is a vital hinge on which turns the work of the Mediator, the incarnate Son, our Redeemer in all his offices.

The ascension signals both end and beginning, completion and inauguration, in the person and work of Christ. Consider its relation to his threefold office of prophet, priest and king:

1. The ascension marks a turn in Christ's prophetic office. It marks the end of our hearing his human voice speak on earth. He is gone. Yet the ascension provides the necessary prelude to the sending of the Holy Spirit, who now brings Christ Jesus' words to us. Because in his flesh he has left us, Jesus can through his Spirit lead us into all the truth of who he is and remind us of all he said while among us (John 16:13; 14:26).

2. The ascension signals the completion of Jesus' priestly act of atonement, the essence of which is seen in the cross, though it includes what Calvin calls 'the whole course of his obedience'⁶ from incarnation through sinless life, atoning sacrifice and resurrection triumph. The ascension is at the same time, though, the beginning of Jesus' priestly appearance on our behalf to bring the offering of his continued, mediatorial human life before the Father, and to intercede for those he now calls his brothers and sisters.

3. The ascension completes the triumph on earth of Christ's resurrection and its demonstration of his kingly glory. His exaltation began on the cross and continued through his glorious rising, reaching a zenith in his ascension beyond the heavens. The ascension also inaugurates Jesus' eternal reign as the divine-human Lord, who is seated in power at

the Father's right hand. Though our king is now removed from sight via the ascension, he yet reigns, and will come again, in the same way that he departed, in glory to judge the living and the dead.

Thus, the doctrine of the ascension dynamically draws our attention to the full range of the present work of Christ. It lifts our eyes and hearts to watch for his promised return. So the ascension changes the way we understand our place in this world. We belong to Jesus Christ who is in heaven. Our true home is there, not here. As we sojourn, we touch the things of this world but lightly. We do not seek an earthly kingdom but a heavenly one, for 'The world and its desires pass away' (1 John 2:17). At the same time, because Jesus remains incarnate, we know that human beings and this world continue to be the object of his concern and redemptive love. It is these enfleshed souls whom he has recapitulated in himself, this earth he will free from its bondage to corruption and subjection to decay (Romans 8:20–1). The church of Jesus Christ, then, is called out of the world in order to lay down her life for the world. We draw apart from the world in its insistence on self-sufficiency. Yet we return to that very world with the offer of the love of the gospel. Our mission is properly defined by the ascended, reigning and returning Jesus.

So, the recovery of the ascension in the life of the church offers a bracing corrective to one of the most prevalent problems we face in the west: an over-identification with the present age. The virtual indistinguishability between much of the church and the culture in the United States and western Europe has crippled our witness. Part I, then, continues by examining the degree to which the church, particularly in its mainline expression, has lost its distinctiveness. With the problem exposed, we may proceed in Part II to articulate a concise, historically orthodox theology of the ascension. Then, in Part III, we will see how a robust doctrine of the ascension and Christ's continuing incarnation can invigorate the church's worship, foster spiritual growth, and lead the church into a proper and fruitful relationship with the world.

How To Use This Book

This book is an attempt to see a doctrine all the way through –
from its biblical source to its implications for the daily life of the
church. Rather than considering the ascension in isolation, we will
strive to drink deeply from the theological well precisely because
the ascension is so pertinent to contemporary ecclesiology.
Theology has got to reach the frontlines where our people
attempt to live out the faith. So, doctrinal, spiritual and missional
theology are integrated. We will consider the particulars of the
local church as well as the universality of the doctrine in the hope
that these are necessary complements. As the reader, though, you
may have more or less use for the different stages of
consideration. Use it as you need for:

- **a fresh window on Christology.** Considering faithfully
  one facet of Jesus' life inevitably leads to seeing how that
  facet relates to the sparkling whole. The ascension, then, can
  rekindle our interest in historic, orthodox Christology. For
  most, the ascension offers a new way to teach the familiar
  story of Christ, and so these doctrinal chapters (2–6) can
  form the basis for a fresh approach to a class on the person
  of Jesus.

- **a compendium of quotations** from the patristic writers,
  Calvin and all the major English works on the ascension. I
  have quoted liberally so that readers will have the benefit of
  research pulled together from many sources, whether for
  teaching, writing, or prayer.

- **a lens on the contemporary western church,** particularly
  as our theological struggles relate to our relationship with
  the culture, and as both relate to shaping and enacting
  mission (Chapters 1, 3, 7–10).

- **a vital path for spiritual growth,** rooted in biblical
  teaching and ancient wisdom, yet fresh and new to many
  contemporary Christians. The quotations alone offer an
  invigorating source for revitalizing our praise and practice.
  See especially Chapters 8 and 10 and the Appendix.

- **practical suggestions** on how the doctrine of the ascension
  may be integrated into the worship, teaching, mission and
  ministry of a congregation (Chapters 6 and 9).

With these ends in mind, let us face head on the cultural situation
in which the western church finds itself, a context crying out for
the recovery of Jesus ascended.

Chapter 1

The World Is Too Much With Us

Nearly two centuries ago, William Wordsworth lamented the encroachment of the secular world on the minds and souls of the people of England. His words were prophetic:

> The world is too much with us; late and soon,
> Getting and spending, we lay waste our powers:
> Little we see in Nature that is ours;
> We have given our hearts away, a sordid boon!
>   .   .   .   . etc   .   .   .
> For this, for everything, we are out of tune;
> It moves us not.—Great God! I'd rather be
> A Pagan suckled in a creed outworn[.][1]

Even in a country long dominated by a Christian framework of thought and practice, the new Industrial Revolution and the rise of unchecked capitalism (fuelled by the Enlightenment insistence on the primacy of humanity) was choking the spirit of the nation. Wordsworth saw Christianity as offering little resistance to this materialism – it had been co-opted by the power of the culture. So he pined that he would rather be a pagan, gleaning at least some heart-stirrings from ancient myths, than a soul-dead modern man, whose faith is only a gloss on a shallow life.

Would Wordsworth have anything more hopeful to say if he could see the church in the west at the beginning of this postmodern, post-Christian millennium? Sadly, I think not. The core problem I identify in my local church situation may, I suspect, be seen across Europe and America: the world is too much with us. While research which supports this claim will be cited further on, we will consider first how the church officers at the First Presbyterian Church in a small town in North Carolina came to this very conclusion. The particular may reveal the general. Indeed, as Lesslie Newbigin writes, 'the local church is not a branch of something else. The local church is the catholic Church.'[2] Theology must be done in the context of the parish because that, all across the world, is where the church universal exists. The congregations which gather at a particular place are, each and all, at the crossroads between the world with all its demands and need and the Lord who is still present with us by his Spirit.

A Letter to the Angel

The book of Revelation records seven letters sent from Christ to the angels of churches in specific locations. Each letter follows a similar pattern. It begins with a descriptive identification of the author, the 'Son of God' (2:18), who is also 'someone like a son of man' (1:13), 'the First and the Last, who died and came to life again' (2:8). Then Christ, the author, goes on to describe the angel of each church in the local context beginning with a phrase such as 'I know your deeds' (2:2; 2:19; 3:1). In five cases, the Lord praises the angel of the church for works of faithfulness. Curiously, the addressee is always spoken to in the second-person singular, though the deeds of the whole church are described. The single angel, therefore, somehow represents the collective congregation. Next, Jesus identifies an area of weakness in the church and follows that with a prescription for correction which includes a promise or threat.

Walter Wink has interpreted the angels of the churches to be the corporate spirit of each congregation, the interior reality or personality of the local body of Christ.[3] Though Wink's eschewing of the angels as actual, personal beings is problematic, I have found the Bible study Wink developed on these letters to be a very helpful tool in discernment.[4] Three times in my decade at the Lenoir church, our officers have worked through this study to hear what the Spirit of Christ might be saying to our church in the present hour.

We studied the passages together, making particular note of what external characteristics of a church might reveal its inner personality. Then, each participant prayerfully wrote a letter he imagined Christ might be addressing to our angel. The letters followed the pattern of identification and praise for Christ as author, an affirmation of the church that begins with 'I know your deeds . . .' followed by a specific response to the words 'But I have this against you . . .' The letters closed with a call to a particular correction and the promise that follows obedience. Then, we gathered again as a group, and read our individual letters aloud. Each time, we were amazed at the common themes which emerged. This study has been a powerful means of discernment for our officers as they articulate our mission and plan our goals for the future. Their letters went right to the heart of the problems afflicting the church, with insights that are confirmed through further reading of experts on the state of the church today.

At a winter planning retreat (during the earliest stages of ascension research), our elders, deacons and staff created this composite letter, comprising actual phrases from their work:

To the Angel of the Church on Kirkwood Street, write:
These are the words of him who has the sharp-edged sword – the Amen, the faithful and true witness, the ruler of God's creation.

I know your deeds – your spiritual worship, faithfulness, and compassion. You worship in spirit and in truth. You are eager to hear Scripture, sing sweet notes of praise, have a rich tradition of worship, and glorify my name in worship. You are faithful, a beacon of light, committed and devoted disciples. You show faithfulness through difficult times and are a remembering people. And you are a caring and compassionate people: a leader of compassion for the poor, caring of my people, faithful in mission overseas, a shepherd to God's people. In you, love flows among all in the church body and your concern for others is warming to my heart.

But I have four things against you. First, you have lost your passion and first love for me. You have not prayed with passion and regularity. I do not hear your earnestness in prayer. You have lost zeal for the love of Christ and your witness to my abiding love lacks vigor and spirituality. You have lost the heart of passion and the fire of faith. You only dimly reflect Christ's light.

Second, you have become too comfortable with the present. You choose to remain safe while allowing the world to creep in in small places. You have become too comfortable with the present. Beware present-day idols: elaborate lifestyles, power and prestige.

Third, your comfort has produced complacency: in teaching the Word to your children and youth, in giving routinely out of habit, and in tending the needs of my sheep. You have become too comfortable in the grace of God, taking it for granted.

Fourth, your comfort and complacency has caused you to become self-focused. Your doors are open only to those who knock – who dare to approach you. You wrap your arms only around your own, not seeing the people who are not a part of this. You are caught up in the urgency of the moment and fail to recognize the agony and loneliness of many you pass. You forget that my Father is the one to be worshipped and keep your faith to yourselves. You have lost part of the flock. And I do not hear a great repentance.

So be earnest and repent. For in those who overcome, I will shine with the light of the sun, casting out darkness and driving out the evil one. For those with ears to hear, then: remember who is your head, kindle active faith, and look outward with faithful action. I am the Head of the Church. Seek first the kingdom. Do not allow the world to dictate any of what you speak and teach. Do not apologize for your belief in me or surrender any part of it. Be humble and quiet in your deeds. Reach out to the needy in *my* name. Let *my* name be on your lips at all times and in all places; do all things in remembrance of me. Remember the true source of your every breath and tell others. Kindle active faith, renewing your zeal for my mission. I want you to restate what it means to be a Christian and form a vision that will excite your members and bring in new members to my body. Pray for the fire of the Spirit to ignite wonder and wildness in the life of Christ. Stand strong! And finally, look outward and act faithfully: use your affluence and influence, throwing open your doors to reach out and welcome all of God's people. Be a light and a strength to those who would wonder and doubt. Extend yourselves. Spread the Word. Tend the sheep – chase away the wolf. Minister to the youth of your church and city. Let the Spirit guide you – these experiences are far from routine.

I am the light of the world ... you are the light of the world! To the one who has an ear to hear – hear what the Spirit has to say to the church.

Our officers were daring enough to speak bracingly about the church they cherish. We love Christ and minister to the world, but we know that our passion has been tempered and our mission dulled by an over-identification with the culture. Our very strength has become our weakness. Success in the world, which makes so much ministry possible and gives us such influence in the community, has also made us dangerously comfortable. Our vision of the kingdom to come gets clouded by the urgent business of the present age. Our edge in mission is dulled when comfort makes us complacent about reaching those outside our immediate sight. We evaluate our lives too easily, by the standards of the world. And too often, even in our good works, we do not go with the name of Christ on our lips.

John's first epistle applies to us:

> Do not love the world or anything in the world. If anyone loves the world, the love of the Father is not in him. For everything in the world – the cravings of sinful man, the lust of his eyes and the boasting of what he has and does – comes not from the Father but from the world. The world and its desires pass away, but the man who does the will of God lives forever. (1 John 2:15–17)

In this world we hear the insistence that we look no higher than ourselves nor beyond any moment but the present as we determine our course of action. Here we act as if we were our own gods. We are ruled by the cravings of the sinful flesh, which sees itself as a consumer needing to be filled by ever-increasing amounts of pleasure and activity. We measure our worth in terms of the pride of life. The world, in this sense, is hostile to the worship of God and the working out of his purposes in us. This is the context in which the church has always lived, and the struggle against its constant tidal pull towards living as if it were all there is remains with us until the return of Christ.

The very world (*cosmos*) that God so loved (with *agape* love) is a world set up in rebellion against him. Yet, the world we are *not* to love (with that same *agape* love) is the very one to which God gave his Son. In this juxtaposition is the crux of our situation. Lesslie Newbigin has written: 'We must always ... be wrestling with both sides of this reality: that the Church is for the world against the world. The Church is against the world for the world.'[5] The world sets itself up as independent of God, as if its own reality were ultimate. Yet the church goes in Christ's name to the world with a different story. We bring a counter-claim, a word of a different and higher identity than the world acknowledges. And so we are locked in a conflict of love. As Douglas Farrow writes, the church is 'wrestling with the world to the bitter end in hope – a well grounded hope! – of redeeming the time'.[6]

In Chapters 7 through 9, we will explore further how the doctrine of the ascension relates to the way the church is sent into the world. But now our attention is focused on the problem of being so closely identified with the world that we may actually lose any sense of this conflict. When we lose our distinctiveness, we become no good to the world or God.

As the Pastor Sees His Flock

I am the pastor of a church filled with 550 perfectly nice people. For the most part, they believe the historic doctrines of the faith. They look after one another with heartfelt concern and great diligence. They are leaders in the community and have the common good in mind as they coordinate nearly every significant ministry in this small southern US town. Sunday mornings, the church is filled with well-dressed, smiling, happy people. Success is upon their brows, and they do not mind reasonably sharing their bounty with others. They treat their pastor with great respect and provide for him a lifestyle that very few others in the history of ministry have enjoyed. Only a complete fool could fail to be happy and successful here with all the support that is given to the minister. Our buildings are beautiful and our budget is robust – stewardship is always easy. The church staff is large in proportion to the membership, hard working, well paid and even better loved. We rarely fight. We seldom hesitate to seize opportunities. We might well be described as 'vibrantly stable'.

Yet, I wonder. If it cost my people something precious to be Christians, would they still come? If there were no tax deduction for giving, would the pledges be as high? If being a member of

First Presbyterian Church were a social stigma instead of a star of prestige, would they keep joining? In other words, how different are we really from the culture around us? We are all infected with the pluralism of the age, constantly breathing the air of consumerism and the culture of disbelief. The sweet breaths of the far country of heaven which we receive in spite of our faults in worship and study just barely keep us hoping that we are meant for more than the world around us offers.

As I began this study, four symptoms emerged which point to the disease of the 'sordid boon' of the world being too much with us:

First, our people are breathless with busyness: late and soon, getting and spending, we have laid waste our powers. It takes an enormous amount of time and energy to manage our prosperity. We have so many things to maintain. Moreover, we have such huge expectations for our children that we keep them running on the hamster wheel of 'good' activities. There is no time for family life, and only a terror of being left together with nothing to do. Our children are too busy to have time to serve others in any consistent and meaningful way. Most of our people see only that this is the usual state of things, and so they complain that they are tired all the time.

Second, we do little or no evangelism. We give plenty of money to social ministries and happily sit on boards of organizations which help those less fortunate than us. It has been a tremendous relief to our members that our worship services are broadcast on television and that for a year the ministers gave a daily radio message. We get high visibility and 'buzz' in the community without anyone actually having to initiate a conversation about Jesus Christ. There is no urgency for the spiritually lost. The claims of Christ fit so loosely upon us that we cannot imagine they would be binding on others.

Third, we are uncomfortable with the assertion that Christ Jesus is the true and only path to God, and that the Bible is the authoritative guide for faith and practice. Our success in business in a multicultural nation and world depends on our being adaptable and open to many points of view. Commerce rules, and whatever might jeopardize commerce must be avoided. Our low-profile Christianity keeps us from challenging the pluralism that is in the very air we breathe. We have learned to hold many contradictory ideas in our heads at once. Also, we want to get along with our neighbours. As we would prefer to be left alone, we leave others alone, letting faith be their business. If pressed, then, we prefer to talk of how Christianity is 'true for me'. Seeming to impose one view, insisting that it is right, would be distasteful. Hence, our church has been relatively silent on issues such as homosexuality and abortion, as those tend to raise strong opposing feelings when discussed. But we are strong in non-controversial areas such as hospices, adult day care, and food for the hungry.

Fourth, many of our people feel a sense of separation between their church life and their business, school or private life. Church is soothing after a rough week. People say it helps put things back into perspective. They get reoriented at church, and then go back into the world where a different set of values reigns. By the end of the week, they have lost their spiritual footing and feel soul-weary. Very few view their work and home lives as a mission field in which they have been placed by God as lights in the darkness. Fewer still consciously shape decisions at work or school based on the values contained in scripture.

These symptoms, as seen in the letter to the angel of the church, manifest themselves in the church in a series of seemingly contrary pairs of facts:

1. Enthusiasm about the church and its worship is strong, yet attendance levels remain flat. Slightly less than half our membership attends church, and we cannot get over the hump. People love their church, but there are just so many things to do that a lot of us miss a lot of Sundays.

2. Giving is high and increases steadily while membership stays about the same. Commitment is high among those who are active. Yet, the number of these highly motivated people is not great. We gain just enough to replace

inevitable losses when people die or move. Nearly everyone is comfortable with this.

3. Our members speak positively about their church to friends and co-workers but speak little about Jesus Christ. Members are proud of their church and its fine record of service to the community. They are enthusiastic about our programmes and staff. Yet we have had so little experience telling the gospel story that we feel unprepared and shy in doing so.

4. We sit on many boards of groups doing ministry to the needy but few of us get our hands dirty in the actual mission. We write more cheques than we donate hours.

5. The social composition of our membership is strikingly homogeneous. We are willing to welcome anyone, we say, but generally the only visitors who stay are the ones who are like the rest of us.

All of these signs point to a membership composed of committed Christians who are living in the grip of a world that has claimed them as its own. I do not believe my people are consciously trying to serve two masters. Generally, I do not think they even realize the contradiction between our beliefs and our life as a church. They are kind, happy, forgiving, dear church folk. Their pastor, however, knows himself to be compromised, realizes that he, too, has 'the world is too much with us' disease, and wants to get better. The cure means change, and a certain amount of surgery in our lifestyles that will be painful.

Voices from a Comparable Age

It is interesting that during one of the few periods when significant writing was devoted to the ascension, each of the writers of these major works identified the struggle with worldliness as a key issue for the church. This occurred at the turn of the twentieth century, during what has become known as the Gilded Age in Europe and America. This was an age of relative prosperity when the myth of human progress had not yet been shattered by the First World War.

In Aberdeen, Professor William Milligan in his Baird Lectures
warned of

> the pretences and superficialities of an outward religiousness, the
> vain shows of wealth, or the self-indulgent luxury of so large a
> portion of the professing Church[.][7]

How closely this mirrors the warning in the letter to the angel at
Lenoir: 'Beware present-day idols: elaborate lifestyles, power and
prestige.' Milligan's further analysis, with a slight change in
writing style, could be found on bookstore shelves today:

> The world is around us in its misery. The ear is pained, the heart is
> sick, with its tales of wrong and infamy, with its dark places the
> habitations of horrid cruelty, with its oppressions that make wise men
> mad, with its myriad of innocent children trained up in every form of
> vice and steeped in wretchedness. Worse than this, the very Church
> of Christ to which we would naturally turn for help seems powerless;
> the light of men, but her light dimmed; the salt of the earth, but the
> salt with its savour lost; hardly to be distinguished from a world that
> cares for little else than the newest luxury or folly; often ignoring if
> not denying the most characteristic doctrine of her faith, and eager to
> make the best of both worlds which seldom has any other meaning
> than making the best of this world, and letting the next world take its
> chance, while at the same time her different sections are busier
> contending with one another than with the common foe, without
> mutual forbearance, or sympathy, or helpfulness, or love.[8]

The quest to be the first people successfully to serve both God
and mammon is not new to our age. Contemporaneously with
Milligan, Andrew Murray, a Dutch Reformed pastor in South
Africa, whose father was a Scot, wrote:

> The power of the world, the spirit of its literature, the temptations of
> business and pleasure, all unite to make up a religion in which it is
> sought to combine a comfortable hope for the future with the least
> possible amount of sacrifice in the present.

> We have here the great cause of the weakness of faith in our days.
> *There is no separation from the world.* So many Christians seem to have
> as much of its pleasure and honour and riches as they possibly can,
> consistently with their profession of religion. In such an atmosphere,
> faith is stifled. Many hardly believe, or never remember, that the
> world, with its arts and culture and prosperity, amid all its religious
> professions, is still the same world *that rejected Christ.*[9]

A few years later, Henry Barclay Swete, the Regius Professor of Divinity at Cambridge University, concluded his work on the ascension with these reflections, which, as we shall see, remarkably presage George Barna's research a century later:

> Belief in the Ascended Christ inspires a deep sense of personal responsibility. Few things are more necessary at the present time. In a self-pleasing, self-asserting age responsibility is apt to sit very lightly on many, or to be wholly ignored. Men and women, nay, even children, claim the right to be arbiters of their own conduct. This is not so only with the very rich, but with the poor and dependent; in all classes of society the question which men put to themselves is not, 'What is my duty?' but, 'How can I get the greatest enjoyment out of my life? How can I best succeed in evading its burdens?'[10]

Each of the above identified the same problem we have noted, and each directed our attention, as we shall see later, to the ascended Christ as an antidote.

A Current Study

In his book *The Second Coming of the Church*, church researcher George Barna provides evidence that our local church is by no means unique in its struggle against over-identification with the world. We are merely participating in an attitude that affects our whole nation. He writes:

> To increasing millions of Americans, God ... exists for the pleasure of humankind ... we live by the notion that true power is accessed not by looking upward but by turning inward. The focus of our faith has shifted from the transcendent to the mundane.[11]

In this inward focus, people create hybrid religions that blend various parts of different traditions according to their personal tastes. Barna, reflecting Swete's words a century earlier, declares that we are

> A nation hooked on syncretism – the blending of ... perspectives into an entirely new and heretical mixture of faith ... we have enthroned ourselves as the final arbiters. ... Americans align themselves with values that give them control.[12]

The church has been infected with this consumer-oriented spirituality. Barna's studies show that we think and behave no differently from anyone else. We watch nearly as much MTV as non-Christians, yet may actually give less money to the poor. Our divorce rate is actually higher, though we file about as many lawsuits and take prescriptions for depression at about the same rate as non-Christians.[13] Thus we, too, may compose a syncretistic religion for ourselves that is partly Christianity and partly soupy pop spirituality. We do not care for the environment any more than anyone else. We uncritically adopt an evolutionary worldview along with the culture. We create just as much garbage and buy just as many useless things. Commitment to church activities is little more than an accent on the good life. The local church, then, has become part of a cafeteria of choices for meaning and pleasure in a modern life. It is all we can do to get ourselves there one Sunday in four. Thus, we are kept so busy that we never have time to think of the church as anything more than a place where 'I can get some peace one hour a week'.

Barna surmises that this blending is based on the underlying belief that God exists to suit our pleasure. Hence, as pragmatic Americans, we want to blend beliefs and practices according to our right to choose those which we believe will make us happy. He writes:

> When asked to describe the ends they live for, the top items most American Christians reported were good health, a successful career, a comfortable lifestyle and a functional family. The average Christian assumes that when we are happy, God is happy ... a large majority of Christians contend that the true meaning of our earthly existence is to simply enjoy life and reap as much fulfillment as we can from our daily pursuits.[14]

In other words, we may well think, albeit unconsciously, that God is the accent to the lives we have chosen for ourselves. He is the icing on the cake. Amidst prosperity and the pleasant whirr of daily activities that keep us occupied, we add a dash of God to give us some joy, and maybe some Jabez-sized blessings. We will offer occasional thanks and hope that in return, when things get dodgy, God will give us a bit of peace. The Lord's ultimate goal is to help us be content in the lives we have chosen for ourselves.

When the church is indistinguishable from the culture, people with no hope who arrive at our door find nothing different to give them hope. We have squandered our riches for the pig pods of the culture. There is no will to be different from the world. Many churches survive now by habit and convention, but draw few new people, and even fewer non-Christians, because we have lost our saltiness and our light is dim.

So, the blandness in our churches, with so little difference in attitude between the Christians in our pews and the people outside our walls, has arisen from this chilling reality: 'Most Christians have plentiful exposure to God's truths and exhortations, but few have actually been pierced by the truth, principles and meaning of the Christian faith.'[15] This is the cultural situation in which our local churches are struggling to be faithful to the gospel. We live and work amidst a very loud, insistent story. The culture tells us incessantly that we are individuals whose decisions belong to the individual alone. It is up to each of us to pursue our happiness in ways we choose, and for those who are 'spiritual', God, and even Jesus, are but possible options for maximizing fulfilment now in this present world.

The Antidote

My premise is that the church – our local church and the churches of the west – needs to recover the meta-narrative of the gospel as a counter-story, indeed a better story to the one the world tells. As we noted in the Introduction, the second article of the Apostle's Creed is a narrative of a dozen dramatic movements. One of those episodes, the ascension, has been sorely neglected in the church's telling of the story. The silence about this episode cuts us off from the present work of Christ in heaven and from the conclusion of the story – his coming again to judge the living and the dead. Recovering a proper and robust doctrine of the ascension can reconnect us to a sense of our true citizenship in heaven and the implications of that identity for life in the world.

In his book *The Gagging of God*, D. A. Carson writes:

> For our materialistic culture, passionately focused on the comforts of
> this life and the pleasures of the now, this calls for the urgent
> restoration to our vision of the ultimate importance of heaven. ...
>   There is a primacy to preparing people to meet God which,
> though its horizon is eternity, will also change how people live in the
> here and now.[16]

A solution to the world's being too much with us is an increased
awareness of how much our true identity and life's destination is
located in heaven, followed by the change in life here on earth
that comes from the transformation in vision.

Swete specifically considers the ascension as a vital part in
recovering the church's identity:

> The Ascension and Ascended Life bear witness against the
> materialistic spirit which threatens in some quarters to overpower
> those higher interests that have their seat in the region of the
> spiritual and eternal. They are as a *Sursum corda* – 'lift up your hearts'
> – which comes down from the High Priest of the Church who stands
> at the heavenly altar, and draws forth from the kneeling Church the
> answer *Habemus ad Dominum* – 'we lift them up unto the Lord.' Faith
> in the ascended Christ was S. Paul's remedy for the sensuality which
> he encountered in the Greek cities of Asia Minor ... in the early days
> of the faith, when men lived in full view of the Ascended Life, they
> knew how to live in the world without being of it.[17]

The church can reclaim the fullness of its story, with spectacular
results. Andrew Murray understands the ascension to be one of
the four cornerstones on which a revived church is built:

> Faith has in its foundation four great cornerstones on which the
> building rests – the Divinity of Christ, the Incarnation, the
> Atonement on the Cross, the Ascension to the Throne. The last is
> the most wonderful, the crown of all the rest, the perfect revelation
> of what God has made Christ for us. And so in the Christian life it is
> the most important, the glorious fruit of all that goes before.[18]

The doctrine of the ascension is a powerful remedy for a church
caught up in the spirit of the age. It enables us to realize that we
are not at home in this old order that is passing away. We are on
our way to the new heavens and the new earth. Yet for now we
live here. We conduct our business, rear our children, worship our

God and work out our salvation on *this* earth. So, here, too, is our mission field. This is the very world to which we are sent even as the Son of God was sent. So we have identified the need to be more sharply separated from the world in order that we might be properly sent to give our lives *for* it, not *to* it. Next, to reclaim the ascension for the transformation of the church, we must spend some significant time exploring this episode of our salvation drama, unearthing it from under the layers of neglect.

PART II

Toward a Concise Theology
of the Ascension

Chapter 2

The Ascension as Public Truth

In the same body in which he was crucified, Jesus Christ rose from the dead, and in that very flesh he ascended into heaven.[1] Immediately we have questions, even doubts. Where did Jesus go? A human body cannot possibly live outside of the atmosphere, gravity, sunlight and sustenance of earth. How did he go? We can hardly take seriously some kind of space voyage to the outer reaches of the universe, as if heaven could be reached that way if only we had the right conveyance. Acts 1:9 tells us that Jesus was 'taken up before their very eyes, and a cloud hid him from their sight'. That is rather enigmatic. What really happened? If we do accept that the human Jesus is alive away from the earth, in what form is his humanity now? These are the pressing questions that must be addressed in order to establish the doctrine. For an ascension in the flesh from earth to heaven is simply difficult to apprehend.

This has always been the case. In New Testament days, the Jewish Sadducees would have claimed that life on earth as an ensouled body is the extent of our existence. Their denial of the resurrection of the body would have rendered the further question of the ascension absurd. Many contemporary Greeks would have been aghast at the assertion that corruptible flesh went into the realm of spirit. For them, only the rational soul could go on to the noumenal realm when it finally slipped away from the prison of the material body. Flesh and heaven simply do not mix.

The patristic writers encountered the same resistance, as a sampling of their writings will show. For example, Justin (d. 165) had to assert Jesus' resurrection and ascension in 'the flesh in which He suffered' against the idea that flesh in heaven is 'impossible'. Tertullian (d. 225) combated those who would have 'excluded from ... the court of heaven itself, all flesh and blood whatsoever' by boldly asserting that 'Jesus is still sitting there at the right hand of the Father, man, yet God ... flesh and blood, yet purer than ours.'[2]

Origen (d. 254) was anathematized in the sixth century for implying, among other things, that 'after the resurrection the body of the Lord was ethereal'.[3] His actual writings seem in conflict on this issue, asserting a real incarnation, resurrection and ascension at one point, yet also paving the way for what would later become known as the ubiquity of the person of Christ:

> He Himself is everywhere, and passes swiftly through all things; nor are we any longer to understand Him as existing in those narrow Limits in which He was once confined for our sakes, i.e., not in that circumscribed body which He occupied on earth, when dwelling among men, according to which He might be considered as enclosed in some one place.[4]

This spiritualizing of the ascension would become a constant challenge to the Church through the ages.[5] Two centuries after Origen, we see the struggle reflected in Augustine (d. 430), who freely admits that Jesus' rising and ascending in the flesh was 'incredible', particularly since the story was first advanced by men 'of mean birth and the lowest rank'. Though sceptics are not persuaded by the miracles of either Jesus or these uneducated apostles, all these works but confirm 'that one grand and health-giving miracle of Christ's ascension into heaven with the flesh in which he rose'.[6] The move from earth to heaven in the body was an enormous, splashy, mind-scrambling miracle − on which our very lives depend.

In the east, John Chrysostom (d. 407), preaching on Acts 1, recognizes how interconnected affirming the ascension in the flesh is with accepting the resurrection, the incarnation and even creation. Incredulity over the ascension, because the account asserts it to be such a visible, outward event, exposes those who also doubt whether the entire Christian worldview could be true, because of its emphases on the goodness of creation and the importance of matter. Chrysostom preached, 'For the two denials go together: the denial that God creates anything from nothing, and the denial that he raises up what has been buried.' Thus, the assertion that matter is eternal actually limits the possibilities for human existence. The assertion that God did *not* create out of nothing keeps us limited to the finite world, and so denies the possibility of transformation from the carnal to the spiritual. This leaves us on our own, searching for 'spirituality' however we may find it. Chrysostom's sermon, then, articulates how the ascension directs us immediately to the scandal of the incarnation, and he recognizes that the very notion of 'God's entering into a body' is 'shocking' to many. Yet he also notes that those same sophisticated sceptics who rejected the offence of the Christian story might readily believe some spiritual nonsense as absurd as 'God in the onion!'[7]

Even during the Reformation, a certain amount of scepticism about the ascension can be detected. While Reformed theologians challenged the Lutherans about spiritualizing the nature of the ascended body of Christ, as we shall see below, some also rejected the dramatic flourishes in Catholic liturgy that had come to be associated with Ascension Day. In a work rather pejoratively entitled *The Bee Hive of the Romish Church*, we read this description of an ascension celebration:

> Likewise upon Ascension Day, they pull Christ up on high with ropes above the clouds, by a vice devised in the roof of the church, and they haul him up as if they would pull him up to the gallows: and there stand the poor priests, and look so pitifully after their God, as a dog for his dinner![8]

Evidently, enacting the story literalistically made it seem all the more absurd, and overstressed the absence of Jesus to the detriment of celebrating his triumph. The mind simply struggles to conceive of the ascension in the flesh, let alone re-create it in a drama. The renewal of Christian theology in the Reformation and the period immediately following included entering into the

perennial theological struggle to express how Jesus, fully God
and fully human, could be a man in heaven and yet everywhere
present as God.

Today, we may routinely count on Bishop John Spong and his
Scottish counterpart, Richard Holloway, to reflect the spirit of the
age. On this issue, they do not disappoint. Among the twelve
theses he believes will bring about a new reformation, Spong
includes:

> 7. Resurrection is an action of God. Jesus was raised into the meaning
> of God. It therefore cannot be a physical resuscitation occurring
> inside human history.
>
> 8. The story of the Ascension assumed a three-tiered universe and is
> therefore not capable of being translated into the concepts of a post-
> Copernican space age.[9]

Mixing a New Age spirituality with a nineteenth-century
scientism, Spong thus dismisses the ascension as impossible to
grasp in our day. His colleague Holloway addressed the corollary
to the ascension, Christ's return in the flesh, in his column for the
Scottish nation at the beginning of the new millennium:

> Jesus is not coming back; and the best way to honour him on his
> birthday is to look for him not in the skies, but in the streets of our
> own town.[10]

The story of Jesus is reduced to an ethic, and we now approach
the record of it as if reading the diary of fellow strugglers along
the way of life. The only meaning in the ascension is as an interior
event.

While few in our church would be so bold as these bishops, we
must admit that ascension in the flesh challenges our credulity. It
would be very easy simply to assert that Jesus ascended to
heaven bearing the *essence* of our humanity though not necessarily
bearing glorified flesh and blood into the heavenlies.[11] For our
minds are spared the conflict if we collapse the story into a
transition of Jesus from one *state* to another, rather than insisting
that Jesus moved locally, from one *place* to another.

Yet, as we shall see, these negotiations are not an option for us.
Rather, a deeper understanding of the ascension on its own terms

is needed in order to proceed to consider the meaning of the doctrine for the life of the church. So, we must quickly deal with the gauntlet the ascension throws down before the world, and some of the pressing questions that arise about the *nature* of the ascension should one dare to pick up this challenge of God's triumph and consider it as an event that really happened.

Public Truth

The ascension, then, in all its glaring physicality, brings the Christian claims about Christ right into the open market of real events in space and time. We believe that the truth of Jesus Christ is what Lesslie Newbigin calls *public truth*, the truth about what is the case.[12] Today, a false dichotomy between public and private truth is often drawn. The world of facts, of science and carpentry, accounting and clothes washing, comprises the realm of public truth. What is true can be known, articulated, measured and accepted by all reasonable people. The world of feelings, of religious belief, of values and opinions, is placed in the arena of private truth. So we may hear people say, 'These statements of faith may be true for me but I certainly would not impose them on your view of the world.' But Christianity has always created upheaval by declaring that Jesus is the eternal Son of God come down to our world of dust and swiftly passing time, to the external, physical world where we actually live. He spoke in a human voice that could be heard by listeners. He healed the sick in the presence of witnesses. He was tried in a public court of law, such as it was, and crucified on the open hill where anyone could see. But more, this crucified Jesus rose from the dead and appeared, in the same flesh in which he had been executed, to many witnesses. We claim that this is public truth, a fact in the real world. We insist as well that he was taken up to heaven in that same body and that there were many who saw him depart.

For Newbigin, the resurrection is the central fact around which all other facts, and all other claims to truth, must be arranged: 'Indeed, the simple truth is that the resurrection cannot be accommodated in any way of understanding the world except one of which it is the starting point.'[13] The Christian rule of truth has always resisted any spiritualizing of the resurrection, and the account of the ascension dramatically rules out any thought of resurrection as only an interior spiritual event in the believing church. Jesus, who rose from the dead in a body, ascended in the same body. This fact appears in history as a great stone, around which all other streams of thought break. One may build on the stone or break against it, but it will not go away. Nevertheless, as believers, we have questions. Beginning to address these questions makes it possible to consider the meaning of the ascension further on.

When Did Jesus Ascend?

The obvious time of Jesus' ascension is forty days after his resurrection, as specified by Luke in Acts 1:3. Surely that marked his physical departure from earth, never to be seen again in the flesh until his return when 'the time comes for God to restore everything' (Acts 3:21). Yet passages such as Luke 24:51 seem to imply an ascension on Easter Day. After appearing to the disciples in the Upper Room in Jerusalem on Sunday night, Jesus led them out towards Bethany and lifted his hands to bless them. 'While he was blessing them, he left them and was taken up into heaven.' Has Luke written two different accounts? Is he in conflict with himself, supposedly correcting his gospel story with the information in Acts? Or are we dealing with a corrupted text in Luke 24:51?[14] Perhaps Luke meant us to read the events of Chapter 24 as occurring during the forty days between resurrection and ascension.[15] Or maybe he simply conflated the time elements as he closed his first account.

This raises the possibility that there were more than one ascension to heaven, the one in Acts being the final departure, or the 'ascension proper'.[16] Indeed, the evidence from John's gospel suggests this. In John 21:17, Jesus tells Mary Magdalene not to touch him because he has not yet gone up, or ascended, to his Father. But then he instructs her in 21:18 to go to his brothers and tell them 'I go up to my Father and your Father'. The verb there is *anabaino*, in the present, active indicative, which denotes an action that is occurring or will occur imminently. Then, when Jesus next appears, he breathes on the disciples, saying 'Receive the Holy Spirit' (John 20:22). Though discussion of the timing of the sending of the Spirit is beyond the scope of this book, we may nonetheless see here the thread of the argument for an ascension prior to the fortieth day. Since Jesus had said the Spirit could not come until he had gone away (John 16:7), this breathing out of the Spirit assumes a going up to the Father on Easter Day.

With these considerations in mind, theologians such as Peter Toon have argued 'that there was a secret ascension on Easter morning, and then on the fortieth day there was a symbolic demonstration of that ascension by Jesus for the benefit of his disciples'.[17] This view solves the problem of where Jesus was during the forty days between resurrection and departure – he was in heaven with his Father, returning when he wished to appear again to his disciples. Following this argument too far, however, could lead to serious problems of speculation about both the method and propriety of Jesus' dropping in and out of our world. Douglas Farrow rejects the Easter Day ascension, primarily because 'it still refuses to take [Jesus'] leaving as seriously as the going. In biblical terms, the ascension involves a real departure of Jesus of Nazareth.'[18] Ultimately, the question of the time of the ascension is neither our concern nor our priority. For it is with the final departure of Jesus from this world that the ascension is primarily concerned, and all the benefits we shall consider which arise from the ascension have to do with the arrival of the God-man in heaven, where he remains until the parousia.

How Did Jesus Go?

Two main words are used in the New Testament for Jesus' return to heaven. One implies an active going. *Anabaino* means to go up. It is something one does oneself. Thomas Torrance notes that the Greek *anabaino* renders the Hebrew *alah*, which, while it also means to go up or ascend, has definite cultic significance.[19] One ascended both to Jerusalem and to the Temple. So we note many 'Psalms of ascent' (e.g. Psalms 120 to 134) for pilgrims making their way to the great festivals. In the Septuagint translation of our Psalm 24, a form of *anabaino* is used in the question, 'Who may ascend the hill of the Lord?' as David asks us to consider how we may approach the Lord of all the earth. The word also implies the very enthronement of God, his taking of his rightful place as divine sovereign.

As we noted above, Jesus used *anabaino* in speaking to Mary in John 21. He also used it in John 3:13 and 6:62 when referring to his ascension as a return to the heaven from which he came (and in fact never left). The word gives us the sense of an active ascension accomplished *by* the will and power of Jesus himself.

The word used more often by others to describe Jesus' ascent, however, implies an action done *to* Jesus. *Analambano* means to take up, or lift up. In Acts 1:2, 11, 22 and 1 Timothy 3:16 the word is used in the passive voice. Jesus was taken up to heaven. He did not so much go up as he was picked up. This, of course, was the perspective of the disciples who saw him go. He did not flap his arms and fly under evident human power. He was taken up in the sky until the cloud hid him from their sight. In this *shekinah* cloud of glory, Jesus was removed from his disciples and this world. He was translated from the earthly sphere of being to the heavenly one.

But the contrast in voice between these two verbs raises an interesting theological question. In what way did Jesus ascend on his own and in what way was he taken up to heaven by the Spirit? H. B. Swete helps us here:

> The 'going up' of the Son of Man into heaven was also His 'being taken up,' the Ascension was an Assumption; and the words answer to two complementary aspects of the event. The one represents Jesus Christ as entering the Presence of the Father of His own will and right; the other lays the emphasis on the Father's act by which He was exalted as the reward of His obedience unto death . . . as seen by the spectators, the ascent was bounded by the sky, but viewed in the light of the Spirit, it carried the Lord beyond all bounds of space.[20]

The ascension was an act of the Triune God, just as the

incarnation, baptism, ministry and resurrection involved all three Persons in the work of the Son. Jesus ascended because he had triumphed. As the Son of God he returned to his Father by his power and will. As the Son of Man, ever obedient, he allowed himself to be taken up by the Spirit under the decree of the Father to the place of exaltation given to him, not seized or demanded, as a result of his obedience. In this way, we are pointed towards our discussion of spiritual ascent in Chapter 8, for Torrance notes that *analambano* directs us to the lifting up of the human heart and will in worship and prayer.[21] This ascent is a distinctly human participation in the triune life of God, a willingness to be borne up by the Spirit into the will of God for us.

The biblical writers were very spare in their descriptions of Jesus' ascension. We are nowhere led into metaphysical speculations or explanations of celestial transport. Charges that the accounts reveal a naïve belief in a three-storied universe cannot be substantiated.[22] As Farrow succinctly writes, 'space travel was never in view'.[23] How did Jesus ascend? Simply, as he had always lived, in active passivity, exercising his will and power in perfect cooperation with the actions of the Father and the Holy Spirit.

Where Did He Go?

Jesus ascended into heaven. He went to the 'place' where God is. As K. C. Thompson has written, 'What makes heaven Heaven is the immediate and perceptible presence of God.'[24] Or, as Barth puts it, 'He returns to heaven, which is the dwelling of God in His creation.'[25] It is as simple and as difficult as that. We know that the biblical writers understood 'heaven' in a multi-layered way. It is, first, the dome of the sky above us, then the vast region of the stars beyond our world, and also the realm of God beyond all sense perception.[26] The word is used, then, in a variety of contexts. But never did Christians believe Jesus had gone to a 'place' we could locate if only we had the right visual equipment. Calvin quips, 'What? Do we place Christ midway among the spheres? Or do we build a cottage for him among the planets?

Heaven we regard as the magnificent palace of God, far outstripping all this world's fabric.'[27]

The Triune God, of course, cannot be limited to heaven, or circumscribed by any 'place', or realm of creation, since he is always more than and beyond, as well as present with, his creation. Yet, heaven is the 'place' where God tells us he dwells, the realm where we, in our finite capacities, are to think of his being. Heaven is the place where the presence of God meets his creatures. As Moltmann writes, 'Heaven is the sphere of creation which already totally corresponds to God because it is totally pervaded by his glory.'[28] Though available to the angelic beings, perception of this place is prohibited to fallen humanity this side of our deaths – except through divine revelation across the divide of our sin and mortality. And even so, we have been given only limited information about heaven now.

Thus, much as Nicene Christians regard the ascension in the flesh to be a real event, we also recognize that the language used to describe the ascension necessarily points to realities beyond human comprehension and of a greater weight than our words can bear. So these realities are described with a measure of symbolism. H. B. Swete invited his readers not to allow the symbolism in which the 'ascended life of our Lord is draped to interfere with ... the actuality of the things that it represents'. He writes:

> With symbols, then, we must be content in this high region of Christian faith. Yet the symbolical need not be fanciful, and in the teaching of the Spirit we are assured that it is not so; here it presents to us certainties as substantial as the physical or historical facts which can be described directly in terms of common experience.[29]

To say that language about heaven is symbolic is not at all to say it is untrue or inaccurate. Rather, we are recognizing that human language is inadequate fully to describe realities of a higher order than we can comprehend. Yet, the biblical language is divinely inspired, and our frail capacities are not an insuperable obstacle to God's revelatory intent. God, therefore, perfectly employing our imperfect words, points us beyond ourselves to realms best described as 'above' our present experience.

With his usual clarity, C. S. Lewis notes how the biblical writers were not naïve about their use of language, but rather were reflecting accurately the way God has designed both us and the world:

> They never thought merely of the blue sky or merely of a 'spiritual' heaven. When they looked up at the blue sky they never doubted that there, whence light and heat and the precious rain descended, was the home of God: but on the other hand, when they thought of one ascending to that Heaven they never doubted He was 'ascending' in what we should call a 'spiritual' sense.
> It is a fact, not a fiction, that light and life-giving heat do come down from the sky to Earth. The analogy of the sky's role to begetting and of the Earth's role to bearing is sound as far as it goes. The huge dome of the sky is of all things sensuously perceived the most like infinity. And when God made space and worlds that move in space, and clothed our world with air, and gave us such eyes and such imaginations as those we have, He knew what the sky would mean to us. And since nothing in His work is accidental, if He knew, He intended. We cannot be certain that this was not indeed one of the chief purposes for which Nature was created; still less that it was not one of the chief reasons why the withdrawal was allowed to affect human senses as a movement upwards. (A disappearance into the earth would beget a wholly different symbolism.)[30]

That Jesus went *up* to heaven we understand intuitively as the direction of transcendence 'hard-wired' into human understanding. We need not worry which 'up' from our spinning, orbiting earth actually reaches toward God's realm. Heaven is higher than we, not lower. It is beyond us, not beneath us. It is without, not within; more than our capacity to hold, not less. Heaven transcends us as a greater, truer, more splendid reality.

We also recognize that Jesus 'has gone through the heavens' (Hebrews 4:14) to be exalted at the right hand of God. We await his return to us from heaven (Philippians 3:20; Acts 1:11), but know that not even the heavenly realms can be said fully to contain him. Jesus has taken his place in the glory of the Triune God. God 'seated him at his right hand in the heavenly realms, far above all rule and authority, power and dominion, and every title that can be given, not only in the present age but also in the one to come' (Ephesians 1:20–1). And here we may say that sitting at the right hand of the Father in no way implies inactivity, but is rather a reference to being exalted to the position of authority and rule,[31] where, as we shall see below, Christ Jesus is most definitely at work.

What Kind of Body?

The man Jesus, risen from the dead, ascended into heaven, where 'in our name and for our comfort' he still lives and acts. But what kind of body does he have that can exist apart from the earth? Again, the answer is deceptively simple. Jesus has a glorious resurrection body, fully human yet perfectly fitted for heaven. He has the same kind of spiritual body which he is going to give to us (Philippians 3:21), so it is not something unrecognizable as human. The Lord Jesus is embodied, yet 'in him all things hold together' (Colossians 1:17). This is no different than in the days of his sojourn among us, except that now that he is absent in body from us, he nevertheless declares 'I am with you always' (Matthew 28:20). The disciples from the beginning understood that the Lord Jesus is present to us through his Spirit. At the most basic level, this should not be a problem.

Augustine comments on the nature of this ascended resurrection body and the limits on human enquiry about it:

> But by a spiritual body is meant one which has been made subject to spirit in such wise that it is adapted to a heavenly habitation, all frailty and every earthly blemish having been changed and converted into heavenly purity and stability ... But the question as to where and in what manner the Lord's body is in heaven, is one which it would be altogether over-curious and superfluous to prosecute. Only we must believe that it is in heaven. For it pertains not to our frailty to investigate the secret things of heaven, but it does pertain to our faith to hold elevated and honorable sentiments on the subject of the dignity of the Lord's body.[32]

The ascended body of Jesus has been 'adapted to a heavenly habitation', and so shall our bodies be. All 'frailty and every earthly blemish' have been transformed. Christ Jesus the man is in heaven with God, still incarnate in a spiritual body, yet in a realm beyond our perception. To speculate further on the details of life in heaven would be 'altogether over-curious and superfluous'. It is enough to know that Christ Jesus is in heaven, still fully human and ever fully God.

Yet early on, influenced by the scandal of the appearance of flesh in heaven, theologians have struggled to understand the limits of the ascended body of Jesus. As we noted above, Origen could not imagine Jesus 'existing in those narrow Limits in which He was once confined for our sakes', nor 'as enclosed in some one place'. There is a human tendency to reduce the tension created by contemplating a man in heaven by over-spiritualizing our understanding of the ascended Lord. These attacks on orthodox simplicity make further reflection on the nature of Christ's spiritual body, Augustine's warning notwithstanding, a necessity.

Gregory Nazianzen (d. 389) refutes two mistaken notions with a powerful affirmation of the continuing incarnation:

> If any assert that He has now put off His holy flesh, and that His Godhead is stripped of the body, and deny that He is now with His body and will come again with it, let him not see the glory of His Coming. For where is His body now, if not with Him Who assumed it? For it is not laid by in the sun ... nor was it poured forth into the air and dissolved, as is the nature of a voice or the flow of an odour, or the course of a lightning flash that never stands. Where in that case were His being handled after the Resurrection, or His being seen hereafter by them that pierced Him, for Godhead is in its nature invisible. Nay; He will come with His body ... If anyone assert that His flesh came down from heaven, and is not from hence, nor of us though above us, let him be anathema.[33]

The Godhead is not stripped of humanity, but adorned with it. The incarnation was not a lightning strike that is brilliant one moment but gone the next. No – though he is in heaven, he remains one of us, wearing the clothes of flesh he acquired on earth, even unto eternity.

Once more, C. S. Lewis sparkles when handling our subject. Considering the nature of the resurrection body of Jesus, he writes:

> He goes 'to prepare a place for us.' This presumably means that He is about to create that whole new Nature which will provide the environment or conditions for His glorified humanity and, in Him,

for ours ... It is the picture of a new human nature, and a new Nature in general, being brought into existence. We must, indeed, believe the risen body to be extremely different from the mortal body: but the existence, in that new state, of anything that could in any sense be described as 'body' at all, involves some sort of spatial relations and in the long run a whole new universe. That is the picture – not of unmaking but of remaking. The old field of space, time, matter, and the senses is to be weeded, dug, and sown for a new crop. We may be tired of that old field: God is not.[34]

The ascended body of Jesus belongs to the new creation. This is full humanity, but untainted by mortal corruption, freed from our bondage to decay and from subjection to futility (Romans 8:20–1). We have to look beyond the paltry limits of our unresurrected flesh but not so far as to look beyond the limits of a human body, glorified and transformed.

If Jesus is in Heaven, How Can He Be With Us?

Our problems, however, are not solved. The difficulties of a man being in heaven resurfaced with vigour during the Reformation. Dispute over the nature of Jesus' ascended body erupted into a full-scale theological battle, with Calvin and his successors against the Lutherans. Following the thorough analysis by James Wagner, we may briefly summarize it. The Reformed position took a literal view of Christ's movement from earth to heaven. The ascension,

with regard to Christ's humanity ... signifies literal, physical translation to the heavenly world; with regard to his divinity, the manifestation of the heavenly majesty in and through the glorified human nature ... The literal, local elevation of the physical body of Christ from earth to heaven is the central concept of the Reformed understanding of the ascension as event.[35]

This understanding follows what I have been arguing throughout: Christ Jesus retains a truly human, albeit glorified, body. The sixteenth- and seventeenth-century theologians went on to delineate that body by saying that it retains all 'essential properties' of humanity, such as 'circumscription, visibility and palpability', while no longer bearing such 'accidental properties' as 'hunger, fatigue, passibility and mortality itself'.[36]

By contrast, the Lutherans believed the Calvinists had become absurdly literalistic about the ascension. The Lutherans agreed that Jesus was locally elevated into the clouds (the 'visible terminus' of the ascension) according to scripture. But they rejected the idea that the ascension could be understood 'in terms of progressive physical movement' from the clouds to the heavenly realm. Rather, Christ returned to his Father, to 'the ineffable glory and majesty of the spiritual world'.[37]

Both sides insisted on the full humanity of Christ being retained and no longer encumbered by mortal frailty and the limits of earthly existence. Both wanted to emphasize how the ascended Christ could be present with his people now. Both held to a 'real presence' of Jesus in the Lord's Supper. Still, exaggeration of the weaknesses of the other's point of view occurred in both camps. Generally the Reformed accused the Lutherans of dissolving the body of the ascended Christ into a ubiquitous omnipresence. John Walvoord summarizes:

> The Lutheran church, following Martin Luther, has generally maintained the doctrine that the body of Christ is omnipresent in contrast to the general position in Reformed theology that Christ is omnipresent only in His deity and is local as far as His body is concerned.[38]

The struggle between the 'ubiquity' of Christ and his 'localized' ascended body worked itself out particularly in regard to the theology of the Lord's Supper, and how Jesus is present to us in that sacrament.

Today, theologians such as Thomas Torrance and Douglas Farrow have enabled us to see that the whole dispute was founded on a faulty conception of space.[39] Calvin's successors as well as his opponents failed to see that he was working towards a *relational* understanding of space in which distance is collapsed by the Holy Spirit.[40] This stunning theological insight outstripped the science of the day, and only makes cosmological sense after the discoveries of modern physics. It deserves considerable attention.

What Kind of Space?

Calvin works out his doctrine of the Lord's Supper on the basis of his doctrine of the ascension, and, in turn, his understanding of the ascension refers repeatedly to the meaning of the Supper. For the nature of the body of the ascended Christ has a direct bearing on how Jesus can be present to us in the sacrament he ordained. Calvin affirms that 'it is the true nature of a body to be contained in space, to have its own dimensions and its own shape'.[41] But this in no way limits Christ:

> For though he has taken his flesh away from us, and in the body has ascended into heaven, yet he sits at the right hand of the Father – that is, he reigns in the Father's power and majesty and glory. This Kingdom is neither bounded by location in space nor circumscribed by any limits. Thus Christ is not prevented from exerting his power wherever he pleases, in heaven and on earth. He shows his presence in power and strength, is always among his own people, and breathes his life upon them, and lives in them, sustaining them, strengthening, quickening, keeping them unharmed, as if he were present in the body. In short, he feeds his people with his own body, the communion of which he bestows upon them by the power of his Spirit. In this manner, the body and blood of Christ are shown to us in the Sacrament.[42]

The ascended Jesus, confined by space, is yet unlimited in his power to communicate all his blessings to his people. The Christ who departs from his people on earth ever sends his Spirit to them. The Holy Spirit, in turn, unites Christ and his church. This is possible because the Holy Spirit is able to relate bodies separated by even vast distances of space:

> Even though it seems unbelievable that Christ's flesh, separated from us by such great distance, penetrates to us, so that it becomes our food, let us remember how far the secret power of the Holy Spirit towers above all our senses, and how foolish it is to wish to measure his immeasurableness by our measure. What, then, our mind does not comprehend, let faith conceive: that the Spirit truly unites things separated in space.[43]

So, rather than make Jesus everywhere present in his humanity along Lutheran lines, a proper doctrine of the Holy Spirit as the bond of the Trinity and the ground of our union with Christ solves the problem. As Farrow succinctly affirms, 'The ascended Lord is not everywhere ... but he *is* everywhere accessible.'[44] Jesus can be both locally circumscribed in a body, though a far greater and more glorious body than we can imagine, and yet related in immediate presence through the Spirit to the entire body of his people.

Calvin goes on to distinguish 'the essence of the flesh from the power of the Spirit, by which we are joined to Christ, though we are otherwise separated from him by a great distance in space'.[45] The Spirit thus relates what is apart. Without any worry of being separated from him by the distance between heaven and earth, between what we know as the physical and spiritual realms, or by any distance in time, we may grasp the full glory of the ascension in the flesh for us:

> In short, let them either deny the resurrection of the flesh or grant that Christ, clad in heavenly glory, did not put off the flesh, but that, since we are to have a common resurrection with him, he will make us partners and companions of that same glory in our own flesh ... But how weak and fragile that hope would be, if this very flesh of ours had not been truly raised in Christ, and had not entered into the Kingdom of Heaven![46]

The continuing humanity of Christ is the pattern and guarantee of the glorified humanity which awaits us. The Spirit links us now to this future as the guarantee of what we await. So, as Paul says, 'hope does not disappoint us, because God has poured out his love into our hearts by the Holy Spirit whom he has given us' (Romans 5:5).

On this basis, Calvin goes on to assert the paradoxical reality that in the Supper, Jesus really feeds us from the substance of his physical body, but he does so spiritually, that is by means of the Spirit. The energy and vigour of the ascended Jesus are poured into us by the conveying work of the Holy Spirit in the sacrament. Calvin avoids any idea of the literal body of Christ being in the elements of bread and wine. But, from the literal body of Christ in heaven there comes to us by means of the Spirit the life-giving virtues of his flesh. Thus we may be assured that Jesus is really present to us in the Supper. He spiritually gives to us from his physical, glorified body!

With remarkable clarity, Calvin explains his stunning understanding of the mystery:

> My conclusion is that the body of Christ is really, to use the usual
> word, i.e. truly given to us in the Supper, so that it may be health-
> giving food for our souls. I am adopting the usual terms, but I mean
> that our souls are fed with Him; or, what amounts to the same thing,
> that a life-giving power from the flesh of Christ is poured into us by
> the medium of the Holy Spirit, even though it is at a great distance
> from us, and is not mixed with us.
>
> Only one problem remains: how is it possible for His body, which
> is in heaven, to be given to us here on earth? Some people think that
> the body of Christ is boundless, and is not confined to any one place,
> but fills both heaven and earth, like the essence of God. That notion
> is so absurd that it does not need to be refuted ... But the sharing in
> the Lord's body, which, I maintain, is offered to us in the Supper,
> demands neither a local presence, nor the descent of Christ, nor an
> infinite extension of His body, nor anything of that sort; for, in view
> of the fact that the Supper is a heavenly act, there is nothing absurd
> about saying that Christ remains in heaven and is yet received by us.
> For the way in which He imparts Himself to us is by the secret power
> of the Holy Spirit, a power which is able not only to bring together,
> but also to join together, things which are separated by distance, and
> by a great distance at that.[47]

In Chapter 8, we will consider Calvin's thought on how
partaking of the still-incarnate Christ through the Supper is vital
to our spiritual ascension. For now, we need simply see Calvin's
passion for his understanding of Jesus ascended as absolutely
essential to Christian theology:

> The whole of Scripture proclaims that Christ now lives His glorious
> life in our flesh, just as surely as it was in our flesh that He once
> suffered; indeed if this foundation is overthrown, our whole faith falls
> into ruins, for what ground is there for our hope of immortality
> except the evidence we have now in Christ? Righteousness was
> restored to us by Christ's fulfilling of the Law in our nature and
> abolishing the disobedience of Adam, and life is restored to us in the
> same way by Christ's opening up to our human nature the Kingdom
> of God from which it had been banished, and by His giving it a place
> in the heavenly habitation. Thus unless we still recognize Christ's
> humanity, all the assurance and comfort that we should have in Him
> perishes. But we do in fact know Christ in His flesh as true man and
> our brother, but we do not know him carnally, for our trust is based
> only on a consideration of His spiritual gifts. He is spiritual to us, not

because He has laid aside the body and been changed into a spirit, but because it is by the power of His Spirit that He regenerates and governs His own.[48]

Holding together the spiritual and the physical, Calvin leapt ahead of his contemporaries, and his thought could not actually be appreciated until a century ago when science began to see past the old dualisms.

With the understanding in physics that the relations between things or persons constitute an essential part of what they truly are, the way was opened for theologians to consider the implications of relatedness in our understanding of God. In his *Space, Time and Resurrection*, Thomas Torrance makes a specific connection with the ascension. He argues that the incarnation represents a coming of God from the place where God is to the place where humanity is. The ascension, then, marks the return of the incarnate Son from 'our place' to 'God's place'. By *place*, however, Torrance means us to think relationally rather than spatially. He cautions us against a 'receptacle' view of space as necessarily containing, or circumscribing, all of Christ. (This was the very mistake made in the Reformed–Lutheran debate on the presence of Christ.) Rather, in a relational sense, God in Christ crosses the divide to enter our existence, our way of being. Then, through this union, Jesus returns, still bearing his humanity, to the place of relation described as the Father's right hand, the 'place' of honour, glory, power and dominion. Thus, heaven as a relational place is where God has 'room' for his divine life and activity in ever-deepening communion with humanity. And humanity (present now in Jesus our ascended head, but one day as his whole assembled body) has 'room' in heaven for an eternal life of relational union with the Triune God.[49]

Still, because a body necessarily occupies space, the spatial distinction is not merely metaphor, but a reality. There is a place where the human Jesus is. There is a heaven in which spiritual bodies occupy space, a created realm in which creatures are, to the limits of their capacity, in the immediate presence of God. Of course, here we are beyond the limits of language and the three-dimensional thinking of our world. What matters is that we hold together the reality that Jesus remains enfleshed, in a glorified, transformed body, with the reality that 'where' he is, in heaven, is a realm beyond our perceptions, beyond our understanding of space and time, yet in the presence of God who is as near as our next breath. The ascension, therefore, represents the departure of the incarnate Son of God back to the place where God is, taking human nature where it has never gone before. As Calvin grasped, by the Holy Spirit we on earth may now be intimately related, in the closest union, with our ascended, yet embodied Lord in heaven.

How Does the Ascension Cause Us to Regard Jesus Now?

One more gem from Torrance's study shows how the withdrawal of Christ from physical contact with us actually sends us back to the historical Jesus as the way in which we are to relate presently to our ascended Lord:

> The withdrawal of Christ from visible and physical contact with us in our space-time existence on earth and in history means that Jesus Christ insists on making contact with us, not first directly and immediately in his risen humanity, but first and foremost through his historical involvement with us in his incarnation and crucifixion. That is to say, by withdrawing himself from our sight, Christ sends us back to the historical Jesus Christ as the *covenanted place* on earth and in time which God has appointed for meeting between man and himself. The ascension means that our relation to the Saviour is only possible through the historical Jesus ... to all eternity God insists on speaking to us through *the* historical Jesus. Just because it is the historical and risen Jesus who is ascended, what Jesus says to us, the Jesus whom we meet and hear through the witness of the Gospels, is identical with the eternal Word and Being of God himself. *Jesus speaks as God and God speaks as Jesus* ... Thus the ascension means that we cannot know God by transcending space and time, by leaping beyond the limits of our place on earth, but only by encountering God and his saving work within space and time, within our actual physical existence.[50]

The ascension of the physical, historical Jesus removes him from our immediate grasp. We cannot simply go and find Jesus somewhere. And yet, it is the same Jesus who was here who has gone to heaven, still himself, still God and man, still enfleshed. That means there is not some other, new Christ to know. So, we are driven back to the place where he was when we could see him, back to the words he spoke when we could hear him with our ears. The Spirit who brings Jesus to us from heaven in mystical, spiritual union is bringing us none other than the Jesus of the gospels. Through means of Word and sacrament, prayer and worship, the Holy Spirit presents the historical, ascended, and still advent Jesus to us freshly in the present moment. So, far from separating us from Jesus, the ascension makes the historical, yet living Jesus, the man in whose face the light of the glory of God shone (1 Corinthians 4:6), our perennial meeting place with God until he returns.[51]

A great many words have been spilled to lay a foundation for considering the meaning of the ascension for the life of the church. Two more brief quotations can pull the threads of the discussion together. First, from Professor Milligan:

> But whatever men beheld in Him then they may still behold in Him, though in indefinitely increased measure, and with means of easier application to their wants. If, as the Lamb that had been slain, He bears upon His Person the marks of Calvary, He bears also in His heart the memories of Cana of Galilee, of Simon's house, of the spot outside the little town of Bethany where Mary wept beside her brother's grave and He wept with her.[52]

And next from Professor Swete:

> But the exaltation and glorification of the Sacred Manhood of our Lord, the exercise by Him of all authority in heaven and on earth, the certainty of His final triumph over sin and death, are facts, and the most potent facts in the life of the human race.[53]

Indeed, the Lord Jesus Christ has ascended into heaven in the selfsame body in which he lived, died and rose in our midst. Glorified now, Jesus wears the flesh which is our inheritance. Though fully human still, and thus embodied, Jesus is yet fully God and able to communicate himself to the members of his body across all distance of realms, dimensions, hours or miles. This is accomplished by the work of the blessed Holy Spirit, who is able, beyond comprehension, to connect those who seem impossibly separated. As we prepare to consider six important themes that arise from the meaning of the ascension in the flesh and the continuing incarnation of the Son of God which it has established, we may agree with Swete that the facts related to this doctrine are 'the most potent facts in the life of the human race'.

Chapter 3

The Triumph of Jesus

The ascended Jesus is the reigning Jesus. Of all the meanings of the ascension, this one is pre-eminent: Jesus has gone up to the right hand of God the Father, exalted above every name and power. He reigns. Jesus is Lord and there is no other. This is the earliest Christian confession, made right in the teeth of the Roman empire. While the boots of the soldiers of the most powerful army in the world resounded in the streets of occupied Jerusalem, an uneducated fisherman from the north of Palestine declared, 'God has made this Jesus, whom you crucified, both Lord and Christ' (Acts 2:36). The man Jesus of Nazareth has been taken to heaven in glory, where he is now exalted as the Son of the Most High God. The meaning of a continuing incarnation is revealed in all its splendour: in the person of the eternal Son, the Triune God has taken up humanity into his being for ever. Jesus is God, and God is nothing apart from or contrary to who he is revealed to be in Jesus. The ascension climaxes in an enthronement. Jesus, the triumphant Word made flesh, takes his place as the regent at the Father's right hand. Now, as Christopher Wordsworth wrote in his hymn, 'Man with God is on the throne.'[1] Retaining his humanity, the Divine Son reigns over the world he has created, and whose re-creation he has established in himself but not yet completed. So the Son 'must reign until he has put all his enemies under his feet' (1 Cor 15:25). In the triune economy, the Son will defeat the last enemy, then hand over the kingdom to God the Father so that 'God may be all in all' (1 Corinthians 15:24–8).

Now, however, as we know all too keenly, is the time of the Already and the Not Yet, the time of the church's sojourn in a world on its way to judgement and re-creation. These are the days of the church's mission to that world. Jesus has vanquished Satan and death, yet these defeated enemies are not yet quiet. Thus, the Son may be 'seated' at the Father's right hand but he is far from sedentary. Rather, he is actively engaged in strengthening his people and subduing the enemy. Though Jesus parts from our sight in the ascension, he does not withdraw from the exercise of his authority or his continuing labour for our renewal.

The greatness of a king has always been known through the generosity of the gifts he bestows on his people. One of the first acts of the enthroned Jesus was to open the treasure trove of his love and bring forth a gem of inestimable value. In his bountiful rule, the King of kings showers a priceless gift from his infinite largesse upon his subjects. He receives the Holy Spirit from the Father and pours him out upon the disciples (Acts 2:33). The Spirit, who gives himself to be so poured, becomes the bond between the still-incarnate Son in heaven and his people still sojourning on earth. By this boon, the physically absent King establishes a living tie between himself and his subjects. The head pours his life-giving energies and constant direction throughout his body (i.e. into his people) through his Spirit. Thus, his servants proclaim the good news of the kingdom of God, preaching the 'times of refreshing' which come through turning in repentance to the forgiving King. They pray and wait for the day when Jesus 'who must remain in heaven' returns physically to the world, when 'the time comes for God to restore everything' (Acts 3:20–1).

Jesus himself understood his departure from his disciples as involving entry into a kingdom. He began his parable of the ten minas, 'A man of noble birth went to a distant country to have himself appointed king and then to return' (Luke 19:12). Swete comments, 'The Kingdom was received at the Ascension, the far journey which carried Jesus from earth to heaven. This was at once realized by the Apostles, so soon as they came under the teaching of the Spirit.'[2] Jesus reigns and we understand that the King will come again to ask for an account from his servants.

The King's story has placed his people under tension. He is not here for us to see, yet he is always about to return. The church is under pressure, by the breath of his Spirit, both as an updraft and a downdraft. On the one hand, we are pushed upward by the commands of the sovereign to look to him as we enact mission in his name. We surge into the future on the wind of his triumph as we live and proclaim the gospel. But, on the other hand, our work is never finished, never to be seen as complete in itself. We are demonstrating the kingdom on earth but not creating the final realm. So, the church labours under the downward pressure of a future that draws nigh, shaping the church, encouraging her in times of resistance and persecution with the promise that the new heavens and the new earth are on the way.

We have noted the human tendency to spiritualize the ascension. At first thought this seems a result of our metaphysical concerns about the seeming split between the spiritual and material realms. But in fact, the mind's balking at Jesus' going up in the body may well result from the revolt in heart and will against the sovereignty of Jesus which his ascension implies. We may desire to reduce the 'eschatological tension' of his absence and imminent return by dismissing his continuing incarnation. Douglas Farrow has paraphrased Cyril of Alexandria in saying that 'The mystery of iniquity is the raising up of more or less plausible alternatives to the rule of Jesus.'[3] Farrow notes that if we spiritualize the ascension, and get Jesus safely diffused and dissolved into the heavens, then he no longer seems a threat to the rulers of the world. Rather, we can neatly divide the regions of authority between the spiritual and the worldly. We can build the wall between public and private truth which protects us from the claims of God. A spiritualized Jesus allows the kings of the world to run free without restraint from the church, and allows the church to run after the things of the world without the downdraft pressure of the return of the embodied Jesus.

A continuing incarnation, however, enthrones Jesus in direct relationship to the world and its rulers. There is a real, human king who reigns over the world from heaven. A man who once walked among us is on the throne, and he is not aloof from the affairs of his realm below. All other powers on earth, therefore, are merely temporary and derived. As Paul asserted, 'there is no authority except that which God has established' (Romans 13:1). This, then, is truly a threatening message to any who make claims of their own sovereignty.[4] It is no wonder that earthly rulers wish to silence the church with violence. Farrow asserts that by the ascension 'the rulers of this world are deprived of their direct authority. They render service as a provisional government while waiting for the true King to appear.'[5]

Jesus in ascending has been crowned as the sovereign of this world. Cleaving to this reality, the church has from the beginning been able to thrive amidst the worst persecution. So an old man exiled on a barren island could send comfort to suffering congregations in the name of 'Jesus Christ ... the firstborn from the dead, the ruler of the kings of the earth' (Revelation 1:5). A Roman official who intercepted a copy of the book of Revelation might have mocked such audacious claims by such an insignificant people. But the Christians understood that the supposed rulers of this world could but exercise 'the last impotent rage of powers that are passing away'.[6] Such faith gave them courage to speak and serve, preach and live against all apparent odds.

With this understanding, the church cannot simply go after the world in its pursuit of the pleasures of the moment, nor can the church let the world go unchecked in its injustice and destructiveness. Today, even as the church loses its voice in the culture, we may recover the understanding of the ascension as a triumphant enthronement. In this way, we may strengthen our identity as citizens of heaven in exile, acting now as loving subversives for the kingdom of Christ, a subject we shall consider further in Chapter 7.

Jesus Glorified in Scripture

Of course the Son of God did not receive any glory at the ascension which he did not already have as the Word begotten from all eternity. Yet as the God-human Jesus, he who was humbled unto death and hell has been lifted up to the highest heaven, to take human nature where it has never gone before. His ascension completed his triumph over sin, death, and the forces of evil. This battle began with his incarnation and continued through the whole course of his obedience. John's Gospel highlights for us that his victory, which leads to his glorification, began with his crucifixion.[7] His ascension in triumph includes his being lifted up in the glory of the shameful cross. Thus Thomas Torrance declares, 'the glorification of Christ begins not with his actual ascension or resurrection, but with his crucifixion and indeed with his ascent to Jerusalem and Calvary for sacrifice'.[8] Though they are separate and distinct events, there is a clear unity between crucifixion, resurrection and ascension which makes them inseparable in understanding the exaltation of Jesus. The triumph of Jesus in the ascension never obscures the path of Jesus' utter oblation. As Matthew Bridges has written in the familiar hymn, 'Behold his hands and side, / Rich wounds, yet visible above / in beauty glorified.'[9] Retaining his flesh, and the marks of its wounding, the Lord demands that his glory, and ours, always be understood in relation to his consecration.

The ascension is not explicitly mentioned in every book of the New Testament, yet each writer assumes it as a fact, and each would answer the question 'Where is Jesus?' with a clear affirmation that he is ruling at the right hand of the Father until the day he returns in glory to this world. Just a sampling of passages provides a lovely cascade of praise to the exalted Lord.

First, from the gospels, Jesus himself anticipated his ascension and exaltation when he said to his disciples in Matthew 19:28, 'I tell you the truth, at the renewal of all things, when the Son of Man sits on his glorious throne, you who have followed me will also sit on twelve thrones, judging the twelve tribes of Israel.' And his closing remarks in that gospel indicate the extent of his power: 'All authority in heaven and earth has been given to me' (Matthew 28:18). In Mark, we hear the High Priest ask Jesus, 'Are you the Christ, the Son of the Blessed One?' and he replies, 'I am, and you shall see the Son of Man sitting at the right hand of the Mighty One and coming on the clouds of heaven' (Mark 14:61– 2). That Gospel concludes, in its longer ending, with 'After the Lord Jesus had spoken to them, he was taken up into heaven, and he sat at the right hand of God' (Mark 16:19). Luke, who records in Acts both the ascension story in detail and its repeated affirmation in the sermons of the apostles, also quotes Jesus responding to the council with the affirmation that 'from now on, the Son of Man will be seated at the right hand of the mighty God' (Luke 22:68). Jesus repeatedly declares in John's Gospel that he is returning to his Father (e.g. Luke 14:12; 17:11; 20:17), and from there he will send the Holy Spirit to teach and encourage his disciples until he returns to take them to the place he has prepared for them (John 14:3).

Our High Priest, Jesus the Son of God, has 'gone through the heavens' according to Hebrews 4:13, and indeed that entire epistle revolves around the work of the exalted Jesus. While James does not mention the ascension of his brother, he does affirm the Lord's return (James 5:7–9), as does Jude (Jude 14, 21), which presupposes a departure in glory. Peter eloquently declares that Jesus 'has gone into heaven and is at God's right hand with angels, authorities and powers in submission to him' (1 Peter 3:22). Some of scripture's most glorious descriptions of the ascended, reigning and returning Jesus are found in John's Revelation, and the book is full of praise to him who is the Alpha and the Omega (Revelation 1:8), 'the ruler of God's creation' (Revelation 3:14). There is no doubt that the New Testament writers understood their glorified Lord to be reigning in heaven.

No one, however, exalted the Lord Jesus higher than Paul, he who once would have thought it the height of blasphemy to consider a human being as having in any sense equality with God. He includes the ascension as an essential part of the 'mystery of godliness' which is a synopsis of the acts of the Son of God who 'appeared in a body' and later was 'taken up in glory' (1 Timothy

3:16). Paul's Christological hymn in Philippians narrates the self-emptying obedience of Christ Jesus, who 'being in very nature God, did not consider equality with God something to be grasped, but made himself nothing' (Philippians 2:6). From the place of utter dereliction on the cross, God exalted Jesus 'to the highest place and gave him the name that is above every name' so that all should confess that 'Jesus Christ is Lord, to the glory of God the Father' (Philippians 2:10–11). In Ephesians, we hear how the Father exerted his 'mighty strength' when he raised Christ 'from the dead and seated him in the heavenly realms, far above all rule and authority, power and dominion, and every title that can be given, not only in the present age but also in the one to come' (Ephesians 1:20–1). Here the ascension (implied, and even required, but not explicitly stated) represents the movement from the nadir of humiliation to the apogee of exaltation begun in the resurrection.

Paul also expresses the glorification of Jesus in terms of triumph over the powers of evil. In Colossians, he links the seeming humiliation of the cross with the disarming of the powers hostile to us through the victory of Christ's sacrifice, the foolishness of God that shames the wisdom of the world. He writes, 'And having disarmed the powers and authorities, he made public spectacle of them, triumphing over them by the cross' (Colossians 2:15). The allusion is to a Roman victory parade, in which a triumphant general would lead his captives through the streets so all could see the spoils of victory. One cannot miss Paul's juxtaposition of the Romans' most shameful method of demoralizing a population through the gruesome use of the cross with Christ's victory rally in winning by dying. The cross of defeat is the triumph of God's love. Yet we know that this metaphor would make little sense if there had been no resurrection in which death's grip on Jesus was snapped, and if the ascension were not the necessary completion of Christ's rising. So we are not surprised to read that in Ephesians 4:8 Paul quotes from Psalm 68: 'This is why it says: "When he ascended on high, he led captives in his train"', for Christ Jesus 'ascended higher than all the heavens, in order to fill the whole universe' (Ephesians 4:10).

The Ascension as Enthronement

Paul's use of an Old Testament passage in relation to the ascension echoes the rest of the New Testament. Indeed Psalm 110 is the Old Testament passage most frequently quoted in the New. Peter quotes from it in his Pentecost sermon. We can see the clear reference to enthronement by examining in larger context a passage to which we have already referred:

> Exalted to the right hand of God, he has received from the Father the promised Holy Spirit and has poured out what you now see and hear. For David did not ascend to heaven, and yet he said, 'The Lord said to my Lord: "Sit at my right hand until I make your enemies a footstool for your feet."' Therefore let all Israel be assured of this: God has made this Jesus, whom you crucified, both Lord and Christ. (Acts 2:33–6)

Peter surely remembered Jesus' own use of Psalm 110, recorded in all three synoptic gospels. Jesus had raised the question of how the Christ could be the son of David: 'If David calls him "Lord," how can he be his son?' (Matthew 22:45). Jesus implied that the Messiah's father is his Father, the eternal God. An inspired Peter grasped that the moment of exaltation at the right hand of the Father had indeed occurred through the ascension.

J. G. Davies has cited research into the Psalms linking the Hebrew New Year's festivals to a liturgical enactment of the enthronement of Yahweh. There were four elements to these celebrations: (1) a procession in which the worshippers ascended the hill of the Temple, perhaps escorting the Ark of the Covenant; (2) a dramatic presentation of the Lord's triumph through his anointed over the powers of evil; (3) a re-enthronement of the Lord as King and that through the person of the current king; and (4) the marriage between God and his people.[10] Davies found a parallel with this pattern in the ascension of Jesus, who ascended into the heavenly Temple after despoiling the powers of evil. He has taken his place as the ruler and prepares for the wedding feast of the Lamb with his bride.

With this background in mind, we may see how the enthronement psalms were used by the church fathers to develop the themes of Christ's triumph in the ascension. The fathers expanded their vision of the ascension by combining elements from these psalms with increased reflection on the relationship between Jesus and the angelic beings of an order beyond our usual sight. Swete gathers up the ideas we shall consider in his vision:

> We see the King's Son, invested with the King's authority, passing through the ranks of the great nobles of the heavenly order; and as He passes, every one of these spiritual powers does obeisance, while from the whole assembly there rises the creed of the primitive Church, *Jesus is Lord.*[11]

These psalms provided a rich source of energy and joy in celebrating the ascension. All the way from Justin to Leo, the patristic writers employed Psalms 24, 47, 68 and 110, among others, to describe the meaning of Christ's entry into heaven. It meant a triumph over the powers of evil, the freeing of humanity from sin, and the opening of heaven, which had once been closed to mortal flesh.

The Victor's Procession in the Fathers

In his *Dialogue with Trypho*, Justin Martyr sought to show how the Old Testament prefigured Jesus Christ. After quoting Psalm 24 in its entirety, he goes on to claim that 'the King of Glory' could not possibly be a reference to Solomon but certainly meant Jesus:

> When our Christ rose from the dead and ascended to heaven, the rulers in heaven, under appointment of God, are commanded to open the gates of heaven, that He who is King of glory may enter in, and having ascended, may sit on the right hand of the Father until He make the enemies His footstool ... For when the rulers of heaven saw Him of uncomely and dishonoured appearance, and inglorious, not recognising Him, they inquired, 'Who is this King of glory?' And the Holy Spirit ... answers them, 'The Lord of hosts, He is this King of glory.'[12]

Justin did not envision the ascension as an instantaneous translation from earth to the right hand of the Father, but rather as a procession that led to the gates of heaven, where angelic sentinels guarded the way to the precincts of God's presence.

Jesus arrived with 'uncomely and dishonoured appearance', caused by his taking up of our humanity and by his passion. Thus still arrayed in our flesh, he was unrecognized by the watchers. Their enquiry, however, was answered by the Holy Spirit, who declared that the still incarnate Jesus is indeed the Lord, the King of Glory.

Justin's speculation that the Son of God, by continuing his incarnation, also continued to bear marks of his humiliation, is echoed in contemporary writers. Barbara Brown Taylor, for example, mentions Jesus' arrival in heaven with our 'ruined flesh'.[13] We sense the passion of this reality in worship when a pastor prays in the name of him who 'took his thorns and wore them as a crown'.[14] In his lovely book *The Return of the Prodigal Son*, Henri Nouwen meditates on Jesus' parable in conjunction with Rembrandt's famous rendering. In the painting, the returning son is on his knees. We see one foot bare and the other barely covered by a tattered shoe. The son's head is shaved – he is utterly stripped of his youthful glory. He buries his face in his father's robes, his eyes closed in exhaustion and relief. The old man has embraced him, and his hands, lit with Rembrandt's signature illumination, gently draw the son towards him in full welcome. Nouwen wonders if this scene could be a symbol not only of our return to God, but also of Jesus' return to the Father, in our name and on our behalf, after going to the far country of the lost world. Completely prodigal in his love for us, the Son spent all he had. He faced complete humiliation and the dereliction of being cut off even from the sense of his Father's presence on the cross. Then, in the ascension, he returned home, ragged from his sojourn with us. The Father embraced him with joyful relief and acceptance, enfolding the Son's humanity into the robes of his presence.[15]

Now we might not want to build our doctrine on this image. The ascension, after all, was a triumph and Jesus went up in a glorified body, no longer subject to mortal infirmity and decay. Yet, Justin and Nouwen have grasped an essential truth. The foolishness and disgrace of the cross became the wisdom and triumph of God. Jesus retains an affinity with our frailty even now. Recognition of Jesus' humility deepens our understanding of his continuing humanity. As George Herbert has written,

> Thy life on earth was grief, and thou art still
> Constant unto it, making it to be
> A point of honor now to grieve in me,
> And in thy members suffer ill.[16]

The ascension was surprisingly different from any worldly victor's parade. For Jesus did not break the bruised reed of our humanity. He repaired it. The ascension in the flesh assures us that he eternally condescends to be bone of our bone, knitted to us in the most intimate union. His conquest does not deprive us but enriches us; does not humiliate us, but ennobles us. The humility of the ascension's triumph is foolishness to a world in rebellion, but life and health and peace to those who follow in his train.

The Stronger Strong Man

Just slightly after Justin, Irenaeus (d. *c.* 200) saw the triumph of the ascension in images of a great war with the enemy of humankind. In *Against Heresies*, he linked his essential concept of recapitulation to the ascension:

> He has therefore, in His work of recapitulation, summed up all things, both waging war against our enemy, and crushing him who had at the beginning led us away captives in Adam ...
> And therefore does the Lord profess Himself to be the Son of man, comprising in Himself that original man out of whom the woman was fashioned, in order that, as our species went down to death through a vanquished man, so we may ascend to life again through a victorious one; and as through a man death received the palm of victory against us, so again by a man we may receive the palm against death.[17]

Because Jesus comprises both 'the original man' from whom all humanity was born and the Son of God by whom all things were made, he is able to save us. His death became our death, and his rising our rising to new life. Thus, the ascension is a great triumph to which we are joined in union with Jesus by the Holy Spirit. In Christ, we have exchanged death's palm of victory against us for

Christ's palm of victory over death, that we might join the chorus
of those who cry 'Hosanna, blessed is he who comes in the name
of the Lord!'

Irenaeus explains further by considering how Satan, the strong
man (alluded to by Jesus in Matthew 12:29), had bound humanity
by enticing us to transgress the law of God. When sin entered the
world, we were enthralled. Humanity entered the 'bondage to
decay' and became 'subject to futility' (Romans 8:20–1). We could
not keep the law nor in any way please God on our own, so we
could not break free of our own accord. Rather, we required
another man to keep the law for us, thus taking our chains and
binding Satan the strong man with them. Irenaeus employs Psalm
68 to describe the triumph:

> The Strong Man proves him to be a fugitive from and a transgressor
> of the law, an apostate also from God. After the Man had done this,
> the Word bound him securely as a fugitive from Himself, and made
> spoil of his goods, – namely, those men whom he held in bondage,
> and whom he unjustly used for his own purposes. And justly indeed
> is he led captive, who had led men unjustly into bondage; while man,
> who had been led captive in times past, was rescued from the grasp
> of his possessor, according to the tender mercy of God the Father,
> who had compassion on His own handiwork, and gave to it
> salvation, restoring it by means of the Word – that is, by Christ – in
> order that men might learn by actual proof that he receives
> incorruptibility not of himself, but by the free gift of God.[18]

In this exposition, it is Satan who is the 'captivity led captive', our
captor now enthralled to Christ. For our Man, the 'right man on
our side', as Luther said, is the true Strong Man. For us, he has
taken on the captor and defeated him. We human beings were the
stolen goods in the claws of an evil possessor, but those claws have
been pried open. He who bound us has been bound by the God-
man, and now we are free. So we also are 'the captivity' now freed
to be Christ's bondservants. For Irenaeus, then, the ascension is the
victory of Jesus, in which he passes through an audience in earth
and heaven, openly displaying the spoils of his victory.

Around the same time, Tertullian added another dimension to
this imagery by interpreting the captivity as the power of death
and our slavery to sin:

Now hear how he declared that by Christ Himself, when returned to heaven, these spiritual gifts were to be sent: 'He ascended up on high,' that is, into heaven; 'He led captivity captive,' meaning death or slavery of man.[19]

In Christ, as Paul quoted, ' "Death has been swallowed up in victory." "Where, O death, is your victory? Where, O death, is your sting?" ' (1 Corinthians 15:55). The ascended Christ reigns. The power of death is broken and the final death of Death is assured: 'For he must reign until he has put all his enemies under his feet. The last enemy to be destroyed is death. For "he has put everything under his feet" ' (1 Corinthians 15:25–7). Freeing us from death, the victorious Christ then sent the Holy Spirit with his manifold spiritual gifts to the apostles.

Though Tertullian also makes reference to Psalm 24, his more striking contribution comes in his imagery of the way to heaven being opened by the ascending Jesus. In the *Scorpiace* he writes:

> Heaven lies open to the Christian before the way to it does; because there is no way to heaven, but to him to whom heaven lies open; and he who reaches it will enter... know that both *that way of ascent was thereafter leveled with the ground, by the footsteps of the Lord, and an entrance thereafter opened up by the might of Christ*, and that no delay or inquest will meet Christians on the threshold, since they have there to be not discriminated from one another, but owned, and not put to the question, but received in.[20]

Here the way of ascent, impossibly steep for unaided humanity, has been levelled by the victorious procession of the incarnate Lord from earth to heaven. Jesus ascending 'paves the way' for us to follow. In the ascension, Christ Jesus opens heaven. As he passes through the gates, the way is made for human beings, in him, also to pass into that communion heretofore blocked by sin and mortal frailty.

The Glorious Entrance

In the fourth century, as the Christological conflicts moved to the fore, Athanasius (d. 373), not surprisingly, used the occasion of Christ's triumph to comment on the meaning of the Word ascending *as flesh*. In this important passage about what Christ has done *for* us by being united *to* us, Athanasius draws out the meaning of Psalm 24:

> And as He Himself, who sanctifies all, says also that He sanctifies Himself to the Father for our sakes, not that the Word may become holy, but that He Himself may in Himself sanctify all of us, in like manner we must take the present phrase, 'He highly exalted Him,' not that He Himself should be exalted, for He is the highest, but that He may become righteousness for us, and we may be exalted in Him, and *that we may enter the gates of heaven, which He has also opened for us*, the forerunners saying, 'Lift up your gates, O ye rulers, and be ye lift up, ye everlasting doors, and the King of Glory shall come in.' For here also not on Him were shut the gates, as being Lord and Maker of all, but because of us is this too written, to whom the door of paradise was shut. And therefore in a human relation, because of the flesh which He bore, it is said of Him, 'Lift up your gates,' and 'shall come in', as if a man were entering; but in a divine relation on the other hand it is said of Him, since 'the Word was God,' that He is the 'Lord' and the 'King of Glory'. Such our exaltation the Spirit foreannounced in the eighty-ninth Psalm, saying, 'And in Thy righteousness shall they be exalted, for Thou art the glory of their strength.' And if the Son be Righteousness, then He is not exalted as being Himself in need, but it is *we* who are exalted in that Righteousness, which is He.[21]

The Word himself did not need to be exalted, 'for He is the highest', but for the sake of our exaltation, the Word as a man was glorified in the ascension. Similarly, the gates of heaven were never closed to the 'Lord and Maker of all', but they were closed to us. Therefore, 'because of the flesh which He bore', the cry comes out to open the gates, and he who never left heaven as the eternal Word returns and enters in as the fully human one. The ascension itself, then, was on our behalf, and represented Christ's triumph *for* us.

While still other fathers, including Gregory Nazianzen and Cyril of Jerusalem,[22] discussed the ascension in terms of exaltation psalms, none approach Ambrose of Milan (d. 397) in his passion and sense of drama. In his *Exposition of the Christian Faith*, Ambrose, unlike Justin, does not envision the returning Jesus as uncomely and disfigured, but as magnified and glorious in his triumph:

Angels, too, stood spellbound in wonder at the heavenly mystery. And so, when the Lord rose again, and the heights of heaven could not bear the glory of His rising from the dead, Who of late, so far as regarded His flesh, had been confined in the narrow bounds of a sepulchre, even the heavenly hosts doubted and were amazed.

For a Conqueror came, adorned with wondrous spoils, the Lord was in His holy Temple, before Him went angels and archangels, marveling at the prey wrested from death, and though they knew that nothing can be added to God from the flesh, because all things are lower than God, nevertheless, beholding the trophy of the Cross ... and the spoils borne by the everlasting Conqueror, they, as if the gates could not afford passage for Him Who had gone forth from them, though indeed they can never o'erspan His greatness – they sought some broader and more lofty passage for Him on His return – so entirely had He remained undiminished by His self-emptying.

However, it was meet that a new way should be prepared before the face of the new Conqueror – for a Conqueror is always, as it were, taller and greater in person than others; but, forasmuch as the Gates of Righteousness, which are the Gates of the Old and the New Testament, wherewith heaven is opened, are eternal, they are not indeed changed, but raised, for it was not merely one man but the whole world that entered, in the person of the All-Redeemer.[23]

Ambrose echoes Peter's assertion that the wonder of salvation had been hidden for ages, searched for diligently by prophets, and had created intense curiosity among the angels. In his dying, rising and ascending, Christ amazed all the heavenly powers and they marvelled at 'the prey wrested from death'. Though 'they knew nothing can be added to God from the flesh', still they rejoiced that he was returning with a defeated Satan and a rescued humanity among his spoils.

In a new twist on the imagery of the gates, Ambrose likens them to the Old and New Covenants. These gates, made of all the imperatives of grace, still remain as the means of entry into heaven. They are closed to the sinful, that is, to all of us. Yet in Christ Jesus, the righteous requirements are fulfilled. So the gates may open; they are not replaced but raised. Now, in him, the world may pass through because 'it was not merely one man but the whole world that entered, in the person of the All-Redeemer'. The victorious Jesus is a mighty conqueror indeed, earning the title of All-Redeemer. His triumph is complete and the spoils of his victory are the salvation of the world.

Though he asserted that the Victor's embrace was all-encompassing, Ambrose was not a universalist. In his exposition, he ran right up against the questions with which the church has struggled for years. Can there be a universal atonement without universalism? What role do I play in a salvation wrought all by Christ? Ambrose seems to have no trouble here affirming both sides at once. The whole world entered the gates in the person of the All-Redeemer. And yet, our ascent into heaven requires faith in Christ. Eight paragraphs later, he writes:

> What shall we do, then? How shall we ascend unto heaven? There, powers are stationed, principalities drawn up in order, who keep the doors of heaven, and challenge him who ascends. Who shall give me passage, unless I proclaim that Christ is Almighty? The gates are shut, – they are not opened to any and every one; not every one who will shall enter, unless he also believes according to the true Faith. The Sovereign's court is kept under guard.[24]

Faith in the universal Saviour is a necessary requirement for entry into his courts.[25]

From the same era, an ascension sermon based on Psalm 24 (spuriously attributed to Chrysostom) adds a lovely thought to the scene of Christ's arrival at the gates:

> For He overcame the enemy; He armed Himself against the tyranny of the devil in a human body, and extinguished his fiery darts, and being nailed to the Cross, and having tasted death, being immortal, He spoiled Hades, and, being manifested as a victor, rose from the dead. Then, having converted the erring sheep, behold He comes up bearing him upon His shoulders to the ninety and nine who had not gone astray, who were in the mountains, i.e. who were feeding in the heavens.[26]

The ascending Lord, strong and mighty in battle, is also the good shepherd who had come looking for his lost lamb, the human race. Within the martial beat of Christ's ascension triumph may be heard the sweet tones of Henry Baker's 'The King of Love', particularly the verse, 'Perverse and foolish oft I strayed, / But yet in love He sought me, /And on His shoulder gently laid, / And home, rejoicing, brought me.'[27] The Victor's medal is the bedraggled lamb round his neck.

Who Was Set Free?

Interestingly, as we have seen in the different shades of meaning in Irenaeus and Tertullian, succeeding fathers had varying thoughts on the meaning of 'he led captivity captive'. Ambrose asserts that it was our affections which needed liberation, as he writes:

> But why should I hesitate to say that the Holy Spirit also is given to us, since it is written: 'The love of God is shed forth in our hearts by the Holy Spirit, Who is given to us.' And since captive breasts certainly could not receive Him, the Lord Jesus first led captivity captive, that our affections being set free, He might pour forth the gift of divine grace.[28]

Shortly thereafter, Ambrose's most famous student, Augustine, would ask in a sermon,

> What is, 'He led captivity captive'? He conquered death. What is, 'He led captivity captive'? The devil was the author of death, and the devil was himself by the Death of Christ led captive.[29]

Death and the devil had held us captive but Christ took Satan captive in his triumph. Chrysostom would have agreed, for he proclaimed, 'And of what captivity does he speak? Of that of the devil; for He took the tyrant captive, the devil, I mean, and death, and the curse, and sin.'[30] In every case, we humans were also the captives, whose very affections had been corrupted, and it took a mighty triumph to subdue our enemies and restore us from the inside out.

In the next century, Maximus of Turin (d. c. 475) also considered the procession of the captives in the victor's train. The bishop from northern Italy may well have had occasion to see such parades down in Rome:

> It was customary, as they say, for the procession of the captives to precede the chariot of the triumphant kings, but the glorious captivity did not precede the Lord when He went into heaven and was not led before the conveyance but itself conveyed the Saviour. For by a certain mystery, while the Son of God carried up the son of man to heaven, captivity itself both carried and was carried.[31]

As Jesus is both the priest and the victim, the lamb and the king,
so in his ascension, he himself was both captor and captive. He as
Son of God carried up captive humanity represented in himself,
the Son of Man.[32]

Reason for Celebration

As the triumphant victory procession of Jesus, the ascension has
provided the occasion for joyful celebrations in the church.
Indeed, the scope of the rejoicing has been quite broad at times.
Professor Davies, in his Bampton Lectures, uncovered yet another
sermon mistakenly ascribed to Chrysostom. This one not only
links the ascension to Christ's victory over the devil, but also ties
it to the blooming of the earth in spring:

> The day of the Lord's Ascension makes the devil lament, but the
> faithful to brighten with joy. For now the pleasant spring comes forth
> and the beautiful young buds grow up: the vine shoots appear heavy
> with fruit: the olive trees come into flower: the fig trees bear early
> fruits: the closely sown fields are stirred by the west wind, imitating
> the billows of the sea: all things rejoice with us at the Lord's
> Ascension. Come now and I will sing you the words of David, which
> he himself proclaimed for us on account of the Lord's Ascension: 'O
> clap your hands, all ye people, shout unto God with the voice of
> triumph; the Lord has gone up with the sound of a trumpet' to where
> He was. He has been received up whence He had not been separated.
> For He who descended is He who ascended above the heavens.[33]

Given the nature of Christ's victory, the very earth itself can
flower, the people leap and the angels shout. The ancient motif of
the greening of the earth under the reign of the true and just King
has come to glorious reality.

In another sermon for Ascension Day, Maximus evokes the joy
inherent in the festival. The heart of the miracle is not just that the
Son of God returned whence he came, but that in doing so 'He
brought to the Father the manhood which He had assumed from
the earth'. This releases a flood of joy in the whole creation itself,
both in heaven and earth:

> The earth rejoices at the Son of God having descended from heaven,
> but heaven is glad no less at the Son of man having ascended from

the earth. 'He sits,' it says, 'at the right hand of the Father.' This was necessary, beloved, in order that the flesh of man, which, when sin was in authority, had been captivated for a long time, might receive the freedom of living there whither sin could not penetrate.[34]

As he ascends, creation is healed. The gulf between heaven and earth caused by human sin is bridged; the rift of our ancient wound is closed. The 'flesh of man' is able to go where it was always intended but had ever been prevented since the Fall – into the courts of heaven and the immediate presence of God. This is the foretaste of 'the glorious freedom of the children of God' in which the entire creation will be 'liberated from its bondage to decay' (Romans 8:21). The ascending, triumphant King is the firstfruit of the new creation. Such is the victory procession of the ascension!

Writing about the same time as Maximus, Leo (d. 461) captured the essence of the thought that had preceded him, as he did so often on the eve of the empire's fall, and so preserved it with clarity for those who would come after. Speaking of the disciples' joy at the ascension, he writes:

And truly great and unspeakable was their cause for joy, when in the sight of the holy multitude, above the dignity of all heavenly creatures, *the Nature of mankind went up*, to pass above the angels' ranks and to rise beyond the archangels' heights, and to have Its uplifting limited by no elevation until, received to sit with the Eternal Father, It should be associated on the throne with His glory, to Whose Nature It was united in the Son. Since then Christ's Ascension is our uplifting, and the hope of the Body is raised, whither the glory of the Head has gone before, let us exult, dearly-beloved, with worthy joy and delight in the loyal paying of thanks. For to-day not only are we confirmed as possessors of paradise, *but have also in Christ penetrated the heights of heaven, and have gained still greater things through Christ's unspeakable grace than we had lost through the devil's malice.* For us, whom our virulent enemy had driven out from the bliss of our first abode, the Son of God has made members of Himself and placed at the right hand of the Father, with Whom He lives and reigns in the unity of the Holy Spirit, God for ever and ever. Amen.[35]

We have gained in Christ more than we lost in Adam! Christ Jesus in his ascension penetrated the heights of the heavens and opened the way for us. He bore our nature, as the hymn says, 'Through all ranks of creatures, / To the central height, / To the throne of Godhead, / To the Father's breast'.[36] The triumphal procession of Jesus has carried us along in his victory train. Our 'vigorous, virulent enemy' has been emasculated! Now Jesus reigns. One day, the victory will be fully realized.

Finally, much nearer to our own age, Swete, with his worshipful style, describes the ultimate goal of the triumphant, ascended Lord:

> The Son, having entered creation by taking our flesh, and having in that flesh overcome Sin and Death, completes His mission by receiving the submission of all creatures to Himself as the father's Representative and Plenipotentiary. But the submission completed, or the enemies that refuse submission destroyed, He will no longer retain the authority which He received as the Christ; and as the Incarnate Son, He will lead Creation in the final subjection to the Father, which fulfills the purpose of the Christian economy. Then the great end will have been reached, and *God* will again be *all in all* – *God*, not the Father alone, but in the fullness of the Divine Name – Father, Son and Holy Spirit; His Name hallowed, His Kingdom come, His will done as in heaven so on earth.[37]

The victory of Jesus, celebrated in the ascension, inaugurates his reign as the God-human enthroned at the right hand of the Father. This economy will continue until the entire creation in Christ Jesus, led by Christ Jesus, submits to the Father and the Triune God again fills all in all. The ascension, then, is the promise of a more complete victory. Our King has gone forth to his throne; he will come again in splendour. In this hope, the church has found its identity in the world, and the more the church has embraced the place of its ascended Lord, the more it has advanced his kingdom.

Chapter 4

The Ascension and the Person of Christ

We have established that the ascension of Jesus means the continuing incarnation of the Son of God as also fully Son of Man.[1] Retaining his humanity is essential for our salvation. Now we must consider that the obverse is vital to theology and the life of the church as well: the doctrine of the ascension ensures that we realize that Jesus of Nazareth continues in his divinity.

Nicene, historically orthodox Christianity understands that the second person of the Trinity came to us *as* a human being. He did not simply enter into a particular man already living. Nor did he merely *appear* to be in a human form as an audio-visual aid to divine communication. The eternal Word took to himself flesh and came among us as one person – one Jesus – in two natures, divine and human. He was truly a man, flesh of our flesh and bone of our bone. But Jesus was never a man apart from or before the eternal Son took human being to himself in the womb of Mary.[2] Once incarnate, however, the union between the divine and human natures in Jesus endures. This reality is disclosed by the doctrine of the ascension, in the ancient affirmation that the risen Jesus of Nazareth was taken up to heaven where he is exalted as the reigning Son at the Father's right hand. Thus, the ascended Christ not only retains his humanity, but the exalted man continues in the fullness of his divinity. And so the very ground of our salvation endures in the one person of Jesus; God and humanity are brought together, and remain together, in him and through him.

Once again, then, the ascension leads us to realize that in knowing Jesus, we know God. In hearing his words preserved in scripture by the inspiration and providential care of the Holy Spirit, we are hearing God speak to us. Professor Andrew Purves has clearly illuminated the thought of his mentor, Thomas Torrance, in writing:

> God is none other than who he is in Jesus (not reducible to Jesus, though this Word is Jesus) and never other than who he is toward us in Jesus. For the person of faith, who knows and loves God in Jesus Christ, there is no hidden God, or some aspect of God now unknown, that will confound us and of which we should live in terror ... who we see God to be for us in Jesus Christ is who God is antecedently and eternally in himself.[3]

This understanding was dearly won by the church in the first centuries after Christ. But before we trace the role of the ascension in patristic considerations of the person of Christ, we should pause to reflect on how urgent their discussion is for us today. For the church's capitulation to culture is not only the result of the attacks of pluralism and materialism from without, but also of the resurgence of ancient challenges from within our ranks.

Urgent Challenges

In our pews, at our church assemblies, and within our seminaries, essential questions are being raised: is the Christ enshrined in our creeds and confessions really anything like Jesus of Nazareth? Or can we find some 'true Christ' who has been hidden for centuries under the agenda of the church? The church today is under the increasing influence of those who would attempt to disentangle the 'real' Jesus from the gospels.

Far more than just the contemporary Marcions, such as the Jesus Seminar, have been raising these issues. For years now, our mainstream seminaries have been graduating ministers who have little confidence in the texts of scripture they are to preach. Our historical-critical methods have deconstructed the texts but we have failed to put them, and our students, back together again. These new pastors leave seminary unsure of what Jesus said and did, and suspicious of the epistles which reflect on the theological meaning of the Jesus presented in the gospels. They have been saturated with trendy reinterpretations but lack an in-depth knowledge of our heritage.

This ignorance has opened the way for ancient heresies to return with new vigour in the church. Many contemporary ministers and Christians function with an adoptionist Christology. That is, we read and hear that Jesus was a man who connected with God so deeply and lived so authentically that he has been called the Son of God. He was not really God incarnate. Rather, Jesus the man discovered 'the divine within' and related to it deeply. He is now an example and guide of what we can be in ourselves, as we, too, are 'Christ-ed' by the influence of the divine.

So, we might read of David Spangler asserting that Jesus was 'the *first* being to become incarnate by the Christ'. Thus, praise for Jesus arises because 'it would have been impossible for the Christ to have accomplished His purpose if Jesus had not made his body available for the three years that the Christ needed it'.[4] The ascension of Christ was, for Spangler, an 'ascension of consciousness' which filtered over the earth. Or we might more readily hear of Professor Marcus Borg interpreting Easter as not 'about literal resurrection but experience of an exalted Jesus as a living reality after his death'.[5] The ascension story would then be an extension of this exaltation of the 'living reality' of Jesus in the life of the church. Under this influence, many of our ministers and teachers have yielded to the ancient temptation to spiritualize what Douglas Farrow has succinctly called 'Jesus-history'.[6]

When such Christology is paired with the search for a Christ behind the gospels in popular biblical scholarship, we are left with a Jesus, and a God, who are ultimately unknowable. Hence, we are back to ancient Gnosticism where only the expert few have enough knowledge to disentangle the texts, read the clues and tell us who Jesus is. Of course, the results of such enquiries may well offer a Jesus strikingly similar to the interests and ideologies of the enquirers! So, distressingly too often, we have considered Jesus to be special, but really no more than a mere man, albeit a rather disturbing subversive peasant.

In my own denomination, the Presbyterian Church (USA), the self-described 'progressive theology' may be understood succinctly in the assertion that 'There is more to the Christ than we know in Jesus.'[7] Of course, the eternal Son cannot be wholly contained in the man Jesus. But, as we will see below, the church has always affirmed that the person of Jesus is wholly God as well as wholly human, and truly reveals the essence of the Triune God, to the fullest extent human capacity can receive. Inserting the definite article between 'Jesus' and 'Christ', while technically correct, comes filled with Christological implications. The article provides a wedge that separates the oneness between Jesus and the eternal Son. Thus, we read that 'Jesus the Christ is fully divine, but God is still more than this,'[8] or, to put it more starkly, 'Jesus is not God, but God is fully incarnate in Jesus.'[9] Into the gap created by such assertions is posited a great ocean of mystery. Within that dark sea, there may be a God who does not require the historic, biblical understandings of atonement, and thus the whole subject of sin may be recast. In those murky waters may well be other revelations from the divine that can free Christians from the sharp edge of the claims arising from the public truth of Jesus-history. So, not surprisingly, the adherents of this theology generally line up behind a social, ethical agenda that would move the church closer to conformity to rather than distinctness from our postmodern culture.

When any denomination of the church can do little more than reflect the values of the society in which it exists, the saltiness of its message and mission is replaced by a bland vagueness. Motivation for evangelism diminishes. Our social pronounce-ments are ignored by a culture that finds us no threat. So today, there is an urgent need to recover a theology that will invigorate us to preach the truth about who Jesus is, and thereby be of use to a world languishing in darkness. The visible ascension of Christ has played an important role in the consideration of his nature and person from the beginning. Tracing the arguments of the patristic writers, we may see how crucial this doctrine is to today's discussions about Jesus.

Biblical and Patristic Texts Relating the Ascension to the Person of Jesus

That Jesus ascended to heaven evokes contemplation of the corollary: he descended from heaven. Who is he, then, that came down to be where we are? This has been the vital question in all of the attacks on the church through the centuries, and especially in the years leading up to and surrounding the Nicene-Constantinopolitan Creed of the fourth century. The theologians summoned to the defence of the truth have had to battle Gnostic heresies denying the physicality of Christ as well as the Arian heresy placing Christ exclusively on the side of the creation. Moreover, they have had to define the relationship between the human and divine natures of Christ to defend against Nestorian confusion. Three texts in particular have historically played an important role in the link between the doctrine of the ascension and the person of Jesus Christ:

1. John 3:13: 'And no man hath ascended up to heaven, but he that came down from heaven, even the Son of man which is in heaven' (Authorized Version).
2. John 6:62: 'What if you see the Son of Man ascend to where he was before!'
3. Ephesians 4:10: 'He who descended is the very one who ascended higher than all the heavens, in order to fill the whole universe.'

The passage from John 3 is especially important, and we shall see it cited throughout the patristic writings.[10] As we move through the teachings of the fathers, we note that theological precision requires saying several things at once and saying those several things together each time. Though difficult to read, the gift of this precision is the accrual of understanding. Thus, many of my quotations will be lengthy, in the hope that the destination will prove worth the rigours of the journey.

In his refutation of the teachings of Noetus, Hippolytus (d. 236) defended the rule of truth against the modalists, who claimed that God the Father only temporarily took the form, or mode, of the Son as he appeared among us. In so doing, Hippolytus employs the ascension to distinguish between the persons of the Father and the Son. Moreover, he sharpens the definition of Christ as the Word incarnate:

> When the Word was made incarnate and became man, the Father was in the Son, and the Son in the Father, while the Son was living among men. This, therefore, was signified, brethren, that in reality the mystery of the economy by the Holy Ghost and the Virgin was this Word, constituting yet one Son to God. And it is not simply that I say this, but He Himself attests it who came down from heaven; for He speaketh thus: 'No man hath ascended up to heaven, but He that came down from heaven, even the Son of man which is in heaven.' What then can he seek beside what is thus written? Will he say ... that flesh was in heaven? Yet there is the flesh which was presented by the Father's Word as an offering, – the flesh that came by the Spirit and the Virgin, and was demonstrated to be the perfect Son of God. It is evident, therefore, that He offered Himself to the Father. And before this there was no flesh in heaven. Who, then, was in heaven but the Word unincarnate, who was dispatched to show that He was upon earth and was also in heaven? For He was Word, He was Spirit, He was Power. The same took to Himself the name common and current among men, and was called from the beginning the Son of man on account of what He was to be, although He was not yet man, as Daniel testifies when he says, 'I saw, and behold one like the Son of man came on the clouds of heaven.'[11]

Hippolytus asserts that the eternal relationship between the Father and his one Son in the Spirit did not change but rather continued when the Son, the Word, became flesh. The oneness in their being endures unabated by the incarnation, when the Word was 'dispatched' to the earth, yet without leaving heaven. The Word's return to heaven still incarnate, however, created a scandal for Hippolytus' Greek readers, from which he did not shy away. He baldly affirms that flesh is now in heaven. Before the incarnation, this could not have been true. But now, the Word made flesh, offering himself to his Father, has ascended to heaven. The Son came down to earth as a man while yet remaining in heaven. The person of Jesus, then, is both the Son of Man with a 'common and current' name, and the Word of God who was from the beginning. The hinge for this understanding is Jesus' declaration of his ascension, which demands both a descent from heaven and a continuing presence there.

A short time later, Novatian (d. *c.* 258) undertook a more precise and systematic exposition of the faith. He, too, would use John 3:13 in defining the person of the Redeemer. In his great work on the Trinity, Novatian writes:

> Who can shrink from declaring without hesitation that He is God, especially when he considers the evangelical Scripture, that it has associated both of these substantial natures into one concord of the nativity of Christ? For He it is who 'as a bride-groom goeth forth from his bride-chamber; He exulted as a giant to run his way. His going forth is from the end of the heaven, and His return unto the ends of it.' Because, even to the highest, 'not any one hath ascended into heaven save He who came down from heaven, the Son of man who is in heaven.' Repeating this same thing, He says: 'Father, glorify me with that glory wherewith I was with Thee before the world was.' And if this Word came down from heaven as a bride-groom to the flesh, that by the assumption of flesh He might ascend thither as the Son of man, whence the Son of God had descended as the Word, reasonably, *while by the mutual connection both flesh wears the Word of God, and the Son of God assumes the frailty of the flesh*; when the flesh being espoused ascending thither, whence without the flesh it had descended, it at length receives that glory which in being shown to have had before the foundation of the world, it is most manifestly proved to be God.[12]

Novatian has beautifully woven the imagery from Psalm 19 of the bridegroom coming from his chambers with the descent and ascension. The eternal Son of God came from the 'ends of heaven' to find his bride, humanity, and united himself to her. He descends as the Son of God and assumes 'the frailty of flesh', espousing it to himself. Then, he ascends as the Son of Man, returning to his bride-chamber in heaven fully united to his beloved. Our feeble humanity now wears the Word of God, not only as our bridal gown but as our eternal marriage gift. The 'mutual connection' between God and man, Word and flesh, in the one Jesus Christ is not only vividly illustrated through his unique descent and ascent, but also dynamically enacted with all its saving implications for us.

In the next chapter, Novatian adds John 6:62 to further his reflection. Here he is concerned that some adoptionists might consider Christ Jesus to be a man only:

> If Christ is only man, why does He say, 'What if ye shall see the Son of man ascending thither where He was before?' But He ascended into heaven, therefore He was there, in that He returned thither where He was before. But if He was sent from heaven by the Father, He certainly is not man only; for man, as we have said, could not come from heaven. Therefore as man He was not there before, but ascended thither where He was not. But the Word of God descended which was there, – the Word of God, I say, and God by whom all things were made, and without whom nothing was made. It was not therefore man that thus came thence from heaven, but the Word of God; that is, God descended thence.[13]

Once again, the ascension illuminates the person and nature of Christ. Christ went up to heaven in our flesh. But Jesus said that the Son of Man would be 'ascending thither where He was before'. There was no flesh in heaven before the incarnate Son ascended. Yet his coming to the Father was not a new trip; it was a return. Only God could have been with God. So, when we look upon Jesus, we are seeing 'God descended thence', the fully human, fully divine one.

Further on, Novatian directly refutes the modalists by employing another key ascension text, Ephesians 4:10. Denying that it was the Father himself who descended to the Tower of Babel and refuting the notion that angels 'scattered abroad the children of Adam', Novatian declares flatly:

> Neither, therefore, did the Father descend, as the subject itself indicates; nor did an angel command these things, as the fact shows. Then it remains that He must have descended, of whom the Apostle Paul says, 'He who descended is the same who ascended above all the heavens, that He might fill all things,' that is, the Son of God, the Word of God. But the Word of God was made flesh, and dwelt among us. This must be Christ. Therefore Christ must be declared to be God.[14]

The essential narrative of the Son of God in relation to humanity depends on his descending to us and then ascending *with* us. The days of Jesus on earth, so ordinary in terms of their brief span, are extended into eternity when we understand that the man Jesus is, in one person, also the Son of God. No one witnessed the descent; it occurred in the secrecy of Mary's womb. Yet the ascension was visible and attested by many. This, then, is the event which enables us to see the life of Jesus of Nazareth in the eternal life of the Triune God. By it, we articulate the wonder of Jesus' days with us – his miracles, his teachings, his crucifixion and resurrection – in terms of the divine–human union. 'Therefore Christ must be declared to be God.'

Advancing a century and a half, we see the argument picked up by the two giants of east and west. In his homilies on John, Chrysostom proclaimed:

> Touching him [Nicodemus] therefore very severely, Christ goes on to show that He knoweth not these things only, but others also, far more and greater than these. And this He declared by what follows, when He said, 'And no man hath ascended up to heaven, but He that came down from heaven, even the Son of Man which is in heaven.'
>
> 'And what manner of sequel is this?' asks one. The very closest, and entirely in unison with what has gone before. For since Nicodemus had said, 'We know that Thou art a teacher come from God,' on this very point He sets him right, all but saying, 'Think Me not a teacher in such manner as were the many of the prophets who were of earth, for I have come from heaven but now. None of the prophets hath ascended up thither, but I dwell there.' Seest thou how even that which appears very exalted is utterly unworthy of his greatness? For not in heaven only is He, but everywhere, and He fills all things; but yet He speaks according to the infirmity of His hearer, desiring to lead him up little by little. And in this place He called not the flesh 'Son of Man', but He now named, so to speak, His entire Self from the inferior substance; indeed this is His wont, to call His whole Person often from His Divinity, and often from His humanity.[15]

Chrysostom interprets Jesus as asserting himself to be not only greater than all the prophets, but of a different order. Enoch and Elijah's ascension notwithstanding,[16] Chrysostom has Jesus declaring that no prophet has really ascended into the heavenly place where God is. Jesus, however, dwells there constantly.

Anticipating a problem which others would state more explicitly, Chrysostom also comments on why Jesus spoke of the Son of Man, a creature, as being in heaven, since until the ascension proper no flesh had entered heaven. For our sake, for our understanding, Jesus often named 'His entire Self from the inferior substance'. So great is the humility of the Son of God and so close his identification with us that he will speak of himself at times entirely from the human point of view.

This passage from Chrysostom also affirms a truth Hippolytus only hinted at: while he was on earth as God incarnate, Christ was yet in heaven, fulfilling his relationship as loving Son of the Father and sustainer of all creation. And more: 'not in heaven only is He, but everywhere'. The Son of God who in assuming flesh became one particular man yet maintained his omnipresence throughout the universe. With John 3:13 as a base, this doctrine so crucial to a proper understanding of the full divinity and humanity in the person of Christ would be developed extensively by the fathers.

Simultaneous Presence

In the west, Augustine also provided a detailed commentary on the reality of the Son of God's simultaneous presence in the flesh and in heaven, in a sermon on John 2:2. Here is sheer theological poetry:

> He departed not from the Father; and came to us. He sucked the breasts, and He contained the world. He lay in the manger, and He fed the Angels. God and Man, the same God who is Man, the same Man who is God. But not God in that wherein He is Man, God, in that He is the Word; Man, in that the Word was made Flesh; by at once continuing to be God, and by assuming man's Flesh; by adding what He was not, not losing what He was. Therefore henceforward, having now suffered in this His humiliation, dead, and buried, He has now risen again, and ascended into heaven, there He is, and sitteth at the right Hand of the Father: and here He is needy in His poor.[17]

Again, the ascension is a driving force in gaining the theological insight. Because Jesus has gone to the right hand of the Father in our flesh, the continuing reality of his being the Son of God and the Son of Man urges us to consider in what way he was two natures in one person during his days on earth. 'By adding what he was not, not losing what He was', the incarnation meant that Jesus fully took up our humanity while retaining not only the essence but the very same relationships, functions and activities of his divinity.

In the Middle East, the mystical Semitic writer Ephraim (d. 373) reflected on this glorious reality. Though the nativity rather than the ascension was Ephraem's inspiration, the richness of his expression is exactly in line with the other Fathers who described the simultaneous presence of Christ on earth and in heaven based on John 3:13.[18] This writer offers, often overlooked in the west, sparkling treasures to contemporary readers:

Glory to that Voice Which became Body, and to the Word of the High One Which became Flesh! Hear Him also, O ears, and see Him, O eyes, and feel Him, O hands, and eat Him, O mouth! Ye members and senses give praise unto Him, that came and quickened the whole body! Mary bare the silent Babe, while in Him were hidden all tongues! Joseph bare Him, and in Him was hidden a nature more ancient than aught that is old! The High One became as a little child, and in Him was hidden a treasure of wisdom sufficing for all! Though Most High, yet He sucked the milk of Mary, and of His goodness all creatures suck! He is the Breast of Life, and the Breath of Life; the dead suck from His life and revive. Without the breath of the air no man lives, without the Might of the Son no man subsists. On His living breath that quickeneth all, depend the spirits that are above and that are beneath. When He sucked the milk of Mary, He was suckling all with Life. While He was lying on His Mother's bosom, in His bosom were all creatures lying. He was silent as a Babe, and yet He was making His creatures execute all His commands. For without the First-born no man can approach unto the Essence, to which He is equal. The thirty years He was in the earth, Who was ordering all creatures, Who was receiving all the offerings of praise from those above and those below. He was wholly in the depths and wholly in the highest! He was wholly with all things and wholly with each. While His body was forming within the womb, His power was fashioning all members! While the Conception of the Son was fashioning in the womb, He Himself was fashioning babes in the womb. Yet not as His body was weak in the womb, was His power weak in the womb! So too not as His body was feeble by the Cross, was His might also feeble by the Cross. For when on the Cross He quickened the dead, His Body quickened them, yea, rather His Will;

just as when He was dwelling wholly in the womb, His hidden Will was visiting all! For see how, when He was wholly hanging upon the Cross, His Power was yet making all creatures move! For He darkened the sun and made the earth quake; He rent the graves and brought forth the dead! See how when He was wholly on the Cross, yet again He was wholly everywhere! Thus was He entirely in the womb, while He was again wholly in everything! While on the Cross He quickened the dead, so while a Babe He was fashioning babes. While He was slain, He opened the graves; while He was in the womb, He opened wombs. Come hearken, my brethren, concerning the Son of the Secret One that was revealed in His Body, while His Power was concealed! [19]

Ephraim's vision beheld Christ Jesus from the womb of Mary through his birth, his life, and his death before returning again to the nativity. Such an amazing use of parallel opposites! Ephraem's language holds together the paradox of the God-man, making us feel the impossible union to be possible:

- 'While He was lying on His Mother's bosom, in His bosom were all creatures lying.'
- 'While a Babe, he was fashioning babes.'
- 'For when on the Cross He quickened the dead'.
- 'He is the Breast of Life, and the Breath of Life; the dead suck from His life and revive.'

We can only wish he had gone on to the ascension during this incredible hymn. I imagine Ephraem adding:

- He went up to heaven, yet undergirds the whole earth with everlasting arms.
- Though He vanished from sight, yet He gives light to every eye that sees by faith.

Thankfully, Augustine did continue from nativity to ascension in his twelfth tractate on John. Our foundational passage from John 3 led him to consider first how Christ was both here and in heaven, and then to his idea of two nativities, (1) the eternal begetting and (2) his birth from Mary:

And He goes on: 'And no man hath ascended into heaven, but He that came down from heaven, the Son of man who is in heaven.'

Behold, He was here, and was also in heaven; was here in His flesh, in heaven by His divinity; yea, everywhere by His divinity. Born of a mother, not quitting the Father. Two nativities of Christ are understood: one divine, the other human: one, that by which we were to be made; the other, that by which we were to be made anew: both marvelous; that without mother, this without father.[20]

As we will consider more fully in Chapter 8, this link to Christ's birth leads to the possibility of our union with his ascension as well:

Come then, brethren! God has willed to be the Son of man; and willed men to be sons of God. He came down for our sakes; let us ascend for His sake. For He alone descended and ascended, He who saith, 'No man hath ascended into heaven, but He who came down from heaven.' Are they not therefore to ascend into heaven whom He makes sons of God?[21]

The person of Christ is our hope of glorification. Because 'God has willed to be the Son of man' we have confidence that he has 'willed men to be sons of God'. United to Jesus who bears two natures in one person, we hope 'to ascend into heaven' as those 'He makes sons of God'.

In a later tractate, Augustine brings in the ascension passage from John 6 to sharpen his articulation of the Nicene doctrine. Comparing the past tense of 'where He was before' in John 6 with the present 'which is in heaven' of John 3, Augustine notes the significance of Jesus' alternating identification as the Son of God and the Son of Man. He comments:

Then what does He mean when He says, 'When ye shall see the Son of man ascending where He was before'? For there had been no question if He had spoken thus: 'If ye shall see the Son of God ascending where He was before.' But since He said, 'The Son of man ascending where He was before,' surely the Son of man was not in heaven before the time when He began to have a being on earth? Here, indeed, He said, 'where He was before,' just as if He were not there at this time when He spoke these words. But in another place He says, 'No man has ascended into heaven but He that came down from heaven, the Son of man who is in heaven.' He said not 'was,' but, saith He, 'the Son of man who is in heaven.' He was speaking on earth, and He declared Himself to be in heaven. And yet He did not speak thus: 'No man hath ascended into heaven but He that came down from heaven,' the Son of God, 'who is in heaven.' Whither tends it, but to make us understand that ... Christ, both God and man, is one person, not two persons ... Christ, therefore, is one; the Word, soul and flesh, one Christ; the Son of God and Son of man, one Christ; Son of God always, Son of man in time, yet one Christ in regard to unity of person. In heaven He was when He spoke on earth. He was Son of man in heaven in that manner in which He was Son of God on earth; Son of God on earth in the flesh which He took, Son of man in heaven in the unity of person.[22]

The very mixing of tenses and titles confirms the unity of the one person of Christ. Jesus is 'Son of God always, Son of man in time'. Yet because of the unity of his human nature with the divine, and because of his unbroken union with his Father in heaven, even during his days on earth Jesus could be understood to be the Son of man in heaven. Augustine arrived at such conclusions, however, because of the doctrine of the ascension. Jesus not only claimed that he would ascend, he did indeed go up to heaven following the glorious triumph of the resurrection.

A few years earlier, Hilary of Poitiers (d. 367), in his great treatise *On the Trinity*, anticipated Augustine in this area. His language is plainer and less vivid than Augustine or Ephraim. Nevertheless, his sobriety warns against excessive speculation even as it affirms the orthodox mystery. With John 6:62 as the ascension text which is the source of his thought, Hilary raises the perennial questions surrounding the virgin birth, then discusses the difficulty of how Christ could both remain in heaven and descend to earth. The paradoxical truth unfolds for us at an intuitive level if we let Hilary take us on his linguistic, theological ride through the reality, letting the scenery roll past us:

For the present I will speak of the Incarnation only. Tell me, I pray, ye who pry into secrets of Heaven, the mystery of Christ born of a Virgin and His nature; whence will you explain that He was conceived and born of a Virgin? What was the physical cause of His origin according to your disputations? How was He formed within His mother's womb? Whence His body and His humanity? And lastly, what does it mean that the *Son of Man descended from heaven Who remained in heaven*? It is not possible by the laws of bodies for the same object to remain and to descend: the one is the change of downward motion; the other the stillness of being at rest. The Infant wails but is in Heaven: the Boy grows but remains ever the immeasurable God. By what perception of human understanding can we comprehend that He ascended where He was before, and He descended Who remained in heaven? The Lord says, What if ye should behold the Son of Man ascending thither where He was before? The Son of Man ascends where He was before: can sense apprehend this? The Son of Man descends from heaven, Who is in heaven: can reason cope with this? The Word was made flesh: can words express this? The Word becomes flesh, that is, *God becomes Man: the Man is in heaven: the God is from heaven.* He ascends Who descended: but He descends and yet does not descend. He is as He ever was, yet He was not ever what He is. We pass in review the causes, but we cannot explain the manner: we perceive the manner, and we cannot understand the causes. Yet if we understand Christ Jesus even thus, we shall know Him: if we seek to understand Him further we shall not know Him at all.[23]

The 'Son of Man ascends where He was before' even as he descended while remaining in heaven. Indeed, 'can reason cope with this? We cannot explain the matter.' The ascension is the corollary of the descent, and both open us to the very heart of the mystery and meaning of the eternal incarnation: 'God becomes Man: the Man is in heaven: the God is from heaven. He ascends Who descended.' Such moving and remaining, remaining and moving can only be understood in terms of the One to which the actions point: the one Christ in two natures. We have leaned on these patristic passages on the simultaneous presence of Christ in heaven and on earth because they are foundational to Christology. This doctrine combats the adoptionism, docetism and Gnosticism resurfacing today. Moreover, these passages are foundational to reclaiming the vital place of the ascension in Christology. By them, we understand that the doctrine of the ascension quite capably grounds, and even establishes, the Nicene Christology on which we rely.[24]

The Ascension and the Pledge

One nuance from the church fathers on the ascension and the person of Christ deserves attention. The passage quoted in Chapter 2 from Tertullian's *On the Resurrection of the Flesh* continues:

the last Adam, yet the primary Word – flesh and blood, yet purer than ours — ... 'shall descend in like manner as He ascended into heaven' the same both in substance and form, as the angels affirmed, so as even to be recognized by those who pierced Him. Designated, as He is, 'the Mediator between God and man,' He keeps in His own self *the deposit of the flesh which has been committed to Him by both parties – the pledge and security of its entire perfection.* For as 'He has given to us the earnest of the Spirit,' so has He received from us the earnest of the flesh, and has carried it with Him into heaven as a pledge of that complete entirety which is one day to be restored to it. Be not disquieted, O flesh and blood, with any care; in Christ you have acquired both heaven and the kingdom of God.[25]

The ascension inaugurates a double pledge of our future in the person of Jesus. The first we recognize easily as the deposit in *our* flesh of the Holy Spirit, who was received from the Father by the ascended Son and then poured out on his disciples (Acts 2:32). But Tertullian discerns that as Jesus went up still wearing our flesh, he now holds in himself the pledge of the resurrection bodies and eternal life in which we will partake. Ascending in the glorified skin and bones of our nature, Jesus guarantees in his very person what we will become, having secured 'an inheritance that can never perish, spoil or fade – kept in heaven for you, who through faith are shielded by God's power until the coming of the salvation that is ready to be revealed in the last time' (1 Peter 1:4, 5). Not only does Christ send the Spirit as a pledge in our hearts, he bears in himself the guarantee of what we will become in union with Christ.

Two centuries later, in still another sermon by an unknown author, yet so close in thought to Chrysostom as to be assigned to him, we hear an echo of Tertullian's formulation:

Above His body, below His Spirit for us ... On account of the flesh which He took up, we are His kinsmen; we therefore have this pledge above, i.e. the body, which He took from us, and below the Holy Spirit with us. And behold the wonder! I do not say that the Holy Spirit came down from heaven and is no longer in heaven, and that having changed places the body is in heaven and the Spirit on earth, but that the Spirit is with us and everywhere and above ... Heaven has the holy body and earth received the Holy Spirit: Christ came and brought the Holy Spirit; He went up and took our body ... We have therefore the pledge of our life in heaven; we have been taken up with Christ.[26]

Christ Jesus went up in our body of flesh, bringing the pledge of our future into heaven. The ascension narrative is the very drama of our assurance. How do we know what our future is in Christ? Because the witnesses saw him go, still in our skin, back to his Father, just as he promised. Moreover, we are not left here as orphans, but bear now in our bodies the Holy Spirit, because Christ has fitted flesh to be a receptacle for him, and in his days among us, as Irenaeus said, accustomed the Spirit to dwell within the human heart.[27] So the ascension inaugurates the double pledge through the person of Jesus. It is the occasion for the taking of flesh to heaven and of the sending of the Spirit to earth. We now have the *arrabon*, the first payment guaranteeing full payment (Ephesians 1:14–15), of all we will receive in union with Christ. By the Spirit of Jesus, we are 'being little by little accustomed to receive and bear God',[28] just as he did on our behalf in his flesh.

The Glory Secured

We may return to Hilary, who illuminates the connection between the person of Christ, his ascension and our hope in him:

> But He Who was the Son of God had become the Son of man also, for the Word was made flesh. He had not lost His former being, but He had become what He was not before; He had not abdicated His own position, yet He had taken ours; He prays that the nature which He had assumed may be promoted to the glory which He had never renounced. Therefore, since the Son is the Word, and the Word was made flesh, and the Word was God, and was in the beginning with God, and the Word was Son before the foundation of the world; this Son, now incarnate, prayed that flesh might be to the Father what the Son had been. He prayed that flesh, born in time, might receive the splendour of the everlasting glory, that the corruption of the flesh might be swallowed up, transformed into the power of God and the purity of the Spirit. It is His prayer to God, the Son's confession of the Father, the entreaty of that flesh wherein all shall see Him on the Judgment-day, pierced and bearing the marks of the cross; of that flesh wherein His glory was foreshown upon the Mount, wherein He ascended to heaven and is set down at the right hand of God.[29]

In taking flesh, the Son of God never 'lost His former being'.

Rather he adds to himself our humanity and prays that that nature 'may be promoted to the glory which He had never renounced'. He ascended still 'pierced and bearing the marks of the cross', the pledge of our inheritance etched in his palms and seared in his side. The unity of the human and divine in Jesus is seen in the ascension to be an eternal reality which gives us an eternal hope.

Returning closer to our age, Andrew Murray has explained:

> What was true of man in promise, we see fulfilled in Jesus: what we see in Jesus, will be made true of man ... His humanity is the revelation of what we can be; His divinity the pledge that we can be it ... It was by his union with us in our life in the flesh, by His identifying Himself with our nature, that Jesus was able to claim and to work out and enter into possession of the glory God had promised to man ... It is when we know that He is one with us and we with Him, even as was the case with Adam, that we shall know how truly our destiny will be realised in Him. His oneness with us is the pledge, our oneness with Him the power, of our redemption.[30]

The person of Jesus is our hope. Redeeming and transforming our nature, he has taken it to heaven where he bears it now faithfully before his Father, in our name and on our behalf. He has come and claimed – reclaimed – the glory intended for humanity but lost in the Fall. Jesus ascended is himself the promise and the hope that we will share in that glory, now in part but one day in full. All depends on our union with his person, our theme in the next chapter.

To conclude here, however, we return to the connection between the ascension, the person of Christ and the theological discussions in our churches. For the present situation of the church, a proper doctrine of the ascension preserves the vital core of historic orthodox Christology: Jesus who walked among us was, and is, truly a man, and also fully God. The ascension provides the narrative structure upon which the clothing of the doctrine may be hung. For the ascension locates our under-standing of the person of Christ squarely within Jesus-history. Our doctrines are not merely speculations imposed on Jesus, but rather arise from reflection upon what happened to Jesus as well as what he said and did. We find, to our relief and felicity, that the historical frame bears the full weight of the Christology.

In fact, the doctrine of the ascension keeps us from collapsing our understanding of the person of Christ into any of the Christological distortions of the present age. For not only does Jesus continue now in our flesh, he continues in his divinity. The fully human Jesus is and ever shall be fully God. The Son of God from eternity, in the fullness of time, took our humanity up into himself as he became incarnate in Jesus. Now, he will keep our humanity in himself beyond all time. So we may joyfully resonate with the doxology of Professor Mackintosh, who frequently declared: 'When I look into the face of Jesus Christ and see the face of God, I know that I have not seen that face elsewhere and could not see it elsehow, for he and the Father are one.'[31] The ascension as an essential part of the story of Jesus protects the doctrine of his person against the pluralizing tendencies of our culture. The ascension was a singular event (as was, of course, the resurrection and indeed the whole course of Christ's sojourn with us) that demands a proper understanding of Jesus to account for it. I believe Professor Mackintosh would agree that not only 'if we regard him as Saviour' but also if we regard Jesus as ascended,

> we must see him at the centre of all things. We must behold him as the pivotal and cardinal reality, round which all life and history have moved. That is a place out of which his Person simply cannot be kept.[32]

When we know the triumphant Jesus as continuing in his full humanity and divinity through the ascension, we are open to the splendour of the riches of understanding him as our head and firstfruits, to which we now turn.

Chapter 5

Union With Christ: The Head and Firstfruits

Jesus' ascent in our flesh to heaven implies a permanent union between his divinity and his humanity in one person. The ascension informs us of the continuing nature of the incarnation. Thus, we have seen that the church fathers worked from the ascension in their discussions of Christ's union with our humanity. The doctrine remained interwoven with the very heart of their theology. Now we turn to consider the obverse: our union with Christ. Because Christ has united himself to us for ever, we may partake of all that he is and all his benefits for us. We are implicated in his life and work. Two important biblical images express this union: Christ Jesus as head and as firstfruits. These have recurred in the patristic discussions of the crucial link between the ascension and our union with Christ. As these twin concepts build on the narrative of the ascension, a rich understanding of the body of Christ emerges. But first, we turn to Athanasius and then the Cappadocian Fathers to lay the foundation.

Just before the passage in *Against the Arians* which we explored in Chapter 3, Athanasius declares:

> Since then the Word, being the Image of the Father and immortal, took the form of the servant, and as man underwent for us death in His flesh, that thereby He might offer Himself for us through death

to the Father; therefore also, as man, He is said because of us and for us to be highly exalted, that as by His death we all died in Christ, so again in the Christ Himself we might be highly exalted, being raised from the dead, and ascending into heaven, 'whither the forerunner Jesus is for us entered, not into the figures of the true, but into heaven itself, now to appear in the presence of God for us.' But if now for us the Christ is entered into heaven itself, though He was even before and always Lord and Framer of the heavens, for us therefore is that present exaltation written.[1]

Since the immortal Word took the form of the servant, both his death and his resurrection occur for the sake of the race of servants, humankind. He died and rose in our flesh so that we may partake of his dying and rising. Moreover, since Jesus entered into heaven still wearing his manhood, he can 'appear in the presence of God for us'. As we saw in the discussion of the triumph of Christ, the eternal Word himself required no exaltation since he is above all. It is therefore on *our* behalf that his exaltation has occurred.

Two sections later, Athanasius continues:

For the fact that the Lord, even when come in human body and called Jesus, was worshipped and believed to be God's Son, and that through Him the Father was known, shows, as has been said, that not the Word, considered as the Word, received this so great grace, but we. For because of our relationship to His Body we too have become God's temple, and in consequence are made God's sons, so that even in us the Lord is now worshipped, and beholders report, as the Apostle says, that God is in them of a truth ... we were exalted because the Highest Lord is in us, and on our account grace was given to Him, because the Lord who supplies the grace has become a man like us. He on the other hand, the Saviour, humbled Himself in taking 'our body of humiliation,' and took a servant's form, *putting on that flesh which was enslaved to sin.* And He indeed has gained nothing from us for His own promotion: for the Word of God is without want and full; but rather we were promoted from Him; for He is the 'Light, which lighteneth every man coming into the world'.[2]

The glorification of the Word in a human body, and the revelation of the Father through that enfleshed one, did not occur so that the Triune God could enjoy something he had not known before by experience. It was all for us! Now, then, 'because of our relationship to His Body, we too have become God's temple'. A mysterious exchange has occurred. The Lord 'has become a man like us ... putting on that flesh which was enslaved to sin'. Athanasius asserts that Jesus fully entered our condition, penetrating even into our humanity that cannot help but sin, thus feeling the full force of our corruption in himself. Yet, from the moment of his incarnation, Jesus was redeeming and cleansing our humanity. For even within our flesh, the Son of God has not become diminished, or stained with our pollution. He wears our sinful skin sinlessly. And so it is we who are changed, 'exalted because the Highest Lord is in us'. Christ's union with us, seen to be eternally perpetuated in the ascension, becomes our hope of glory.[3]

Similarly, the great Cappadocian father, Basil (d. 379), expounds the whole recapitulation of humanity in Christ in the context of celebrating Christ's ascension:

> God showed mercy upon the erring image in creation. What does He do therefore? He fashions again a second Adam, out of nature raising up a patron of nature; and borrowing earth from a Virgin, He gives shape to a new embryo according to a truer image in Himself. He fashions and it remains, and constructing a garment in the womb, as in a royal chamber, He clothes the image in order to veil the nudity of the image. For He displayed Him stronger than deceit and superior to sin; immortal even after death; a deliverer from the tombs who was in a tomb; and crowning Him with immortality, He brought Him back to-day to the heavens, bestowing a decoration upon the whole creation, i.e. the Firstfruits of nature.[4]

The feast of the ascension marks the bringing of the new creation, the new humanity in Christ, back to the heavens. Though the new creation was formed with the stuff of sinful humanity, its association with the Word transformed it from the beginning. This second Adam came from a 'new embryo', which 'borrowed earth' from Mary but was yet by the Spirit a 'truer image' of God than the first Adam. Thus, the Virgin's womb was 'a royal chamber' in which the new man dressed, clothing the nudity of the first, fallen humanity with his glory. 'Immortal even after death', Christ is brought back to heaven by his Father so that the wonderful 'decoration' of this new creation may be bestowed upon the whole of the first creation. In other words, Jesus' return to the Father did not mean the removal of Christ's presence from the earth as if the gift given in the incarnation were withdrawn. Rather, after Jesus ascended, the Father gave the Spirit to the Son, who poured him out on the disciples. Once again we recall this critical passage from Acts in which Peter describes this act of triune self-giving: 'Exalted to the right hand of God, he has received from the Father the promised Holy Spirit and has poured out what you now see and hear' (Acts 2:33). In sending the Holy Spirit, Christ is 'bestowing a decoration upon the whole creation', for the giving of the Spirit is the giving of himself, the new creation of humanity, in union with us. Thus, this decoration is something new and wonderful arriving in the created order. The bestowing of the Spirit not only upon but within us, then, represents the firstfruits of Christ's presence in us as a pledge of the fuller union to come.

Basil's close friend, Gregory Nazianzen, addresses the union of God with us in terms of how Christ Jesus 'ascended into heaven, that He might take you with Him who were lying low'. Again, a marvellous exchange (what Calvin called the *mirabile commercium*[5]) has occurred, whereby through his humiliation we have been exalted:

> Believe that the Son of God, the Eternal Word, Who was begotten of the Father before all time and without body, was in these latter days for your sake made also Son of Man, born of the Virgin Mary ineffably and stainlessly (for nothing can be stained where God is, and by which salvation comes), in His own Person at once entire Man and perfect God, for the sake of the entire sufferer, that He may bestow salvation on your whole being, having destroyed the whole condemnation of your sins: impassible in His Godhead, passible in that which He assumed; *as much Man for your sake as you are made God for His.* Believe that for us sinners He was led to death; was crucified and buried, so far as to taste of death; and that He rose again the third day, and ascended into heaven, that He might take you with Him who were lying low; and that He will come again with His glorious Presence to judge the quick and the dead; no longer flesh, nor yet without a body, according to the laws which He alone knows of a more godlike body, that He may be seen by those who pierced Him, and on the other hand may remain as God without carnality.[6]

Gregory alludes to the theological shorthand formula 'He became what we are that we might become what he is.' Christ's incarnation was complete, thereby applying to 'the entire sufferer', to every part of our lost, defiled, pained humanity. Thus, he could save us in our 'whole being'. Jesus is 'entire Man', yet bears his humanity 'stainlessly'. This union with us was for our sake. Thus, his dying in the flesh was for the sake of our eternal life, and his ascension in the body was so that we could go with him and in him to heaven.[7]

Gregory of Nyssa and the Exaltation of Humanity

Basil's younger brother, and the third of the Cappadocian trio, Gregory of Nyssa (d. 394), also explored what Christ's exaltation means for us through his continuing union with our humanity. Reflecting on the 'mystery of godliness' in 1 Timothy 3:16, he writes:

> He, I say, *was able even to descend to community with our weakness.* Surely, God needs not to be exalted, seeing that He is the Highest. It follows, then, that the Apostle's meaning is that the Humanity was exalted: and its exaltation was effected by its becoming Lord and Christ. And this took place after the Passion. It is not therefore the pre-temporal existence of the Lord which the Apostle indicates by the word 'made,' but that change of the lowly to the lofty which was effected 'by the right hand of God.' Even by this phrase is declared the mystery of godliness; for he who says 'exalted by the right hand of God' manifestly reveals the unspeakable dispensation of this mystery, that the Right Hand of God, that made all things that are … Itself raised to Its own height the Man united with It, making Him also to be what It is by nature. Now It is Lord and King: Christ is the King's name: these things It made Him too.[8]

The infinite love of the Word meant that he simply would not be cut off from us. He came to share all that we are, and so he entered into 'community with our weakness'. He held mortality and infirmity in common with us. Yet, as the Word undiminished, even in such humility he was able to give us his strength. Then, in the ascension, the 'Right Hand of God … raised to Its own height the Man united with It'. The Son of God's enduring union with humanity, far from diminishing his own glory, actually lifts *us* up to the very level of God himself. Christ Jesus as incarnate Son has been exalted to the place he never relinquished as eternal Son of God. Now, the nature he assumed is raised to the heights of heaven. And so, in him, *we* are exalted because he has joined himself to us.

Later on, Gregory of Nyssa clarifies further:

> Since then it was impossible that our life, which had been estranged from God, should of itself return to the high and heavenly place, for this cause, as saith the Apostle, He Who knew no sin is made sin for us, and frees us from the curse by taking on Him our curse as His own, and having taken up, and, in the language of the Apostle, 'slain' in Himself 'the enmity' which by means of sin had come between us and God, – (in fact sin was 'the enmity') – *and having become what we were, He through Himself again united humanity to God.* For having by purity brought into closest relationship with the Father of our nature that new man which is created after God, in Whom dwelt all the fullness of the Godhead bodily, He drew with Him into the same grace all the nature that partakes of His body and is akin to Him.[9]

This is an enormous claim! Our estrangement from God made it impossible that we should ever 'reach' God or enter into communion with him. The incarnate Son, though, in taking our humanity upon himself also took our curse during his sojourn with us. Even so, however, he remained obedient and in 'the closest relationship with the Father'. Gregory declares that by (*a*) his union with us and (*b*) his faithfulness to his Father while among us, the Son 'drew with Him into the same grace all the nature that partakes of His body and is akin to Him'. The relationship Jesus had with his Father while in the world bearing our sinful humanity was the same relationship of perfect oneness he had with him through eternity. His union with his Father thus healed, from the moment of his conception through the whole course of his obedience, the sinful flesh he wore. He slew the enmity between God and humanity. That Father–Son relationship enacted in our skin and in our midst, Gregory asserts, has swooped up humanity in its embrace.

Baxter Kruger explains this understanding of a universal inclusion in the triune life through the incarnation:

The eternal relationship of the Father and the Son in the Spirit has now been *earthed* as Jesus. It has taken shape inside human existence ... The rich and blessed fellowship of the Father and the Son in the Spirit is now and forever a divine-human fellowship.[10]

Because of his kinship with us, all the nature that is akin to Christ's body, that is, all humanity, all flesh, also partakes of that Father–Son relationship.

Before we examine these claims, Gregory has still more to assert, arising from Jesus' conversation with Mary in John 20:17 concerning his ascension, 'Do not hold on to me, for I have not yet returned to the Father. Go instead to my brothers and tell them, "I am returning to my Father and your Father, to my God and your God." ' He writes:

And these glad tidings He proclaims through the woman, not to those disciples only, but also to all who up to the present day become disciples of the Word, – the tidings, namely, that man is no longer outlawed, nor cast out of the kingdom of God, but is once more a son, once more in the station assigned to him by his God, inasmuch as along with the first-fruits of humanity the lump also is hallowed. 'For behold,' He says, 'I and the children whom God hath given Me.' He Who for our sakes was partaker of flesh and blood has recovered you, and brought you back to the place whence ye strayed away, becoming mere flesh and blood by sin. And so He from Whom we were formerly alienated by our revolt has become our Father and our God. Accordingly in the passage cited above the Lord brings the glad tidings of this benefit. And the words are not a proof of the degradation of the Son, but the glad tidings of our reconciliation to God. For that which has taken place in Christ's Humanity is a common boon bestowed on mankind generally. For as when we see in Him the weight of the body, which naturally gravitates to earth, ascending through the air into the heavens, we believe according to the words of the Apostle, that we also 'shall be caught up in the clouds to meet the Lord in the air,' even so, when we hear that the true God and Father has become the God and Father of our First-fruits, we no longer doubt that the same God has become our God and Father too, inasmuch as we have learnt that we shall come to the same place whither Christ has entered for us as our forerunner.[11]

The eternal Son of God became a 'partaker of [our] flesh and blood'. Therefore, he has 'recovered' us. Alienation from the Father is dissolved in Christ's flesh, and now his Father is our Father, and we are his brothers. For Gregory of Nyssa, 'that which has taken place in Christ's Humanity', that is, reconciliation to God and recovery of our relationship to him, is 'a common boon bestowed on mankind generally'. Mixing metaphors, Gregory nevertheless makes his point that the firstfruits have leavened the whole lump of humankind. Because of this union with Christ, where he goes, we go. 'Man is no longer outlawed ... but is once more a son.' So Gregory could declare that as we see Christ enter heaven in the ascension, we know that he went there as our 'forerunner', for we shall follow him to whom we are united.

Gregory of Nyssa's position can be described as *incarnational redemption*, whereby because of the Creator Word's relationship to every living creature as God, what he does in our flesh – living in perfect obedience, dying to and for sin, rising in new life, ascending in glory – becomes a new reality for all of us. His union with us is the very ground of our salvation. George Hendry has explained this tendency in the Greek fathers:

> The gospel, in its simplest terms, is the message of something done by Christ *for* us. To the ancient church it seemed – and rightly – that the vicarious character of the work of Christ could not rest solely upon our subjective appropriation of it ... but must have some prior, objective ground, and they sought this in the idea of an ontological relation between the incarnate Christ and human nature as a whole.
>
> Their chief concern was to insist that the saving work of Christ has an objective reality prior to its subjective appropriation by us ... the work of Christ *for* man was done *in* man prior to its appropriation *by* man and thus to establish an objective ground for the work of Christ in its *vicarious character*.[12]

While there is certainly agreement about the objective work of Christ and its validity prior to its subjective appropriation by us, the relation between the two is a matter of vigorous debate, too extensive to consider here.[13] We may note, however, that even Gregory of Nyssa, perhaps the most universalist of the Cappadocian fathers, nevertheless proclaims in the passage above that Christ's tidings are to the disciples and to 'all who up to the present day become disciples of the Word'. There is absolutely an objective quality to what Christ has done which is completely independent of our response, and there is also a requirement of human response which creates a difference between those who are disciples and those who are not. As Calvin has said, 'as long as Christ remains outside of us ... all he has ... done for the salvation of the human race remains useless and of no value to us.'[14] For our present purposes, we note that Gregory has brought in view the majestic range of what the Word has accomplished in our flesh, and he has directed us towards the heights of where we may go in union with Christ through his ascension.

Our Ascended Head

In his letters to the Ephesians and Colossians, the apostle Paul develops the imagery of Christ as the head, the head of creation and the head of his body the church. Paul declares that God 'placed all things under his feet and appointed him to be head over everything for the church, which is his body, the fullness of him who fills everything in every way' (Ephesians 1:22–3). In Christ Jesus 'dwelleth all the fullness of the Godhead bodily. And ye are complete in him, which is the head of all principality and power' (Colossians 1:9–10, AV). Because Jesus is the last Adam (1 Corinthians 15:45), he is the head of the human race. Because he has been exalted above every name that is named (Philippians 2:9), he is the head of all authority, of all creation. But he has a special relationship as head of his body and bride, the church. Paul asserts:

> Instead, speaking the truth in love, we will in all things grow up into him who is the head, that is, Christ. From him the whole body, joined and held together by every supporting ligament, grows and builds itself up in love, as each part does its work. (Ephesians 4:15–16)

Christ supplies all that the body needs, and we, his members, derive our life and being from him. United to us in a relationship as close as the head and the rest of the body in one person, Christ is truly our life.

Professor Swete explains the necessity of a vital union with the head for the life of the body, both in its members and as a whole:

> He is not only the dominating, directing Power which the Body obeys and follows, but the source of its vitality and of its vital energies ... [.]

From Him comes the principle of growth in the Body, working
through the means of union which connects us with Him in His
ascended life, and operative in each individual member according as
he partakes of the Head's vital power ... The Head of the Ecclesia is
in heaven; but although invisible, He is in the closest union with His
Body, which is on earth. There is a great system of communications
between Christ and the Church, which makes the Head and members
a living unity. Upon the use of this system depends the life or
growth of each member, and the ultimate maturity of the whole
Body.[15]

Jesus our head is in heaven, but he communicates his life through
the Holy Spirit, directing and empowering the members of his
body on earth.

Early in the third century, Irenaeus developed this scriptural
imagery out of a direct consideration of Christ's union with our
humanity. Once again, we find the ascension hidden within a
profound discussion of the person of the God-man and his work
of redemption, working as leaven in our understanding:

For as He became man in order to undergo temptation, so also was
He the Word that He might be glorified; the Word remaining
quiescent, that He might be capable of being tempted, dishonoured,
crucified, and of suffering death, but the human nature being
swallowed up in it [the divine], when it conquered, and endured
[without yielding], and performed acts of kindness, and rose again,
and was received up [into heaven]. He therefore, the Son of God, our
Lord, being the Word of the Father, and the Son of man, since He
had a generation as to His human nature from Mary – who was
descended from mankind, and who was herself a human being – was
made the Son of man. Wherefore also the Lord Himself gave us a
sign, in the depth below, and in the height above, which man did not
ask for, because he never expected that a virgin could conceive, or
that it was possible that one remaining a virgin could bring forth a
son, and that what was thus born should be *'God with us,'* and
descend to those things which are of the earth beneath, seeking the
sheep which had perished, which was indeed His own peculiar
handiwork, and ascend to the height above, offering and commending to His Father that human nature which had been found, making
in His own person the first-fruits of the resurrection of man; that, as
the Head rose from the dead, so also the remaining part of the body
– [namely, the body] of every man who is found in life – when the
time is fulfilled of that condemnation which existed by reason of
disobedience, may arise, blended together and strengthened through

means of joints and bands by the increase of God, each of the members having its own proper and fit position in the body. For there are many mansions in the Father's house, inasmuch as there are also many members in the body.[16]

The incarnation involves a great search and rescue mission. The Word made a foray into the depths of the land of our lostness. He found us, his own handiwork, and returned to heaven bearing us up as a shepherd carries home the lost sheep. He returned as the head of the humanity to which he is joined, offering and commending to his Father that human nature which had been found. As the head rose and ascended, all the 'remaining part of the body', that is, all who are in Christ, will also be taken to heaven. Interestingly, Irenaeus went on to join the metaphor of the many mansions, or rooms, in the Father's house to the image of the many members of Christ's one body. Heaven as the house of God is inseparable from heaven as the one body of Christ at last visibly and completely together.

Ambrose, commenting on 1 Corinthians 11:3, also considers Christ's union with us in terms of his headship:

Christ is indeed, after His divine generation, the power of God, whilst after His putting on of the flesh, He is of one substance with all men in regard of His flesh, excepting indeed the proper glory of His Incarnation, because He took upon Himself the reality, not a phantom likeness, of flesh. Let God, then, be the Head of Christ, with regard to the conditions of Manhood. Observe that the Scripture says not that the *Father* is the Head of Christ; but that *God* is the Head of Christ, because the Godhead, as the creating power, is the Head of the being created. And well said the Apostle 'the Head of Christ is God;' to bring before our thoughts both the Godhead of Christ and His flesh, implying, that is to say, the Incarnation in the mention of the name of Christ, and, in that of the name of God, oneness of Godhead and grandeur of sovereignty.

But the saying, that in respect of the Incarnation God is the Head of Christ, leads on to the principle that Christ, as Incarnate, is the Head of man, as the Apostle has clearly expressed in another passage, where he says: 'Since man is the head of woman, even as Christ is the Head of the Church;' whilst in the words following he has added: 'Who gave Himself for her.' After His Incarnation, then, is Christ the Head of man, for His self-surrender issued from His Incarnation.[17]

Ambrose deftly distinguishes between the absolute equality of the three persons of the Godhead and the understanding of God as the head of Christ, inasmuch as 'Christ' refers to the incarnation of the Son, and his subordination during the time of the economy of our redemption. This Jesus is 'of one substance with all men' because he truly took on 'the reality, not a phantom likeness, of flesh'. He is one with us, and yet our head. He is the first of a new creation as incarnate Son and Lord of all as Son of God. His union with us is organic, and so his headship over his body is real.

Augustine and the Whole Christ

Ambrose's pupil, Augustine, must have loved this image, because he returned to it often. In a sermon based loosely on Matthew 22:42, Augustine proceeds with incredibly clear yet daring theological steps. He segues to a consideration of Paul's pressing on 'for the prize of the high calling of God in Christ Jesus' (Philippians 3:12, AV). This leads him to consider spiritual ascension, which in turn sends him to the oft-cited ascension passage from John 3:13. From there he is able to develop the concept of the whole Christ (*totus Christus*). Only as we are one with the one Christ can we ascend with him. The sermon demands extensive quotation:

> We must journey on then … Run with the heart's affection, journey on with love, ascend by charity. Why do you seek for the way? Cleave unto Christ, who by Descending and Ascending has made Himself the Way. Do you wish to ascend? Hold fast to Him that ascends. For by your own self you cannot rise. 'For no man hath ascended up to heaven, but He that came down from heaven, even the Son of Man which is in heaven.' If no one ascends but He that descended, that is, the Son of Man, our Lord Jesus, do you wish to ascend also? Be then a member of Him who Only has ascended. For He the Head, with all the members, is but One Man. And … no one can ascend, but he who in His Body is made a member of Him … If then the Body of Christ and His members belong to One, do not make two of them. For He left 'father and mother, and clave to his wife, that two might be one flesh.' He left His Father, in that here He did not show Himself as equal with the Father; but 'emptied Himself, taking the form of a servant.' He left His mother also, the synagogue

of which He was born after the flesh. He cleaved to His Wife, that is, to His Church ...

You may know that the Bridegroom and the Bride are One according to the Flesh of Christ, not according to His Divinity (for according to His Divinity we cannot be what He is; seeing that He is the Creator, we the creature; He the Maker, we His work; He the Framer, we framed by Him; but in order that we might be one with Him in Him, He vouchsafed to be our Head, by taking of us flesh wherein to die for us); that you may know then that this whole is One Christ, He said by Isaiah, 'He hath bound a mitre on me as a bridegroom, and clothed me with ornaments as a bride.' He is then at once the Bridegroom and the Bride. That is, the Bridegroom in Himself as the Head, the Bride in the body. 'For they twain,' saith He, 'shall be in one flesh; so now they are no more twain, but one flesh.'[18]

Explanation may only diminish the precision of Augustine's thought, but may at least reinforce what we have heard. We desire the prize of heaven, communion with the Triune God. Our role, which we will consider further in Chapter 8, involves cleaving to Christ. If we desire to ascend with him, we must 'hold fast to him that ascends'.[19] But all our holding and cleaving means nothing without the union Christ Jesus has forged with us, which is mediated to us by the Holy Spirit through faith.

No one can ascend to heaven but the one who descended. No human being has come from heaven except the incarnate Son who has been and ever remains eternally with the Father and the Spirit. Thus, only he may ascend. So how do we ascend? By being united to him.

How do we understand this union? In terms of him who is the head of his body. By becoming what we are, he has united himself to us in the flesh. This union is so close as to be described in the Ephesian terms of the complete intimacy of marital oneness, though even that human image is but a shadow of the reality of Christ's oneness with the Father and his oneness with his body, the church. He is the bridegroom and the head. The only way to God is be part of the whole Christ, who is one Christ, one person in two natures, thus bringing together in himself God and humanity. This occurs through the work of the Holy Spirit who creates the faith in which we are united to Jesus who is united to us.

Other passages clarify this concept even further. Elsewhere, commenting specifically on John 3, Augustine writes:

> 'No man,' says He, 'hath ascended up to heaven, but He that came down from heaven, even the Son of man which is in heaven.' Thus, He says, shall come the spiritual birth, – men, from being earthly, shall become heavenly; and this they can only obtain by being made members of me; so that he may ascend who descended, since no one ascends who did not descend. All, therefore, who have to be changed and raised *must meet together in a union with Christ*, so that the Christ who descended may ascend, reckoning His body (that is to say, His Church) as nothing else than Himself, because it is of Christ and the Church that this is most truly understood: 'And they twain shall be one flesh ...'[20]

Only Jesus Christ can ascend to heaven, because he alone is the man who came from heaven; he alone is God as well as man. So, we must 'meet together in a union with Christ'. That union occurs as Christ, in astounding graciousness, reckons 'His body (that is to say, His Church) as nothing else than Himself'. He became what we are, uniting himself to us, that he may declare us to be one with him. The union was forged in his incarnation. Our participation in that union seems to be based on his royal decree, his reckoning of our position – a creating word by the Word who created all things. This he does by the Holy Spirit whom he pours into our hearts to effect, or actualize, the union he has established.

Further on, Augustine explains that by faith we know that there are not 'two Christs – the one God, the other man – but one and the same God and man'. Therefore, given the unity of his person, how will we not believe that

> His faithful saints become one Christ with the Man Christ, so that, when all ascend by His grace and fellowship, the one Christ Himself ascends to heaven who came down from heaven? It is in this sense that the apostle says, 'As we have many members in one body, and all the members of the body, being many, are one body, so likewise is Christ.' He did not say, 'So also is Christ's' – meaning Christ's body, or Christ's members – but his words are, '*So likewise is Christ*,' thus calling the head and body one Christ.[21]

One Christ, the Son of God, came down to earth. One Christ, the Son of God and Son of Man, ascends to heaven. Those who go with him are no longer their own, but his, their lives 'hidden with Christ in God' (Colossians 3:3), so that the head and body are one.

Swete may here remind us that 'it is of a corporate rather than an individual relation'[22] we primarily speak in discussion of the head and his body. William Marrevee notes the strong influence of Augustine's doctrine of the ascension on his ecclesiology. Christ ascended sends his Spirit to found the church. The head of the church is its cornerstone, and that foundation is in heaven. Thus the church derives its authority and mission not from this world but from above. Though the church, the bride of Christ, may feel like a 'widow', she knows that Christ has actually ascended vested, or clothed, in his church and will return for her on the day of the great marriage supper. Hence, the church on earth tends towards heaven, where the ascended Lord her founder and husband prepares her place.[23]

Christ Jesus is the bridge. In himself, his oneness with the Father extends one way and his oneness with our humanity extends the other. We might almost expect Augustine to draw a picture of the outstretched arms of the Saviour on the cross, bringing God and humanity together in his utter oblation. It is through the ascension that we understand the oneness Christ must have with his body, the church. Since only in him can heaven be penetrated, and only in him is the criterion for ascension met, i.e. that one came down, it follows that we must be united to him in the closest possible conjunction in order to gain what he has for us. As Augustine says elsewhere, the only way we can go up with him is 'as a member fastened into His Body ... therefore this Whole, that is the Head and the Body, is One Christ'.[24] Our spiritual ascension now and future resurrection later is based on his continuing union with us, whereby he has not only created his body the church, but continues to supply its needs, maintaining its very cohesion and constantly sustaining its life as both the proper function of the head, and the loving regard of the bridegroom.

Firstfruits

Another biblical image the patristic writers frequently employed to describe Christ's union with us and developed in connection with the ascension is that of the *firstfruits*. Throughout the Old Testament, the Lord requires this offering of the first, and indeed best, portion of the yield from crops or herds as a sign of our recognition that all things come from his gracious hand. For example, Exodus 23:19 declares, 'Bring the best of the firstfruits of your soil to the house of the LORD your God.' And Deuteronomy 26 describes the offering of the firstfruits as a tangible reminder that it was by the Lord's hand that the house of Israel, his people, were brought out of slavery into the promised land. The people would declare:

> '... So the LORD brought us out of Egypt with a mighty hand and an outstretched arm, with great terror and with miraculous signs and wonders. He brought us to this place and gave us this land, a land flowing with milk and honey; and now I bring the firstfruits of the soil that you, O LORD, have given me.' Place the basket before the LORD your God and bow down before him. And you and the Levites and the aliens among you shall rejoice in all the good things the LORD your God has given to you and your household. (Deuteronomy 26:8–11)

The giving of the firstfruits is an occasion for joy. In returning to God what is his, we are able to rejoice in all we have as a gift from God. The firstfruits are the token of the offering of our very lives to God as a result of realizing that we depend solely upon the loving, sovereign God.

In the New Testament, Paul in particular developed the firstfruits imagery as Christ's triumphant offering of himself to his Father in resurrection as the foretaste and sign of the resurrection that will come to us. We read:

> But Christ has indeed been raised from the dead, the firstfruits of those who have fallen asleep. For since death came through a man, the resurrection of the dead comes also through a man. For as in Adam all die, so in Christ all will be made alive. But each in his own turn: Christ, the firstfruits; then, when he comes, those who belong to him. (1 Corinthians 15:20–3)

Not only Christ's resurrection, but the Holy Spirit in us is part of the firstfruits of all that is to come based on what he has established through his perfect offering to the Father. He sends the Spirit as the pledge, the first flowering, of what will be a glorious harvest. Paul declares, 'Not only so, but we ourselves, who have the firstfruits of the Spirit, groan inwardly as we wait eagerly for our adoption as sons, the redemption of our bodies' (Romans 8:23).

Returning to *Against Eunomius*, we see how Gregory of Nyssa employs the firstfruits imagery in connection with the ascension:

> For men revolted from God, and 'served them which by nature were no gods,' and though being the children of God became attached to an evil father falsely so called. For this cause the mediator between God and man, having assumed the first-fruits of all human nature, sends to His brethren the announcement of Himself not in His divine character, but in that which He shares with us, saying, 'I am departing in order to make by My own self that true Father, from whom you were separated, to be your Father, and by My own self to make that true God from whom you had revolted to be your God, for by that first-fruits which I have assumed, I am in Myself presenting all humanity to its God and Father.'[25]

Christ became what we are and then made himself the firstfruits of all that we will become in him. He, as man, is the first of us, the first-born from the dead, the firstfruits of resurrection. In the ascension, he goes as the firstfruits of 'all humanity' to present us to God, now in him truly our Father.

Further on, Gregory explains a part of how the firstfruits affects the whole harvest:

> Since, then, the first-fruits made the true God to be its God, and the good Father to be its Father, the blessing is secured for human nature as a whole, and by means of the first-fruits the true God and Father becomes Father and God of all men. Now 'if the first-fruits be holy, the lump also is holy.' But where the first-fruits, Christ, is (and the first-fruits is none other than Christ), there also are they that are Christ's, as the apostle says.[26]

Similarly to Augustine's image of the head and body, here the firstfruits affect the whole lump, or harvest. The blessing Christ achieved is 'for human nature as a whole'. By 'means of the firstfruits', Christ's God and Father becomes the Father of 'all men'. Now we may have the same struggle noted above with the universal extent of Christ's union with humanity in Gregory's thought. We may even ask whether this redemptive union is more potential than necessarily actual, and once again wonder about the place of the Spirit's work in effecting the faith necessary for our participation. Nevertheless, we cannot but appreciate the scope of his vision. Christ the firstfruits of humanity is the first of an entirely new harvest of children for the Father. This new crop, the new race, is established by his union with us.

Chrysostom and the Celebration of the Firstfruits

The concept of the firstfruits was particularly beloved of John Chrysostom in his ascension sermons and in those later attributed to him. Professor Davies uncovered this celebratory sermon for Ascension Day:

> But we who appeared unworthy of earth have been led up to-day into the heavens: we who were not worthy of the preeminence below have ascended to the Kingdom above: we have scaled the heavens: we have attained the royal throne, and that nature, on whose account the Cherubim guarded paradise, to-day sits above the Cherubim. But how did this great marvel take place? How were we who had quarreled, who had shown ourselves unworthy of earth and had fallen below our origin – how were we taken up to such a height? How has the strife been brought to an end? How has the wrath been removed? How?
>
> To-day is the foundation of these benefits, *for as He assumed the firstfruits of our nature, so He took them up to the Lord* ... For as it happens in a field of corn, when a man takes a few ears of corn and makes a small sheaf and offers it to God, he blesses the whole cornfield by means of this sheaf, so Christ has done this also, and through that one flesh and firstfruits has made our race to be blessed. But why did He not offer the whole of nature? Because that is not the firstfruits if He offers the whole, but if He offers a little, preparing the whole to be blessed by a smaller amount.[27]

Chrysostom describes the means of offering 'a few ears of corn' in 'a small sheaf' as the firstfruits which 'blesses the whole cornfield'. So Christ Jesus is the one on behalf of the many. By his union with us, what he did as the firstfruits blessed the entire 'crop' of humanity. Chrysostom continues:

> And these things refer to our flesh which He offered. So He offered the firstfruits of our nature to the Father and so the Father admired the gift, and on account of the worth of the offerer and the blamelessness of that which was offered, He received it with his own hands and placed the gift next to Him, and said, 'Sit thou on my right hand.' To which nature did God say: 'Sit thou on my right hand'? To that which heard: 'Dust thou art, and unto dust shalt thou return.'[28]

Now dust sits at the right hand of the Father! As Leo Imperator (d. 911) said on Ascension Day, 'For today our dust is taken up on the shoulders of the cherubim and being received within the inner palace is set upon the royal throne.'[29] In his ascending, the Son offered the firstfruits of our nature and 'on account of the worth of the offerer', we have been received in heaven. What never was in heaven before, human flesh, is now there in Christ, who by virtue of his union with us is the way and the pledge for us.

In a sermon on 1 Timothy, Chrysostom again links our exaltation in Christ, our sharing in the benefits of his ascension, to the firstfruits. It led him to an exceptionally vivid, even stunning, description of Christ's union with us:

> Beloved, see how we are honored! yet some are so unreasonable and so ungrateful as to say, 'Why are we endowed with free will?' But how in all the particulars which we have mentioned could we have imitated God, if there had been no free will? I rule Angels, He says, and so do you, through Him who is the Firstfruits. (1 Cor 15:23.) I sit on a royal throne, and you are seated with Me in Him who is the First-fruits. As it is said, 'He hath raised us up together and made us sit together in heavenly places in Christ Jesus.' (Eph. ii. 6.) Through Him who is the First-fruits, Cherubim and Seraphim adore you, with all the heavenly host, principalities and powers, thrones and dominions. Disparage not your body, to which such high honors appertain, that the unbodied Powers tremble at it.
> But what shall I say? It is not in this way only that I have shown My love to you, but by what I have suffered. For you I was spit upon, I was scourged. I emptied myself of glory, I left My Father and came to you, who hate Me, and turn from Me, and loathe to hear My Name. I pursued you, I ran after you, that I might overtake you. I united and joined you to myself, 'eat Me, drink Me,' I said. Above I hold you, and below I embrace you. Is it not enough for you that I

have thy Firstfruits above? Does this not satisfy your affection? I descended below: I not only am mingled with you, I am entwined in you. I am masticated, broken into minute particles, that the interspersion, and commixture, and union may be more complete. Things united remain yet in their own limits, but I am interwoven with you. I would have no more any division between us. I will that we both be one.[30]

Through the offering of the firstfruits on our behalf, we are seated with Christ in the heavenly places. We are glorified with him. Chrysostom did not want us to doubt one iota the extent of the union the firstfruits has effected. He ran after us in the incarnation and overtook our sinful nature through the whole course of his obedience. Speaking in Christ's voice, John said, 'I united and joined you to myself ... [Now] I not only am mingled with you, I am entwined in you. I am masticated, broken into minute particles, that the ... union may be more complete.' God simply will have 'no more division between us'. Moving from the firstfruits to the sacramental image of the bread and wine, Chrysostom shows how utterly complete is the union of Jesus the God-man with us in our humanity. He allows himself to become completely dispersed within us by the Holy Spirit, as particularly revealed in the sacred supper, that there may be no more separation. He is eaten like a fruit, that his life-giving nourishment might quicken us and raise us up to where he is at the right hand of the Father.

While it would seem that the above passage could not be improved upon, Davies, continuing his unprecedented research, notes an ascension sermon attributed to Chrysostom which urges a response to such glorious conjunction. We are encouraged on Ascension Day to 'leap' and join the preacher in 'a choral dance'. The preacher declares:

> For today our firstfruits ascended up to heaven, and taking up the flesh from us took possession of his Father's throne, in order that He might work reconciliation for His servants, destroy the old enmity and bestow freely upon the men of earth the peace of the powers above. For today he makes available to us a feast in honour of victory over the devil, He makes available the prizes, the crowns and the glory. ... Stand amazed therefore, beloved, at the ingenuity of

the Master, and glorify Him who gives such things freely to thee; for the distinction of the gift surpassed the magnitude of the loss. See, we who were excluded from paradise have even been taken up into heaven itself ... For the Lord of all has ascended, reconciling the Father to the generation of man.[31]

In the ascension are made available 'the prizes, the crowns and the glory'. We who were once excluded from an earthly paradise have now gained entry into 'heaven itself', all because our firstfruits has ascended in our name and on our behalf. The staggering magnitude of our loss in the Fall has been recouped and even more has been given. We have not merely returned to Edenic neutrality but have been granted entrance into heavenly participation in the life of God.

The bringing of the firstfruits to heaven in the ascension has not only freed humanity but vanquished the devil. Another sermon in the style of Chrysostom declares that we ought joyfully to keep the feast of ascension because

> on this day Christ led up the firstfruits of our nature, i.e., the flesh, into the heavens. Wherefore the apostle also said: 'he raised us up with him, and made us to sit with him in the heavenly places in Christ Jesus.' Whence the author and inventor of all evil, the devil, on account of the tumour of pride and the cloud of arrogance, fell down, thither by the greatness of His beneficence, Christ has restored man who had been cast out of paradise by the devil's most evil counsel.[32]

The evil one has been thrown down. And all that is good, all that is joyful and loving in this flesh has been taken up. So dance! Nothing good in our humanity is lost. The memory of a body that works in health is more than recollection: it is now anticipation. The ache of true love once known but now sundered will be filled with glorious reunion. The feeling of the distant memory of Beauty, the ideal of Truth in a fallen world, the longing for Goodness that surfaces amidst the choking thorns of our wickedness, all these will find fulfilment when the firstfruits comes to harvest.

Such hope is born out of what happened when the Son of God, who united himself to us, ascended into heaven still in our flesh. In the next chapter we will consider how our ascended Lord mediates his benefits to us through his continuing High

Priesthood. We give the final word in this chapter to Andrew Murray, who moves us from one topic to the next. Murray sees that because of Christ ascended, we may participate in the heavenly life here on earth:

> And how is this effected? In virtue of His union with us, and our union with Him. Jesus is the second Adam; the new Head of the race. He is it in virtue of His real humanity, having in it the power of true divinity that filleth all. Just as Adam was our forerunner into death, and we have all the power of his sin and death working in us and drawing us on, so we have Jesus as our Forerunner into God's presence, with all the power of His death and His resurrection-life working in us, and drawing and lifting us with divine energy into the Father's presence. Yes, Jesus with His divine, His heavenly life, in the power of the throne on which He is seated, has entered into the deepest ground of our being, where Adam, where sin, do their work, and is there unceasingly carrying out His work of lifting us heavenward into God's presence, and of making God's heavenly presence here on earth our portion.[33]

Jesus has 'entered into the deepest ground of our being'. He is bone of our bone and flesh of our flesh. But that flesh which he shares with us is in heaven, and from there he communicates his heavenly life, the head sending down his vital energies through the Spirit to all the members of his body. Christ's ascension secured not only his place, but by his continuing union with human nature in his glorified flesh he has established for us a dynamic present relationship with him in the heavenlies.

PART III

The Present Implications of Jesus Ascended

Chapter 6

The Priesthood of Christ in the Power of the Holy Spirit

The priesthood of Jesus Christ appears not to be a helpful concept in our churches today. For some, its connection to the Jewish sacrificial system makes the priesthood inscrutable, while others might think that the priesthood of Christ sounds like a medieval Roman Catholic idea. Reformed Christians might dutifully remember the offices of Jesus as prophet, *priest*, and king, though the priest part seems best understood as wholly in the past, as related to Jesus' act of atonement on the cross, and not a living office still exercised by Christ. Nevertheless, to consider the ascension means contemplating his priesthood. The book of Hebrews, above all, links the ascension of Jesus into heaven – even through the heavenlies and into the immediate presence of God – with the ascension of the High Priest into the Temple and even into the Holy of Holies to intercede for all Israel on the Day of Atonement. Without this going into the Most Holy Place with the blood of the sacrifice, the act of atonement could not be complete. Similarly the work of Jesus on the cross would still be unfinished if he had never passed through death and returned to heaven in our name and on our behalf. In fact, the priesthood of Christ helps us see how the act of ascension and the consequent heavenly session of Christ are linked and necessarily always considered together. The ascension, like the High Priest's act of atonement, means that something has been completed (the sacrificial death), and something must go on (the intercession on behalf of the people represented). The priesthood of Jesus, difficult as it is for western minds, is the key to understanding the continuing incarnation. Perhaps a more contemporary story can provide clues for grasping this concept.

In the musical adaptation of Victor Hugo's *Les Misérables*, the protagonist is Jean Valjean, meant to represent Everyman. John the son of John is a man for all of us. Early in the story, Valjean became a factory owner and the mayor of a small French town. In a moment of inattention, however, he allowed a poor single mother to be unjustly sacked from her job at his factory. Desperate to support her daughter, the woman turned to prostitution and was soon taken gravely ill. When Valjean's path crossed hers again, he realized that her suffering was ultimately his responsibility. As she died in his arms, he promised to take her daughter under his protection, raising her as his own.

And so he did, until the day came that his beloved adopted daughter Cossette fell in love with young Marius. Valjean knew then that he would have to let her go, for she was surely meant for more than a cloistered life with a lonely old man. Then, the ill-fated attempt at revolution in France intervened. Marius joined the other revolutionaries on the barricades attempting to face down the French army. Sympathetic to their aims, and hoping to protect Marius, Valjean also joined the rebels. The night before the battle, as the men slept, Valjean gazed at Marius, the young man who won his daughter's heart. He was moved to pray ardently that God on High would spare the boy, even if it meant that Valjean would lose his own life. He pleaded that God would bring him home.

With the dawn, Valjean received the opportunity to be the answer to his prayer. The revolutionaries were massacred. Young Marius was gravely wounded, helpless to flee. Just before the authorities arrived, Valjean hefted the unconscious Marius onto his back and descended into the sewers of Paris. Then Valjean carried the wounded boy through the stinking channels to safety and to a hospital. He did not at first tell Marius who had saved him, but reunited the young man with Cossette, and gave his daughter in marriage to Marius. Hence an older man risked his life to descend into the sewers to carry a wounded man to healing. He passed through the underground, expending all his strength, to haul the man his daughter loved back to her, back to a place of union and love. One man acted on behalf of another, to give his life that the other might live and love.

Valjean is certainly not intended to be an exact allegory for Christ, but we may nevertheless feel the power in the imagery. The Son of God descending became what we are, a man for all men and women. He has passed through the earth to gather his lost and mortally wounded children. Through the sewers of human sin he strode, picking us up, we who were bound for the grave, and carrying us on his back. He walked upstream against the flood of the filthy waters of our defiance and corruption. Jesus brought us through death and into the place of healing and communion. He passed through the veil and into the Father's presence, in our name and on our behalf. He came to us as the representative of God's intentions of love toward us. He returned to his Father, bearing us in his heart, having taken our sins onto his back on the cross, and thus representing us to God. The ascension brings our humanity out of the sewers of sin and into the Father's house, the place of union and communion. This is the essence of priesthood.

The High Priest in Israel

Recalling the Day of Atonement in ancient Israel will open up our understanding of Jesus' priesthood. There were strict divisions in the central place of Hebrew worship, in the days of the moveable Tabernacle as well as in those of the Jerusalem Temple. The Tabernacle, or Tent of Meeting, contained a Most Holy Place, separated by a thick curtain (Exodus 26:33). In this Holy of Holies was the Ark of the Covenant containing the tablets of the law, the rod of Aaron and an urn of manna (Hebrews 9:4). On top of the ark was a mercy seat, with an atonement cover, overlooked by two gold cherubim. This inner sanctuary, then, represented the presence of the Most Holy God, whose name was so sacred it could not be spoken aloud. There were the great gifts of his revelation to his people, the gifts of law and the signs of his everlasting covenant and constant provision for his people. The curtain represented the veil between God and his people, between the Holy One and sinful humanity, between the eternal Lord and frail mortals. No one could go into the Holy of Holies except the High Priest of Israel, and he only once a year.

On the Day of Atonement, the High Priest would dress in sacred garments of linen, over which was placed a breastplate. On that chestpiece were inscribed the names of the tribes of Israel: 'Whenever Aaron enters the Holy Place, he will bear the names of the sons of Israel over his heart on the breastpiece of decision as a continuing memorial before the LORD' (Exodus 28:29). He was going inside in the name of and on behalf of his people. They entered symbolically with him. Calvin comments:

> The high priest used to enter the Holy of Holies not only in his own name, but in that of the people, as one who in a way carried all the twelve tribes on his breast and on his shoulders ... so that they all went into the sanctuary together in the person of the one man.[1]

The High Priest acted as a vicarious man, the one on behalf of the many, taking up all Israel in his person.

The sixteenth chapter of Leviticus details how, before his entry, the High Priest would have to make adequate preparations. Aaron was instructed to bathe himself so that he would be ritually clean before putting on the sacred garments of his office (16:4). Then he had to make personal atonement by offering a bull for the sins of himself and his family (v. 5). In a cloud of incense that kept him from full, immediate and deadly contact with the holy Presence, the priest would enter the Holy of Holies and sprinkle the blood of the bull seven times before the mercy seat (vv. 12–14). These rituals of cleansing, dressing and offering made it clear that he was exercising an office larger than his person. In himself, he could never actually be the one man for the many, but entering the way given by a gracious God, he could, in a sense, step out of himself to be the High Priest for the nation.

The chapter goes on to explain how, once personally prepared, leaving himself behind and entering fully into the office, the High Priest was to sacrifice one of two goats set aside for the Lord (vv. 8–9). The first was offered as a propitiation for the people's sin (v. 15). The High Priest, dressed with the names of his people over his heart and consecrated to his task, would once more enter the Holy of Holies with the blood of the goat. He would take its blood behind the curtain and spread it on the atonement cover of the ark (v. 15). This was enacted intercession. The High Priest served as a mediator between God and the people. For though the scripture texts do not specifically tell us if the priest spoke, or prayed, he knew why he was there. He came as the whole nation, bearing the divinely prescribed sacrifice for sins. His presence was confession of sin. His survival in the presence of the Holy One, who had promised that improper entry into the Holy of Holies would mean certain death (v. 2), was an adequate divine answer: God forgives sin. Perhaps, however, we may go further, following James Torrance in asserting that the High Priest in the presence of God would himself verbally intercede on behalf of all Israel, confessing their sins, recalling the promises of God and claiming his mercy.[2] So he would make an atonement for the sins of all the people.

When he came out from the ark, the High Priest would place his hands on the head of the second goat, the scapegoat. Here, from Leviticus 1–6, we know the High Priest would confess all the sins of the people (v. 21), enumerating their iniquities and thereby putting them onto the goat. Symbolically, then, the priest transferred the transgressions of his people to the scapegoat, which was then sent off into the wilderness. Thus he demonstrated how a forgiving God had removed the sins of the people.

Finally, the High Priest would bless the people. We extrapolate this, not from the actual instructions for the Day of Atonement, but from the actions of Moses and Aaron after the priesthood was instituted. Leviticus 9:22–3 tells us that when they came out from the Tent of Meeting, Moses and Aaron lifted their hands and blessed the people. In Numbers, the Lord gave instructions for how Aaron was to pronounce this benediction, by saying,

The LORD bless you and keep you;
the LORD make his face shine upon you and be gracious to you;
the LORD turn his face toward you and give you peace.
(Numbers 6:24–6)

Then the Lord declared the effect of this blessing: 'So they will put my name on the Israelites, and I will bless them' (Numbers 6:27). Thus, the man who had put the names of the Israelites on his breast as he went into the Holy of Holies then came forth and through his blessing was the means by which the Lord put his name onto all Israel. Invoking the name of the Lord in this benediction transferred the name, the identity and presence, of God onto his people. The blessing was a kind of branding. The people who had had their sins, the defining mark of separation from God, taken away from them now received in return a defining word of acceptance. So the High Priest represented the people to God. And he represented God to the people. He was the bridge, the mediator, the daysman. But all of these symbols were only shadows of the real thing. They were rituals that had to be re-enacted year after year. The people might wonder, even as we do millennia later, how the blood of bulls and goats could actually remove their sins.

Jesus the High Priest

Once we look at the ritual of the Day of Atonement in some detail, we see clearly the trajectories toward the person of Jesus contained in this act that initially appears disconnected from our Christian heritage. Jesus came as our High Priest. Though his words were characteristic of the office of prophet and his lordly miracles bore witness to his kingship, his personal actions revealed his office as priest.[3] The Son of God became a man. He became bone of our bone and flesh of our flesh. He bore our names over his heart. We recall Isaiah's prophecy, 'See I have engraved you on the palms of my hands' (Isaiah 49:16). The ritual garments of his priesthood were the human flesh he cleansed and made pure by the spotless way he wore our fallen humanity. At the beginning of his years of open ministry, Jesus consecrated himself to the task. Though he needed no cleansing as Aaron did, nevertheless the sinless one took a sinner's baptism in the River Jordan as a sign of his identification with us. He lived the life of obedience to his Father until the time came for his ultimate act of faithfulness. He offered the sacrifice for the sins of his people, not a bull or goat, but himself. On the cross, still bearing our names over his heart, he gave himself in perfect consecration. He took upon himself the sins of the world (John 1:29). So Jesus was the scapegoat *and* the sacrifice, both priest *and* victim. Little wonder, then, that the gospels record that at the moment of his death, the great curtain in the Temple separating the people from the Holy of Holies was rent asunder (Matthew 27:51).

Having made a perfect sacrifice, it was time for Jesus to take his offering into the Holy of Holies. Clad now in a priestly garment of glorified flesh, humanity in its fullest, restored unto eternal life,[4] Jesus ascended into the Most Holy Place. So Jesus in his ascension took the offering of his blood into the true Holy of Holies, the presence of his Father.[5] In our name and on our behalf, he offered his perfect life of obedience. In our stead, he offered his sacrifice. And it was accepted. Unlike Aaron, however, Jesus has not yet returned to his people waiting outside. He remains inside 'the inner sanctuary behind the curtain' (Hebrews 6:19). There he continues to intercede for us (Hebrews 7:25), and though he has not yet returned in the flesh to bring the time to consummation, he still blesses us. For, as we have often noted, the ascended Christ receives the Holy Spirit from his Father and pours him out upon the disciples. This blessing, the Spirit, imprints the name and identity of God upon us in an even more potent and dynamic way than the wonderful Aaronic blessing ever could. The Spirit is the living presence of Christ poured out into our hearts (Romans 5:5), uniting us to our great High Priest who has entered behind the veil in our name and on our behalf, and gifting us for his service in the world.

On the basis of all of the above, Hebrews assures us that we may now draw near the throne of God in all confidence of access (Hebrews 4:16; 10:19). Now the Holy of Holies is opened to humanity. The way is clear. By the conveyance of the Holy Spirit, we may go into the presence of God and be accepted if we go under the cover of our priest, Jesus. In his name, that is, in union with Christ, we are, by the Spirit, carried on his back. Such a journey in the present is a spiritual one, but in our resurrection we will, glorified body and soul as one, be taken in Christ by the Spirit to the Father's presence. So Jesus in himself is the new and living way (Hebrews 10:20) to God his Father.

Before we explore in more detail some aspects of this priesthood, we may summarize what has been said so far with an illustration from daily life. Many women, in fact, may be able to feel this journey of our High Priest in their very bodies. A child is conceived through the loving communion of husband and wife. The child grows inside the sheltering womb of the mother. But the wee one cannot live there for ever. He is made for another world, a world of daylight and air, starlight and sky. He will die if he stays past his time. So in the hours of her labour, the mother offers a new and living way. She is rent asunder that a passage might be made from the darkness into the light. The way to life as a human being in the world passes through the curtain of her flesh. Every birth is a kind of death for the mother, and sometimes a literal one. The curtain must be rent that the child might live and reach the daylight world. She is the new and living way. By her pain, the child is born.

Not one of us is here of our own volition or achievement. No one lives in isolation. We are made when two become one. We are born when one spends herself and is torn that we might emerge. We grow because someone gives life to nurture us. So we do not reach God by right, or by human will, or by our own strength. For we are separated from him. By our mortal limitations, yes. But most deeply by our sin. We are blind to God unless he shines his light in our hearts. We are terrified of him unless he reveals his love. We are lost from him unless he makes a way.

Jesus Christ ascending passes through the heavens and goes where no flesh has gone before: into the other realm, into the immediate presence of God. And he goes, as he says in the Fourth Gospel, 'that you also may be where I am' (John 14:3). In his

Father's house are many mansions. He has gone to prepare a place for us, and he will take us there on the day when soul and body are reunited in glorious resurrection.

But now, right now, the way of access to God has been opened. Now, we may draw near to the presence of God, our hearts, as Hebrews tells us, sprinkled clean by his blood (Hebrews 10:22). Our High Priest has made the way. He is the forerunner. He has gone before us. And so we have hope. This hope, we are told, is an anchor for the soul. But more, this hope runs ahead of us and enters the place where Jesus is on our behalf (Hebrews 6:19–20).

Marius was saved because Jean Valjean carried the man with the mortal wound through the stinking sewers of Paris to a healing place. A child is born because a mother is spent and sundered. We feel in our bones the truth of this. We may live through another. We must, for alone we will die. As Calvin discerns, 'there is need of a Mediator to appear in our name, and carry us on his shoulders and keep us bound upon his breast'.[6] Christ has gone before us. He passed through the sewers of human sin and made a way to the healing place. He himself was rent that the curtain might be pierced and a new and living way opened. He is that way. We travel to God the Father in and through him by the power and conveyance of the Holy Spirit.

The Offering and the Intercession

The offering of Jesus once and for all on the cross fulfilled and supplanted the old system of repeated sacrifices for sin. Both priest and victim, Jesus offered himself, once for all time, the one on behalf of the many. Because of the excellency of his sacrifice, the offering up of 'the Lamb of God, who takes away the sin of the world' (John 1:29), no other offering for sin ever needs to be made. Now, seated at the Father's right hand, he ever lives to make intercession for us (Romans 8:34; Hebrews 7:25).

Yet, through the centuries an understanding developed of the sacrament of the Lord's Supper as a bloodless repetition of the sacrifice of Christ. As transubstantiation dominated the medieval understanding of the Eucharist, the elements of bread and wine were considered to become literally Jesus' body and blood. Therefore, what was offered at the altar was really Jesus. This was not a new sacrifice, but a living, present repetition of his self-offering on the cross. The sacrifice of the Mass became necessary for the removal of present sins.[7] Thus a layer of a near-magic rite accrued to the Lord's Supper.

The Reformers saw in this misunderstanding the return of the entire Jewish sacrificial system. Jesus' once-for-all offering was being perceived as not sufficient and people had to rely on partaking of the sacrifice of the Mass for current and true forgiveness. As Calvin observes, the Roman Catholics 'require daily applications through sacrifice for the death of Christ to be efficacious for us, so that there is no difference between Christians and Jews except in the outward sign'.[8] In their return to *sola fidei, sola gratis, sola Scriptura* the Reformers turned our attention back to the sufficiency of the cross. Citing Hebrews 10, Calvin declares, 'The rite of continual sacrifice was done away with by the coming of Christ.'[9] Thus, any idea of a perpetual offering or continuing sacrifice was steadfastly avoided.

As with any strong reaction necessary to counter a dominant ideology, however, one may err in the opposite direction. Hence we may see an understanding of the offering of Christ even today so intent on preserving the once-and-for-all quality of the cross that the entire priesthood of Jesus is considered as a past transaction and, references to Melchizedek's eternal priesthood notwithstanding, its present reality is neglected. This tendency toward an *ab extra* view of Christ's priesthood greatly diminishes our enjoyment of Christ's present work in his continuing incarnation.

Three of the theologians of the ascension we have been following – Milligan, Swete and Torrance – have attempted to recover a fuller understanding of Jesus as our High Priest, a subject surprisingly not well-developed in the patristic writings.[10] Unfortunately, they occasionally have been misinterpreted and wrongly criticized. By examining these objections and then answering them from the writings of the theologians themselves, we may sharpen our understanding of the priesthood of the ascended Jesus.

John Walvoord, in his article on 'The Present Work of Christ in Heaven', objects to the Roman doctrine of perpetual offering of sacrifice being necessary to the perpetual priesthood of Christ. In the process of this correction, however, he links our Protestant theologians with this position. Walvoord mentions that William Milligan 'takes the position that the work of Christ in sacrifice cannot be limited to earth and therefore has an element of continuance in his present ministry in heaven'. He then notes that Swete's understanding of propitiation being continued in Christ's eternal priesthood 'detracts from the concept of the work of propitiation as finished on the cross'.[11]

Peter Toon picks up Walvoord's thread in his book on the ascension. His concern is a too-close combining of the offering with the intercession, so that Christ's once-for-all sacrifice is given a present, continuing dimension. Toon notes first that Christ entered heaven not *with* his blood but *through* his blood (Hebrews 9:12), so that the shedding of blood is completed on earth at the cross. Jesus did not really need to sprinkle his actual blood in the heavenly places in exact parallel to the Day of Atonement rites. Furthermore, the posture of Christ after his ascension, *sitting* at the right hand of the Father, signifies a completed action. There is no more to be done or offered. Jesus is completely and eternally accepted by his Father. Thirdly, Toon notes the emphatic use of *ephapax* in Hebrews 7:27 to mean that Christ offered up Himself 'truly once for all'. These excellent points Toon contrasts with those of Milligan, Swete and Torrance in their various references to Christ's continuing self-offering to the Father. They have, according to Toon, conflated the offering with the intercession, making it continuous instead of completed. His solution is to consider how 'As glorified Man with a vicarious humanity, Jesus prays the prayers of all his people ... Such prayer proceeds because of the accomplished work of Christ on the cross.' The continuing priesthood, then, is the intercessory work of the seated, glorified Son of Man who is also the Priest-King in the presence of his accepting Father. Toon's 'solution', however, is remarkably similar to the actual position of those he criticizes.[12]

When we turn to their writings themselves, however, our understanding of the priesthood of the ascended Jesus deepens. To begin, we must be clear that our theologians of the ascension do emphatically believe in the sole sufficiency of the unrepeatable once-for-all offering of Jesus Christ on the cross. William Milligan writes:

> The penalty for sin once completely paid cannot be paid again. Its stamp remains imperishably on the life now lived by the Ascended Lord. In the presence of His Father He is for ever the Lamb that was slain, and no repetition of His offering can take place.[13]

H. B. Swete is equally clear:

> Neither in heaven nor on earth can there be any repetition of the Sacrifice, but only a presentation before God of the one full, perfect and sufficient Offering. In heaven, this presentation is made by the Ascended Christ Himself.[14]

And, if there were any doubt, T. F. Torrance succinctly declares, 'The reconciliation wrought by Christ has been completed once and for all and by its very nature cannot be repeated.'[15] So, if the idea of a repeated sacrifice is not what they mean, what are these writers after in their understanding of a perpetual offering?

William Milligan directs us to look deeper than the transactions of Jesus on our behalf to what occurs through his very person: 'The foundation of our Lord's Priesthood is the constitution of His person and not regularity of descent from others.' The priesthood and the person are inseparable, making his work as mediating priest even more than an office:

> Whatever our Lord effects for His people in His heavenly priesthood He effects by reason of the very constitution of His nature as the ascended and glorified Lord ... He bears the name of Mediator because He *is* what it expresses. There is nothing arbitrary or artificial in the arrangement of the economy of grace. Its gifts are no other than the natural and necessary result of what He who is its substance *is* in relation to the Father upon the one hand, and to man upon the other. In Himself he fulfils the mediation at which priesthood aims. He is *the* Mediator, the bond in which the mediation is actually accomplished and realised.[16]

Milligan's thought has ancient roots, as we may compare this to Irenaeus:

> He caused man [human nature] to cleave to and to become one with God. For unless man had overcome the enemy of man, the enemy would not have been ... vanquished ... unless it had been God who had freely given salvation, we could never have possessed it securely. And unless man had been joined to God, he could never have become a partaker of incorruptibility. For it was incumbent upon the Mediator between God and men, by His relationship to both, to bring both to friendship and concord, and present man to God, while He revealed God to man. For, in what way could we be partakers of the adoption of sons, unless we had received from Him through the Son that fellowship which refers to Himself, unless His Word, having been made flesh, had entered into communion with us? Wherefore also He passed through every stage of life, restoring to all communion with God.[17]

The essence of Christ's priesthood is the mediatorship between God and humanity forged in the unity of his one person.[18] The sacrifice on the cross was consequent upon his becoming our mediator in his person as the fully human, fully divine one.

As the eternal Son of God, our Lord has from before time been offering himself to his Father in perfect love. We might say he has ever been completely obedient, though the human implication of a hierarchy involved in obedience obscures the reality. The three co-equal persons of the Trinity give themselves to each other so absolutely that the most abject human obedience to another is pitifully shallow in comparison to the depths of such offering of one divine person to the other, and yet all of this is done not in servility but in total freedom. The very nature of the relationship between the eternal Son and the Father involves everlasting offering of one to the other. The incarnation, then, meant the entry into our time and space, even into our humanity, of this eternal offering of the Son to the Father. The Son enacted his love for his Father within our humanity, thus fulfilling the obedient response required of us as well as expressing the perichoretic union that had never been and can never be broken. So we must understand self-offering as part of the eternal person of the Son and as vital to our nature as human beings in relation to the

Triune God. As he offers himself to his Father, as he has ever done from all eternity, the Son of God now offers his humanity – our humanity – for that is an everlasting part of who he is. He offers himself in the present as the one who has accomplished our salvation, who has united himself to us, and who remains constant toward us in that eternal identification of love.

Andrew Murray reflects:

> As Son, Christ alone was heir of all that God had. All the life of the Father was in Him. God could have no union or fellowship with any creature but through His beloved Son, or as far as the life and spirit and image of the Son was seen in it. Therefore, no one could be our High Priest but the Son of God. If our salvation was not to be a merely legal one – external and, I may say, artificial – but an entrance anew into the very life of God, with the restoration of the divine nature we had lost in paradise, it was the Son of God alone who could impart this to us. He had the life of God to give; He was able to give it; He could only give by taking us into living fellowship with Himself. The priesthood of Christ is the God-devised channel through which the ever-blessed Son could make us partakers of Himself, and with Himself of all the life and glory He hath from and in the Father.[19]

The priesthood of Christ does not consist merely of an external, legal transaction of sacrifice, a paying of the bill, so to speak, but also of a reconciliation accomplished in his person and maintained in his person. This is why Milligan insists that 'life, not death, is the essence of atonement, is that by which sin is covered'.[20] The killing of an animal in the Hebrew sacrifices meant the fullest offering of its lifeblood. What was presented to God was not the death, but the life of the creature. Leviticus 17:11 declares, 'For the life of the creature is in the blood.' So 'in the highest conception of offering death has no place. Had man never fallen it would still have been his duty to offer himself together with all he possessed to the God in whom he lived, and moved, and had his being.'[21]

The effect of Christ's priesthood, then, is to accomplish something within us, something that changes us and reconciles us from the inside out:

> Jesus Christ is become a Priest after the power of an endless life. These precious words are the key to the higher life. Jesus lives in

heaven as High Priest in the power of an endless life. And as He lives, so He works in that power ... He works within us *as a life*, as our own life, so that it is our very nature to delight in God and in His will. His priesthood acts as an inner life within us, lifting us up, not in thought but in spirit and in truth, into a vital fellowship with God. He breathes His own life in us. And he works it in as *the power of life*, a life that is strong and healthy, because it is His own life from heaven.[22]

A priest after the order of Melchizedek (Hebrews 9:20), Jesus lives for ever. He does not have his priesthood by virtue of Aaronic descent, and he does not die as all other priests have. Jesus in himself is perfectly suited to be our priest. For while he is fully man, the man in our place, he is yet 'holy, blameless, pure, set apart from sinners', so he 'meets our need' (Hebrews 7:25). Jesus in his manhood is what humanity has always been intended to be. He is what we were meant to be before sin and consequent death diminished us. Jesus now is the most fully human person ever to live. Humanity in its highest capacity, deepest joy, and uttermost fulfilment has been reached in the ascended Christ. This is the man who is our forerunner (Hebrews 6:20), who has passed through the heavens and gone within the veil. Now by the Spirit in prayer and worship (but one day, by the same Spirit, in our glorified flesh), we, too, in his life, have access to the Holy of Holies. As Swete writes, 'It is the abiding life of our High Priest which makes His atoning Sacrifice operative, and is the unfailing spring of the life of justification and grace in all His true members upon earth.'[23]

We recall here that the life of Jesus has ever and is ever lived through the Holy Spirit. The incarnation was accomplished when the Holy Spirit came upon Mary and enabled her to conceive the Son of God (Luke 1:35). Jesus began his public ministry as the Spirit came down upon him when he came out of the baptismal waters of Jordan (Luke 3:22). This same Spirit led him into the wilderness to face and triumph over his temptations (Luke 4:1, 14), and it was the anointing of the Spirit that Jesus claimed when he preached of his ministry to the poor and captive (Luke 4:18). In Hebrews, then, we read that Jesus made his priestly offering by means of the Holy Spirit. Christ shed his blood for us as 'through

the eternal Spirit [he] offered himself unblemished to God'
(Hebrews 9:14). Moreover, the Spirit was an active agent in Jesus'
resurrection (Romans 1:4; 1 Peter 3:18). And while Jesus'
exaltation is only referred to as a work of God (Acts 5:31;
Philippians 2:9), the lack of specificity certainly does not rule out
the Spirit's operation in the ascension of Jesus as well. Thus, Jesus'
relationship to the Father as a man was in and through the Holy
Spirit, as was his entire ministry from the Father to us. In the
glorious dance of the triune relationship, the Spirit even now
remains the bond of the Trinity, and Jesus' perfect, fulfilled
humanity is lived out in the power and joy of the Spirit as it was
on earth.[24]

So we may see why these theologians discuss Jesus' priesthood
in terms of a perpetual offering. It is not that Jesus is sacrificed
again on the cross or that his atonement was insufficient, but that
his very continuing life constitutes our atonement. We require a
constant advocacy, a dynamic ministry of the mediator to hold us
continually in union with him. The sin offering on the cross was
indeed once and for all. But his life of intercession on our behalf
consists of the self-offering he has made continuously from all
eternity and now makes not only as the Son of God but as Son of
Man, eternally incarnate, in the power of the Holy Spirit.

Thus, Jesus' intercessions are not some ludicrous reminder to
the Father of what he once did – as if the Father would ever
forget the sacrifice of his Son! Neither are they the pleading of his
blood before a reluctant Father who might otherwise remain
angry and seek to destroy us.[25] Rather the intercessions of Jesus
represent his role in the Triune God's continual work of
sanctifying us. For reasons hidden in his love, God has restrained
himself in his dealings with us in order to allow room for our
cooperation in his work in us. We are called to 'work out our
salvation' in response to God who is at work in us enabling us 'to
will and to act according to his good pleasure' (Philippians 2:7–8).
This sanctification depends on the dynamic, continual intercessions of the Son at the right hand of the Father as well as the
Spirit within our hearts. So Gregory Nazianzen can say,

He ever liveth to make intercession for us. O, how beautiful and mystical and kind! For to intercede ... is to plead for us by reason of His Mediatorship, just as the Spirit also is said to make intercession for us. For there is One God, and One Mediator between God and Man, the Man Christ Jesus. For He still pleads even now as Man for my salvation; for He continues to wear the Body which He assumed, until He make me God by the power of His Incarnation.[26]

The priesthood of Christ was, of course, conceived in eternity, and enacted when 'the Lamb that was slain from the creation of the world' (Revelation 13:8) entered the world in our flesh. His high-priestly act of atonement occurred on the cross, once and for all. Yet it was in the ascension that he completed that atonement by his triumphant entrance to the Holy of Holies. The ascension also marks the commencement of his ministry of heavenly intercession for us. There is a dimension to his priesthood that has only come after his ascension in the flesh.

This dynamic ministry is described by Thomas Torrance:

It is as our Brother, wearing our humanity, that He has ascended, presenting Himself eternally before the face of the Father, and presenting us in Himself. As such He is not only our word to God but God's Word to us. Toward God He is our Advocate and High Priest, but toward man He is the acceptance of us in Himself. The very Spirit through whom He offered Himself eternally to the Father He has sent down upon us in His high-priestly blessing, fulfilling in the life of His Church on earth that which He has fulfilled on our behalf in the heavenlies ... Christ was once and for all sacrificed in our stead on the Cross but He has ascended into the Holy Place and ever lives to present Himself (and us *in Him* because of Himself *for us*) before the face of the Father. That sacrificial act of Christ once and for all performed and enduring in His endless life in the presence of God, is realised in the life of His people, not by repetition of His substitutionary sacrifice, but by their dying and rising with Christ in faith and life, and by the worship of self-presentation to God.[27]

The priesthood of Christ continues because he is the living mediator. We offer ourselves to God not only based on what Jesus did in the past, but also *in him now* because in our name, Jesus as man offers worship, prayer and even his life in obedience for us. The atoning work continues in his vicarious humanity.

We will consider below the place of the ascended priest in our worship, but we conclude this section by noticing how Calvin himself understood the priesthood of Christ in terms of a continual offering of the blood of Christ, shed once for all on the cross. Commenting on Hebrews 10:19 and 13:20, he writes:

> Since the blood of Christ is not corrupted by any decay but flows continually in unadulterated purity, it will suffice us to the end of the world ... Christ who rose from the dead to give us life pours His own life into us. This is the continual consecration of His life that the blood of Christ is continually being shed before the face of the Father to spread over heaven and earth. ... Christ so rose from the dead that His death was not abolished but keeps its eternal power, as if he had said, that God raised up His Son in such a way that His blood once shed in death has power to ratify the eternal covenant after His resurrection, and brings forth its fruit as though it were always flowing.[28]

How are we to understand this vivid description? Do we imagine that Jesus' blood is literally flowing? If Jesus indeed remains incarnate in a resurrection body, there may be some sense in which blood, transformed and glorified, flows within his incarnate life. But Calvin says this blood is being shed. Symbolically, then, it is 'as though it were always flowing'. For in literal reality Jesus is continually consecrating his life to his Father's will, out of his own love, and on our behalf. His life flows out to his Father in worship and self-offering. His life flows out to us as he pours out the Holy Spirit within us and upon us, uniting us more and more to himself. He pours out his blood in Holy Communion as the Spirit collapses the distance between us on earth and Christ in heaven, making us truly to share in his life. Calvin realized that the intercession flows from the offering, and while the sacrifice on the cross is complete, we need not consider Christ's offering in so narrow a sense as to relegate it only to a past event. Rather his blood is always flowing, bringing forth the fruit of the new covenant that is rooted in his own person.

Worship and the Priesthood of Christ

Though we will specifically consider in Chapter 8 our participation in the ascension of Jesus, two aspects related to his priestly intercession come before us now: worship and prayer.

In a remarkable passage from Hebrews 2:10–13, the author describes Jesus, whom he has already affirmed as the Son of God, as being one with his brothers. The incarnation and course of Christ's obedience are all part of the plan of salvation. But, interestingly, the union of Christ with his people is most fully realized in the context of worship. A stunning set of Old Testament passages are attributed to Jesus:

> In bringing many sons to glory, it was fitting that God, for whom and through whom everything exists, should make the author of their salvation perfect through suffering. Both the one who makes men holy and those who are made holy are of the same family. So Jesus is not ashamed to call them brothers. He says,
> 'I will declare your name to my brothers;
> in the presence of the congregation I will sing your praises' [Psalm 22:22].
> And again,
> 'I will put my trust in him' [Isaiah 8:17].
> And again he says,
> 'Here am I, and the children God has given me' [Isaiah 8:18].

Jesus, the one who makes us holy, and we, the ones he makes holy, are bonded as family. Literally, Hebrews says we are 'all out of one'. We are cut from the same piece of cloth, the humanity we have in common with the incarnate Son of God. We are all of one family now, all of one Father. Jesus has come in the flesh so that he is now our brother. And he claims us as his own kin. The text says that he is not ashamed to call us his sisters and brothers. He has been made like us, so we might be made like him, so we might become part of his family. He came down so he could lift us up and bring us back to God.

This union is revealed through the Old Testament passages which Jesus utters as his own. Jesus the man declares God to his brothers and sisters in the flesh. The priest represents God to the people. But then we hear that Jesus the man will praise his Father in the midst of the *ecclesia*, the church, the assembled, summoned people of God. And he says to his Father in the midst of the congregation, 'Here I am! Here I am and the children I have gathered because you gave them to me.' These passages are not just in the past tense, as something done once long ago. They are present and future tense. They are occurring right now and will continue to do so! This worship as one of us, on our behalf, and with us is an essential part of the intercessory ministry of our ascended High Priest. He is our *leitourgos,* a minister in the Holy Place (Hebrews 8:2), a leader of worship in whom all our earthly worship is gathered up and presented to the Father.

In the television programme *Touched by an Angel,* the lovely Irish angel Monica so often begins her prayers by saying, 'Father, here we are.' It is not that God could not otherwise find us if we did not voice our location. He always knows where we are. But the phrase indicates our willingness to be found. It is an offer of availability, echoing the archetypal biblical reponse to the call of God. The boy Samuel replied to the voice in the night, 'Here I am' (1 Samuel 2:8). In Isaiah 6, God asked 'Whom shall I send?' The humble prophet Isaiah replied, 'Here am I. Send me' (Isaiah 6:8). By contrast, in Eden, when God came looking for Adam and Eve, he called out 'Where are you?' (Genesis 3:8). Our first parents hid in their shame. Now, in recapitulating the human race, Jesus is making a different answer in our name and on our behalf. He offers himself in complete obedience: 'Here I am! And I am not alone. I have brought all of these brothers and sisters with me. They are found in me; they too wish you to see them, regard them and love them.'

Such a passage transforms our understanding of worship, filling us with new layers of imagination as we visualize the unseen reality around us. The glorified, ascended, still incarnate Jesus is in the Holy Place, within the true tabernacle (Hebrews 8:2) of which every earthly house of worship is at best a shadow. Yet in the Holy Spirit he is not removed from us. The Spirit is the Spirit of Jesus, and brings his presence to us in worship, most especially in the preaching of the Word and the administration of the sacraments. And the Spirit lifts us up, spiritually, in our worship to the throne of God where Jesus serves as our advocate, priest, intercessor and worship leader. Through the Spirit, then, the ascended Jesus comes to be in our midst and through the same Spirit we are brought in Christ our High Priest into the Father's welcoming presence.

So in worship, we may visualize Jesus standing in the midst of our sanctuary. His arms are outstretched and his head is raised to heaven. He has gathered us all and he is offering us to his Father even as he offers his praise. In our congregation, his congregation, Jesus sings to his Father: 'Father, here I am. Here with the children, the family you gave me. Father, here I am! Within the gathered church I will lead your praise. To my brothers and sisters I will make you known. Father, here I am!'

This means that in the midst of every sanctuary, Jesus is leading our praise. In the tiniest church in the remotest region to the grandest cathedral in the heart of the city, Jesus is worshipping his Father, bringing his brothers and sisters with him into the presence of God. For the Son of God who became man is still fully human, still in the flesh, still incarnate. As a man he worships God. He has blazed the way before us. He has pioneered the path in his own flesh. And he collects us up, gathers us in his arms and presents us in praise to God the Father as those whom he has cleansed and redeemed and sanctified. All of that is going on in the midst of our sanctuary, when we are there, sitting some mornings like bumps on a log, sleepy, distracted, bored, confused, and waiting for lunch. We may call the people to worship with the astounding news that Jesus is here with outstretched arms declaring to us the name of God, and declaring to God the names of his brothers and sisters assembled.

The church on earth is allowed a share in this ministry of the ascended Jesus. For we have been invited to come along, not just as passive spectators but as participants. God has made us to be storytellers, artists, musicians and preachers. It is given to the likes of ordinary people to raise the song, to paint the picture, to tell the tale, to bring forth into the world the news of the Son who gathers us up in his praise. So the Psalmist has declared,

> Sing to the Lord a new song,
> his praise in the assembly of saints ...
> Let the people of Zion be glad in their King.
> ... praise his name with dancing,
> and make music to him with tambourine and harp.
> For the Lord takes delight in his people[.] (Psalm 149:1–4)

The Father loves to hear the praise of his Son. And he loves to hear our praise. Feeble as it may be, God loves to hear it. We have been granted the gift to make merry in the presence of the Father, to make music for the ears of the High King to adorn the heavenly court. We have been granted to give it our best effort, knowing that it is inadequate but that Jesus the worship leader lifts it up, cleanses it and makes it perfect.

Calvin beautifully summarizes this thought in relation to the priesthood of the ascended Jesus:

> Christ now bears the office of priest, not only that by the eternal law of reconciliation he may render the Father favourable and propitious to us, but also admit us into this most honourable alliance. For we though in ourselves polluted, in him being priests [Revelation 1:6], offer ourselves and our all to God, and freely enter the heavenly sanctuary, so that the sacrifices of prayer and praise which we present are grateful and of sweet odour before him. To this effect are the words of Christ, 'For their sakes I sanctify myself' [John 17:19], for being clothed with his holiness, inasmuch as he has devoted us to the Father with himself (otherwise we were an abomination before him), we please him as if we were pure and clean, nay, even sacred.[29]

Because Christ is our worship leader and the perfecter not only of our faith but also of our worship, we are remarkably free now to come before God's presence in him, with singing, dancing, and great rejoicing.

The Priesthood and Our Prayers

A corollary to Christ's priesthood and our worship is his relationship to our prayers. This is a theme dear to the heart of James Torrance, which he expounds with a lovely pastoral sensitivity in his lectures and writing. Torrance recognizes the feelings of inadequacy we all experience concerning our prayer life: 'We know we ought to pray, we try to pray, but we fail. We do not know how to pray.' On our own, we are inadequate to the task of approaching Almighty God in prayer. The gospel of Christ Jesus comes to our rescue. Torrance writes:

> But God so loves us and longs to draw us into a life of loving communion that he comes to us in Christ to stand in for us, to pray

for us and with us and in us, sending the Spirit of his Son into our hearts crying 'Abba, Father!'

The Son of God takes our humanity, sanctifies it by his vicarious life in the Spirit, carries it to the grave to be crucified and buried in him, and in his resurrection and ascension carries it into the holy presence of God.

That is the message of the New Testament, the secret of our prayer life. Our great High Priest has entered for us sinful men and women into the Holy of Holies leading us by the Holy Spirit to the Father. Therefore we have to hold two things together. First, he has *already* taken our humanity into the Holy of Holies, the presence of the Father in his own person. Second, he comes to us *today* by the Holy Spirit to take us with him into the Holiest of All, to present us 'without stain or wrinkle or any other blemish to the Father.'[30]

The priesthood of the ascended, incarnate Jesus is the key, then, not only to our atonement with God and our worship but also to our daily prayer life. We pray as we participate in the man Christ Jesus' continuing prayers of thanks and intercession to his Father through the Holy Spirit. We enter this participation by faith, consciously appropriating all we know of our High Priest as we make our prayer. Thus, his priesthood in the power of the Spirit is our communion in the life of the Holy Trinity.

Augustine develops this thought in his commentary on Psalm 86. Once again, we see his understanding of the *totus Christus*, the head and the body as one, coming to the fore:

No greater gift could God have given to men than in making His Word, by which He created all things, their Head, and joining them to Him as His members: that the Son of God might become also the Son of man, one God with the Father, one Man with men; so that when we speak to God in prayer for mercy, we do not separate the Son from Him; and when the Body of the Son prays, it separates not its Head from itself: and it is one Saviour of His Body, our Lord Jesus Christ, the Son of God, who both prays for us, and prays in us, and is prayed to by us. He prays for us, as our Priest; He prays in us, as our Head; He is prayed to by us, as our God. Let us therefore recognise in Him our words, and His words in us.[31]

Because we are united to our ascended head, we participate in his oneness and communion with his Father. So we have a triple relation to Jesus in prayer. First, as God the Son, he is prayed to by us; Jesus is the object of our prayer. But second, Jesus also prays for us as our High Priest, reconciling us to the Father, making our prayers acceptable in him. And, third, he prays in us, through the Holy Spirit, who is sent from the head throughout the body, joining all the members as one and joining all the members in vital life and energy to the ascended Lord. Our prayers, then, first, middle and last, are all in Christ.

As Calvin says, 'No man can derive the least benefit from any prayers without the intercession of Christ ... [So] let it be held as a fixed principle, that all the intercessions thus used in the Church must have reference to that one intercession.'[32] In his fourth ascension sermon, Calvin elaborates:

> When we presume to pray to God we shall be rejected unless Jesus Christ is there in our name. Since he is there, He is our Intercessor and presents our prayers there and causes us to be answered, as if we had the privilege of saying what we have to do and to pour out our heart before God ... Also, since Jesus Christ has entered into heaven, and He bears us there, although we are only brute beasts, and also He bears our names before God to show that He has us in His heart; we need not pray to God in doubt, but we may be assured that our prayers will always be acceptable to Him, since we pray through Jesus Christ.[33]

The joy of prayer is the intercession of the ascended Jesus, ever our brother and only mediator. That which we would not dare to presume on our own, we undertake with bold assurance through Jesus.

Ultimately, this means that prayer through the priesthood of Christ is primarily a matter of looking away from ourselves and to Jesus. It is not an expression of our spirituality or an exercise in our religious quest. Prayer is in Christ, through Christ, and for Christ. James Torrance will have the final word:

> In prayer, in our helplessness, we look away to God our Father, to Jesus Christ our High Priest, as he intercedes for us, with us and in us, trusting in his grace to hear and answer our prayers, yielding, surrendering our wills to his will ... As we pray in faith, Christ takes our prayers, cleanses them, makes them his prayers to the Father, presenting us in himself to the Father, and makes his prayers our prayers ... We are summoned all our life to look away in faith to Christ our High Priest, to let him lift us up daily by the Spirit into his prayer life.[34]

The continuing work of the ascended Jesus is to maintain through himself in the power of the Spirit the wonderful exchange, whereby what is ours becomes his and is cleansed, and what is his, even his prayers, becomes ours by grace.

Chapter 7

Citizens of a Far Country

We are now ready to see how a robust doctrine of the ascension in the flesh can influence, and even transform, the life of the present-day church in the west. The very nature of the church is determined by the condition and location of her Lord, the head of his body. Jesus is in heaven, yet we, his people, are here on earth. The church thus exists with a palpable sense of incompleteness in this present world. We are strangers here, but passing through on our way to be reunited with Jesus in heaven. We realize simultaneously, however, that our Christ who has left us here has yet retained our humanity, our very flesh and soul in himself. So though he is absent from sight, we know that he remains interested in this world and these people. He is vitally connected to us through his Spirit; the physically absent Son is present by means of his Spirit whom he pours upon us. The church, while it longs for him in these days of separation, is yet energized by his spiritual presence. He is known to us in the breaking of the bread and the preaching of the Word. Moreover, he has promised to return. Jesus is not finished with us or this world. So we trust that we sojourn here through these difficult years for a reason. Indeed, the church is ever directed to recall her mandate. We have been sent as the body of Christ to this world on the very mission of Jesus to proclaim his gospel and enact his love. This present age, then, is an interim time between the first and second comings of Christ. Our home is in heaven; our work is in the world. A proper understanding of the ascension is crucial to maintaining a proper perspective on Jesus' presence and absence, and therefore the key to a correct, and fruitful, relationship to the world.

As we saw in Chapter 2, Thomas Torrance has explained how the ascension of the risen Jesus in the flesh directs us to find Jesus now through the New Testament witness. His withdrawal from this world prevents our having immediate physical contact with him. We know him as he is now only through meeting him in the power of the Spirit in the sacraments of Baptism and the Lord's Supper which he has left us and in interaction with the inspired record of his time among us. All our worship and prayer pass through these means. All our fellowship and mission have their source in the way we meet Jesus through Word and Sacrament. We may have Jesus no other way until he returns in his glorified person to gather us to himself. For now, our Lord in heaven comes to us by the Spirit in a present, intimate, and personal way through our encounter with what he said and did so long ago and so far removed from us. Thus, we seek no Jesus apart from the historical Jesus, the Lord who has withdrawn but will come again.

Torrance goes on to explain how the ascension shapes the definition of the church:

> The time of the ascension is thus of cardinal importance for a doctrine of the Church and its ministry. The ascension means the establishment of the Church in history with historical structure and form, in which the time of the Church is the time of faith, not yet the time of sight, the time when the realm of *grace* is not yet dissolved by the realm of *glory*. If Jesus during the three years of His earthly ministry had manifested His full divine glory so that men were confronted face to face with the ultimate majesty of God, then they would have been planted at once in the *eschaton*, and historical time within which there is room for free meeting and decision would have been abrogated: the final judgement would have taken place. ... He was holding Himself, so to speak, at arm's length, revealing Himself to men in such a way as not to overwhelm and crush them, giving them time to repent, and room for decision ... The ascension means that Jesus has withdrawn Himself from history in order to allow the world time for repentance. ... That is the time in which the Church exists and carries out its mission, within the succession of history where there is time between revelation and decision, time between decision and act, time between the present and future. It is time

where the present age is already interpenetrated by the age to come, but it is the time when the new age and all its final glory are held in eschatological reserve, in order to leave room to preach the Gospel and give mankind opportunity to meet with God, to repent, and believe the Gospel.[1]

The Son of God came among us in history for a time and in showing his face showed us truly who his Father is. Yet, while that revelation was completely accurate and thoroughly sufficient for us, it was not the entire unveiled fullness of the glory of God which men and women beheld in Jesus. Such a light would have overwhelmed us and brought the present age to a close. So Jesus came to us showing us enough of who he is so as truly to reveal God, yet 'in such a way as not to overwhelm and crush' us. This holding back during his ministry, and the subsequent withdrawal of the risen Jesus through the ascension, leaves us space and time for faith, for choice, for repentance. The Triune God exercises tender loving restraint in order to accommodate our fragility, that our faith might be genuinely human and, while ever the gift of the Spirit, yet mysteriously be truly our own. The ascension stretches out opportunity for the world to come to know God. Jesus' withdrawal makes necessary the mission of the church to the world, but also makes room for the world to receive the mission of the church and come to believe the gospel.

Thus the church enacts the paradox of her earthly existence during the time between the ascension and the return of Christ. We strive to set our minds on heaven at the same time as we plunge into the world with the message of grace. We sojourn as aliens among people not our own, yet for whom we lay down our lives in hope that they will become our own brothers and sisters. We wait longingly for the return of Christ even as we work feverishly to complete our task before the Lord calls us to account.

Psalm 84 offers a lovely paradigm for this dual role. The New International Version renders it,

> Blessed are those whose strength is in you,
>   who have set their hearts on pilgrimage.
> As they pass through the Valley of Baca,

> they make it a place of springs;
> the autumn rains also cover it with pools.
> They go from strength to strength,
> till each appears before God in Zion. (Psalm 84:5–7)

The church has set its heart in pilgrimage to our Lord Christ. We know that our home is with him in heaven. Jesus, however, is not only our destination, but the way as well. United to him, we feel the journey's end in the present moment of sojourn. The joy, the love, the peace of our future home may well break into our worship and our fellowship along the way. Those who partake of our lives here may catch a scent of heaven about us. The psalm describes the blessing of those whose hearts are set on making their way to God – as the New Revised Standard Version translates, 'in whose heart are the highways to Zion'. It is not merely a personal blessing but one which transforms the world around the sojourners. As these pilgrims pass through the dry and arid lands, springs flow and rivers run. Flowers bloom at their feet. For those on their way to Christ and in Christ are not fleeing the earth or trying to escape real life. Rather they are transforming life in this corrupt world as they move towards the home of a new heaven and a new earth. The church sojourns through a world which may well reject her, spreading the life of the heaven for which she quests all along her path.

Three Errors to Avoid

The balance required for properly loving the world as part of the mission for Christ without being co-opted by the world in its resistance to God has never been easy to maintain. At least three errors have regularly been made by the church throughout the centuries: withdrawal from the world, attempting to create the kingdom of heaven here on earth, and conformity to the world. Interestingly, all three of these wrong postures can be related to faulty understandings of the ascended Jesus. Delineating these mistakes is nothing new, yet linking each to inadequate understandings of the ascension is Douglas Farrow's unique contribution and we will especially want to highlight his comments. We will focus most on the error identified in Chapter 1 as a problem particular to the western church at the beginning of the twenty-first century.

Withdrawal from the World

First, the church has always had a tendency to withdraw from this fallen, violent, broken world. Even after the resurrection, Peter and John went back to fishing until Jesus met them on the shore (John 21:3). Perhaps they thought the risen Jesus had simply departed, leaving them on their own. That would have been an ascension without any hope of return. But Jesus corrected their understanding as he gave them the mission of feeding his lambs (John 21:15), being his witnesses to all the earth (Acts 1:8) and making new disciples (Matt 28:18). In these descriptions of Jesus' giving the disciples a mission to enact in the world, we also hear of promises he left them. The departing Jesus is he who said 'I am with you always' (Matthew 28:20), who assured the disciples that he would come again (John 21:22–3) and of whom the angels said, 'This same Jesus, who has been taken from you into heaven, will come back in the same way you have seen him go into heaven' (Acts 1:11). The absence and the presence are always maintained so that the church is sent into the world with hope.

What could cause Christ's people, then, to justify a withdrawal from this world as they wait for his return? Farrow asserts that a spiritualizing of the ascension can have as one of its consequences a shrinking back from the material world into a spirituality of mind.[2] This occurred particularly when the church was influenced by Gnosticism and its disdain for the body and the material world. For example, under such a spell, Origen, as we saw in Chapter 2, began to consider Jesus' ascension as an ascension of the mind, in which he slipped off the body of flesh, making the incarnation merely a 'drop-in' affair and thus 'limiting Christ's bodily humanity to a brief soteriological phase'.[3] We can see such spiritualizing even today, whether it is the extreme of the New Age psychologizing of the entire Jesus story or simply the picking and choosing of aspects of Jesus' life and teaching that occurs in American hybrid spirituality.

But the church also comes to her withdrawal from the world quite honestly. This world is a hard place, and we know it is passing away (1 John 2:17). Its people are hell-bent on rebellion and destruction. Our Lord's name is slandered and his people persecuted. We may well tire of this conflict, and wish to go off with our brothers and sisters, simply to worship and pray until Jesus returns. The attitude among Christians thus becomes 'Let us just wait it out, keeping ourselves as unstained as possible, until we get to the kingdom of God.' These well-meaning Christians may get so wrapped up in spiritual life that they become of little good to anyone. They may remain ostensibly orthodox in doctrine, yet the news of Jesus' continuing enfleshment will seldom be considered. This withdrawing to avoid pain may well go on to weaken the church's doctrinal position, and so the cycle continues to spiral downward.

The neglect of what the ascension means has surely contributed to spiritualizing tendencies even in Evangelical quarters of the church. We simply do not think of Jesus still knit to our humanity, and so we think very little of what that reality means to how Jesus even now values this flesh of ours, these lives of our neighbours, this earth which we consume as yet one more disposable commodity. A weak view, therefore, of the ascension in the flesh and the continuing incarnation of Christ can contribute to a spiritualizing of the Christian life, with an atomistic view of the church that places such stress on individual spirituality that the inevitable result is an indifference to the needs and suffering of the world. Farrow laments, 'The true Gnostic ... denies all obligation to the world ... [because] the spiritual person rises above the affairs of a world destined for destruction.'[4]

Creating the Kingdom Here on Earth

If the conservative error is to neglect the need of the world while concentrating so much on spirituality, the liberal error has typically been to focus too much on transforming the world *now* in such a way that the story of the gospel and the goal of heaven are greatly diminished. This focus on the church as the builder of the kingdom in the present has very ancient roots. Of course it can certainly arise from simple unbelief. Rejecting the story of Jesus at any point after his crucifixion completely skews the understanding of the church. A Jesus who did not truly rise did not triumph over death and thus left us with only an ethic for living which we may try to emulate. A Christ who did not ascend has not established our primary identity in heaven, and he is not returning to bring in the new heavens and the new earth. But pure disbelief while remaining in the church is rare. The readier mistake that leads to this second error is not to deny the ascension outright but to spiritualize it. An ascension of Jesus in the mind, leaving behind his body, could easily lead to an excessive focus on the role of the church in the present age. A spiritualized, or metaphorical, ascension rapidly leads to a neglect of the doctrine of the parousia, thus demanding that all which was once promised for the future should be created now. The job is all up to us, and we are on our own.

Farrow notes how with the rise of Constantine there was 'a conscious attempt to reclaim or sanctify temporal history just as it is'. Even the great Augustine, on Farrow's reading, so emphasized the glory of the ascended Jesus, to the neglect of the humility of his continuing humanity, that the church could easily partner with the state in a triumphalist view of reigning in the world. The more the church focused on the divinity to the neglect of the humanity of the ascended Lord, the more it 'grew bolder in offering itself as a substitute for the absent saviour, and a link to the higher realm he now inhabited'. Thus the church could sometimes actually see itself as an extension of the incarnation. In such thinking the church would erroneously build itself up in worldly wealth and influence to be the kingdom come now into the world. It might consider its primary mission as itself forging the redemption and transformation of the world.[5]

In other words, since Jesus is gone, we will bring the kingdom on earth. Bearing the love of Christ, we might try to realize his love and kingdom now through a mighty human effort. In the past, the church in Europe tried to do this by becoming the most powerful political, social, and artistic force in the world. Though Christendom is long gone, the tendencies still remain. Nowadays we see it when a megachurch becomes everything to people. Why ever leave the church when it will feed us, educate our children, offer exercise for our bodies and nourishment for our souls, and even send us on carefully arranged, safe mission projects? While my Presbyterian denomination has few such churches, we are likely to fall into this same error when we believe that we will bring in the kingdom through our good works. We may operate under the idea that if we just worked hard enough, we could feed the hungry, house all the homeless, rid the world of disease, create peace and save souls – all on our own. But of course, this side of heaven, that vision will not come to be. The church can never be a substitute for Jesus.

Conformity to the World

Far more prevalent today, however, is an over-identification with the present age. The church can be so much in the world that no one can tell the difference between the church and the rest of the world. A Gnostic spiritualizing of Jesus could lead to this error as well as to a withdrawal from the world. For viewing the material world as inferior and irrelevant to the ascension of the mind led to a profligate enjoyment of the pleasures of the flesh. But more pertinent today as a source for this third error is simple disbelief in the ascension in the flesh of Jesus Christ. As we noted in Chapter 2, it simply seems ridiculous that a man still in skin rose up beyond sight to some nebulous heavenly realms. We just think it incredible that Jesus should still be in the flesh. Even many of those in the church who affirm the creeds weekly may mentally be spiritualizing the ascension.

The effects of doing this, of course, are devastating to our understanding of the church in relation to the world. First, we work with a deficient view of heaven as a disembodied place, lacking pleasure or any meaningful exertion. That creepy view of the next world is enough to send any hearty person back to the world to savour what 'real' joy may be had before the end. We thus become as materialistic as our secular neighbours, for the alternatives are not compelling. Second, a spiritualized Jesus more quickly becomes an inspirational figure in our minds and one much less likely to show up here again to call us to account. We then become much more prone to follow whatever has captured the fancy of the culture around us as the way to fulfilment. Third, a spiritualized ascension makes us prone to the two errors noted above: withdrawal from the world and trying to create the kingdom here on earth. On the one hand, we become individualistic in our faith, readily conforming to our culture's emphasis on spiritual quests and faith stories rather than union with the particular man Jesus Christ. On the other, we consider the church in worldly, business-like terms, attempting to develop it as a corporation and increase its influence as though it were a temporal government because we lack a vision of the continuingly incarnate saviour whose rich wounds are still visible above, who still leads by serving, and still brings life through his death.

The Place of Tension

By contrast, the ascension of Jesus in the flesh maintains the church in the tension between two worlds. This position is more difficult than any of the errors to which we are drawn. Yet the very effectiveness of our mission depends on it. We are in the world, not of the world; sent to the world to love it as shepherds seeking wandering sheep, yet not allowed to love it as errant herdsmen enamoured with the high, lost places of their flock. We must give our lives moment by moment for a world that does not deserve them and can never repay us in fulfilment for such service. Douglas Farrow in his exposition of Irenaeus' theology offers a grand vision for the church's mission in relation to the ascension. He writes that the church,

> believing in the renewal of creation, offers an oblation which commits it to a life of responsible engagement with the world for the sake of its transformation. Not that the church can or will accomplish that transformation from below, so to speak, or assist the world to do so. The renewal which it seeks is hid with Christ in God – there is no nascent liberation theology here, nor hint of triumphalism. Indeed, the new possibilities implanted in its oblation by the Word and the Spirit, just because they are eschatological, consistently thrust the church back to the cross as the ground and pattern of its engagement.[6]

Our pattern of engagement is that of the self-giving of the cross. It is given to us by the ascended Lord, who has not slipped out of his everlasting union with us but constantly confirms his commitment to that pattern of sacrifice in the very flesh he wears. Farrow then describes the church as

> the courageous place in which Christians reject *both* of the Gnostic options, often at great personal cost. That is, they refuse either to become irrelevant to the world or to be in conformity with it. Withdrawal and worldliness are alike repugnant to a eucharistic worldview – forsaken not for virtue of moderation, but for the sake of radical love ... Occupying the place of eucharistic stress carved out for it by Jesus, the church is distinguished *from* the world in order to present itself *to* the world as a vehicle for salvation. Which is to say, it is placed in its precarious situation as a community straddling two divergent histories.[7]

An ascension in the flesh is vital to understanding and maintaining this difficult place of tension, of 'eucharistic stress', in which alone the church is of any use to a desperate world. Christ has withdrawn from the world not to forsake the world but in order to give himself to the world in the mission of the church through the power of the Spirit whom he continually pours forth.

Our mission remains that of Jesus:

> by choosing to follow Jesus, the church is still choosing *for* the world and not against it. It is choosing to travel with the world, for the sake of the world, without joining the world. Here then is a continuity that grows precisely by keeping pace with an ever sharper discontinuity. The church, since it belongs to him who ascended in flesh, can neither agree with the world nor let go of it. It can only take up the cross and the offence of the cross, wrestling with the world to the bitter end in hope – a well grounded hope! – of redeeming the time.[8]

We remain distinct from the world in order to present ourselves to the world in the name of Christ. This follows the example of our Lord, who is absent in the glorified humanity precisely so that he may keep on presenting that humanity to the world through the Spirit in the church's witness as the saving, cleansing, redemptive purpose of all creation. Such a mission costs us everything. It also provides the church with a vision of such significance and such high purpose that we may indeed be drawn away from our present over-identification with the world.

Citizens of Heaven

Understanding that we may never in this life withdraw from the epic contest with the world, we may turn to consider our identity with Christ in heaven as the necessary source to sustain us in this mission and save us from the seductions of a world that will seek to defeat our mission by co-opting us far more than it will by trying to persecute us. From scripture onward, the concept of citizenship has galvanized the church for its mission as it sojourns in the world. As Paul wrote to the Philippians, he described the very struggle we have been studying:

> For, as I have often told you before and now say again even with tears, many live as enemies of the cross of Christ. Their destiny is destruction, their god is their stomach, and their glory is in their shame. Their mind is on earthly things. But our citizenship is in heaven. And we eagerly await a Saviour from there, the Lord Jesus Christ, who, by the power that enables him to bring everything under his control, will transform our lowly bodies so that they will be like his glorious body. (Philippians 3:18–21)

Paul is not referring here simply to non-Christians as the enemies of the cross, but to Christians who have fallen into the error of over-identification with the present age. Their minds have turned 'to earthly things'. No fancy terms for sensuality could be more evocative (particularly in a culture as obese as America's) than Paul's simple 'their god is their stomach'. These Christians had become focused on fulfilment in the present time and place to the neglect of their true identity in Christ.

The way to avoid such a trap is a higher vision. Paul reaches toward all believers everywhere as he says, 'But our citizenship [politeuma] is in heaven.' Politeuma is a rich word evoking the sense of the source of one's identity and way of life.[9] The Greek concept of the polis, or city-state, included not just the sense of a locale, but of the whole nexus of relationships, duties, commerce, recreation, worship and service which defined and fulfilled a person. So, our identifying way of life, our heartland, our highest good and finest ways of thinking, derive not from this world but from heaven. We Christians are not defined first by the realm that lives in defiance of God, seeking to be its own master, but by the realm of communion and life that has been opened to us by the saving work of Jesus. This citizenship comes complete with a story of our origins and our destination: we live in the hope that one day our saviour will come riding out of the gates to gather his people from exile. Finding us and retrieving us, he will transform our mortal, decaying frames to be like his glorious, resurrected and ascended body.

We eschew the error of worldliness now because glorying in shame to titillate the appetites of the sinful flesh seems ludicrous in comparison to the true glory that is our inheritance. Why would we spend our energy in macabre play with dead things when real life in communion with the Triune God is available? This lowly body with all its cravings will be transformed. The surety of this hope is the person of the ascended Jesus. If he did not remain in the flesh, our faith might waver. But the image that spurs us onward is of the hand like ours that will open heaven's gates and the face like ours which will greet us in love because we will see with our own eyes that Jesus ever remains incarnate.

Other passages enhance Paul's compact gem on our identity as citizens of heaven. Hebrews describes the great heroes of faith who were able to persist in faithfulness though they never received in this life the fulfilment of the promise. They 'admitted they were aliens and strangers on earth' who were 'looking for a country of their own' (Hebrews 11:13–14). The patriarchs made their way sustained by a vision of 'a better country – a heavenly one'; they sought a 'city with foundations, whose architect and builder is God' (Hebrews 11:10). So Peter could urge us, 'as aliens and strangers in the world, to abstain from sinful desires, which war against your soul'; rather, in view of Christ's coming, we are to 'live such good lives among the pagans that ... they may see your good deeds and glorify God on the day he visits us' (1 Peter 2:11–12). Of course, Revelation 21–22 expands on the vision of Isaiah 60 to describe the glory of the coming City of God as a place where we will dwell in unbroken communion with God, beyond all death and tears.

The understanding of our heavenly citizenship based on the location of our ascended Lord has continued to direct the church in its relation to the world through the centuries. As he concludes his great work on the ascension, H. B. Swete notes how

> The Ascension and Ascended Life bear witness against the materialistic spirit which threatens in some quarters to overpower those higher interests that have their seat in the region of the spiritual and eternal. They are as a *Sursum corda* – 'lift up your hearts' – which comes down from the High Priest of the Church who stands at the heavenly altar, and draws forth from the kneeling Church the answer *Habemus ad Dominum* – 'we lift them up unto the Lord.'[10]

The location of her Lord draws the church to lift her gaze up from the lure and press of the world. Here a thousand thousand competing stories urge humanity to look for the meaning of life in this world, in autonomy and self-interested pursuits. Men and women walk about with the eyes of their minds and hearts cast downwards, blind to greater realities. But the church has a better story to tell. We lift up our hearts to the Lord because he is in heaven, drawing us homeward. In this way, the ascension is 'a safeguard against minimizing estimates of the person and work of Jesus Christ'.[11] A full regard for the greatness of Christ and his work causes the church continually to draw its life from the biblical story, and the narrative of Jesus in particular. This is the story that makes sense of the world and our place in it. In contrast to the stories the world tells to justify its existence and activities, the church lives from a heavenly story and speaks that story into the world through word and work. The ascension of Jesus not only demands but also creates a sense of heavenly citizenship in the church.

Yet Citizens of Earth

At the same time, however, we know that we citizens of heaven make our way in common with the rest of the world. In his research, Swete employed a portion of *The Epistle to Diognetus* to describe the parallel lives we live. The letter, whose author is unknown, may date to as early as AD 150–225. The description of the manners of Christians merits quotation even beyond Swete's use of it:

> For the Christians are distinguished from other men neither by country, nor language, nor the customs which they observe. For they neither inhabit cities of their own, nor employ a peculiar form of speech, nor lead a life which is marked out by any singularity. The course of conduct which they follow has not been devised by any speculation or deliberation of inquisitive men; nor do they, like some, proclaim themselves the advocates of any merely human doctrines. But, inhabiting Greek as well as barbarian cities, according as the lot of each of them has determined, and following the customs of the natives in respect to clothing, food, and the rest of their ordinary conduct, they display to us their wonderful and confessedly striking method of life. They dwell in their own countries, but simply as sojourners. As citizens, they share in all things with others, and yet endure all things as if foreigners. Every foreign land is to them as their native country, and every land of their birth as a land of strangers. They marry, as do all [others]; they beget children; but they do not destroy their offspring. They have a common table, but not a common bed. They are in the flesh, but they do not live after the flesh. They pass their days on earth, but they are citizens of heaven. They obey the prescribed laws, and at the same time surpass the laws by their lives. They love all men, and are persecuted by all. They are unknown and condemned; they are put to death, and restored to life. They are poor, yet make many rich; they are in lack of all things, and yet abound in all; they are dishonoured, and yet in their very dishonour are glorified. They are evil spoken of, and yet are justified; they are reviled, and bless; they are insulted, and repay the insult with honour; they do good, yet are punished as evil-doers. When punished, they rejoice as if quickened into life; they are assailed by the Jews as foreigners, and are persecuted by the Greeks; yet those who hate them are unable to assign any reason for their hatred.[12]

Our heavenly citizenship does not necessarily distinguish us in readily apparent ways. We may well look like ordinary citizens of the world. For Christians live in homes, pay taxes, wear clothes not too out of fashion, walk dogs in the park, and drop children off for school. We work on factory lines and in airplanes; we help maintain roads and run companies. We contribute to the commonwealth of the societies in which we live, quite often with a higher degree of citizenship and sacrifice than others.

All the while, however, when the church is truly living out of the ascended Christ, her members know that they are not really home here. We are fish out of water, while our neighbours think the real meaning of life is actually accumulating the most wealth. We do not repudiate material things; we simply hold them but lightly. These are means, not ends; gifts not possessions. We weep when we lose property and houses but we never say 'I have lost everything', for everything to us is Christ and he cannot be lost. We speak the common language in the marketplace, yet we know that the language of our homeland – the words of worship, the story of God's redemption, the precious scriptures – may well sound like gibberish to our neighbours. We may well live in the same home for decades but we never feel truly home there, for this world is but a stop on the way to the heavenly country. Though the church may not react so charitably to insult as *The Epistle to Diognetus* suggests, we do know there is a higher way than revenge, a more excellent path than the constant jockeying for respect found in the world. We live under the law of love.

Augustine's Vision

In his masterwork, *The City of God*, Augustine envisioned this distinction between residents and pilgrims on earth in terms of two cities.[13] The human race has always been divided along lines of loyalty. Some have served the City of God, putting their allegiance to God above all else. Some have served the City of the World, of Satan, placing their faith in themselves. At first glance, this division of every person into one city or another may seem too simple. But Augustine knew how to take it deeper.

On earth, the two cities are always mixed. Citizens of God and citizens of Satan exist side by side not only in the marketplace but in the church as well. It is only at the Last Judgement that the two will appear plainly revealed. Then all will see the City of God: Jerusalem, and the City of the World: Babylon. Interestingly, the very name 'Babylon' means confusion, and the citizens of Babylon are those who confuse their true identity with the things of this world.

The citizens of the City of God, of the spiritual Jerusalem, live in this world with sighs and longings for another country, a heavenly city, in their hearts. Augustine writes, 'Let us pine for the City where we are citizens. By pining, we are already there; we have already cast our hope, like an anchor, on that coast. I sing of somewhere else, not of here: for I sing with my heart, not my flesh. The citizens of Babylon hear the sound of the flesh, the Founder of Jerusalem hears the tune of our heart.' We endure our existence on earth always sighing for heaven. We are what Augustine calls 'resident strangers'. We live here; we work here; we serve here. But our true home is elsewhere.[14]

In recognizing our distinctive identity as Christians, Augustine did not thereby fall into the error of withdrawal from the world. He was a man of the world, as sophisticated as any aristocrat, as educated as any scholar, as well-connected as any politician of his time. He understood that our life here on earth is always mixed. We long for the shores of heaven. But we live here on earth knowing we have an economy to which we contribute and from which we benefit. We share in the governing responsibilities of our land and in the commonwealth such service creates. We are here to improve the lot of others, to accept God's good gifts with thanks, to be salt and light in the world, not to withdraw from it. Augustine did not say Christians ought to separate themselves and head for the hills. Just the opposite.

The difference is that while we conduct 'our business within this common mortal life', we have an otherworldly longing, a heavenly perspective. God's people live in the world, work in it, love it, care for it but 'refuse to be engulfed' by it, deceived into thinking this is all there is. We strive to maintain our core identity as citizens of heaven even as we interact with the City of Babylon that sets itself up as independent of God.[15]

Augustine understood the allure and beauty of this world. He knew how easy it is to love the world too much. He preached to his congregation, 'I do not blame you; I do not criticize you, even if this life is what you love ... You can love this life all you want, as long as you know what to choose. Let us therefore be able to choose our life, if we are capable of loving it.'[16] The Christian does not withdraw, but strives to maintain a balance in what he or she loves, to give a clear priority to God in the midst of temptations.

The key for Augustine was remembering that God is the giver of all good gifts. He lavishes his kindnesses upon us, even amidst a world torn by sin and wracked with floods and accidents. The citizens of Babylon strive to grasp these things as theirs by right and desert. The citizens of the City of God recognize the Giver. We give thanks. Augustine compares us to a bride with a beautiful ring. We gaze upon this gift with pleasure but we do not for a minute forget the husband who gave it. It is only a token, a symbol. If the gift is this lovely, then how great is the One who loves us.

So Augustine could pray:

These things are Yours, O God. They are good
Because you are in them.
None of our evil is in them. The evil is ours if we love them
At the expense of Yourself – these things that reflect your design.[17]

Interaction with the world, even enjoyment of its good, is not what undoes the church. Our over-identification with the world is not simply because we have common cause with the affairs of the world. Rather our failure to lift up our hearts, to see Christ in heaven and give thanks, is what undoes our mission and compromises our witness. The error of Lucifer was 'he wished no other source of goodness than himself'.[18] He tried to be his own source, and so he fell. This basic denial of dependence is what ruins us. Then we make the world and all that is in it an end in itself. But as citizens of the City of God, we may participate in the life of the world, striving with it, thankful for it, bruised by it, hoping for it, knowing that this is not our truest home. Again, we touch these things but lightly. We do not possess anything and so we possess everything. For we belong to Christ and all things are his (1 Corinthians 3:22–3).

To keep her head above the frenzy of the world's destructive consumption of itself, the church must practise as a whole the spiritual discipline described in the next chapter. We must set our minds and hearts on Christ, who is seated above us in the heavenly places. Our life and mission begins there in him and comes down through the power and presence of the Holy Spirit. As we press forward, the same Spirit leads us homeward. So the church in her pilgrimage passes through the arid lands and springs well up from once-parched ground. Flowers bloom in the desert as she traverses it in faith.

William Milligan summarizes the vision for a church whose mission is drawn from the ascended and still incarnate Jesus:

> The true idea of the Church on earth is ... that of a Body starting from heaven, and so exhibiting, amidst the inhabitants of and things of time, the graces and privileges already ideally bestowed upon it, that it may lead the world either to come to the light or to condemn itself because it loves the darkness rather than the light, its deeds being evil.

> No doubt the Church can never during the days of her pilgrimage execute such a commission to the full ... Nevertheless the Church's ideal state supplies to her the standard of her duty, and to approach nearer to it ought to be her constant effort.

> The Church must be animated by the belief that she is elect not for her own sake, but for the world's; and that her life is to be a priestly life, in the name of the Heavenly Father, for the spreading of that 'kingdom' which, bringing men to God, brings them also to one another, and lifts them into that ideal sphere of the holy, the beautiful, and the loving which is as yet consummated only in the Great High-Priest in heaven.[19]

The church receives its mission from Christ, enacting a priestly life in the power of our High Priest, who is interceding for us and sending us the Spirit to empower our service. We live from above. So with the worship of our hearts reaching to him in heaven, we lay down our lives for the lost here on earth. We take up any human suffering and misery as falling within our care, and lift it as well to the ascended Lord. When the church thus keeps herself fixed on Jesus for her identity and purpose, 'there is no human want or weakness stranger to her. It is her part to heal every wound and to wipe away every tear.'[20] Such a sense of mission frees us from the world's game and empowers our mission to have an integrity the world cannot resist.

If the story and vision of the ascended, ever enfleshed Jesus can be recovered in the church, her people can be liberated from the shallow, enfeebling story of the currently entrenched consumerism. Then we can make our common way with others in this world, knowing that we are subversives. Christians are countercultural revolutionaries in the twenty-first-century west. We are spreading the customs of an alternative kingdom. Neither withdrawing nor capitulating, and never imagining we can do it ourselves, the church engages the world with the gospel. It is a struggle to the death which leads to life, staged amidst ordinary lives as the citizens of heaven seek to turn the world's attention up toward a higher vision.

Chapter 8

Spiritual Ascension

We have considered in some depth the meaning of Jesus'
triumphant ascension in the flesh. By his continuing incarnation,
he reigns with the Father, pours out his Holy Spirit and exercises
his priestly intercession for us while he prepares the place to
which he will bring us after his glorious return. This vision
informs the church of its pilgrim nature as Christ's body on earth
and its servant mission to the world. Now we may consider more
specifically how we partake of the ascended life of Christ. The
theology is meant to shape and invigorate our souls, evoking a
response of faith and gratitude. We find that there is a vital role
for us to play in active participation in Christ Jesus, a part which
includes knowledge, will, affection and action.

In his letter to the Ephesians, Paul sings the praises of God's
eternal plan of redemption now enacted in Christ. In the second
chapter, he describes our place in this story:

> But because of his great love for us, God, who is rich in mercy, made
> us alive with Christ even when we were dead in transgressions – it is
> by grace you have been saved. And God raised us up with Christ and
> seated us with him in the heavenly realms in Christ Jesus[.] (Ephesians
> 2:4–6)

Out of sheer love, when we were no better than a lifeless thing –
spiritually dead, bound by mortality and condemned to eternal
death – God quickened us to new life in Christ. The Son of God
united himself to our humanity in Jesus Christ. If that were not

miracle enough, by his Spirit he unites us to himself in Christ. Thus Paul speaks of what happened to Jesus as what happened to us; we stand in the closest possible relation to the life of Jesus. In using marvellous compound verbs, Paul evokes a sense of joint, perhaps simultaneous, action on God's part. God enlivened us together (*sunezoopoiesen*) with and in Christ, raised us together (*sunergeiren*) with and in Christ, and seated us together (*sunekathisen*) with and in Christ. We who lived *in* the sinful passions of the flesh, whose walk of life was in accord with the spirit that is *in* the sons of disobedience, and who were thus dead *in* trespasses and *in* sins, are now *in* Christ. Our lives are located in a new place; they have their wellspring now in the person of Jesus. We have been created in him (Ephesians 2:10) with the sense of being made anew, and, as Paul says elsewhere, *transferred* from the kingdom of darkness to the kingdom of light (Colossians 1:13). We thus partake of the death, resurrection, ascension and glory of Jesus. This reality is what is meant when 2 Peter 1:4 asserts that through God's 'very great and precious promises' we may 'participate in the divine nature'. Our lives are all in him. His life is ours.

Throughout the centuries, one of the most striking ways to speak of such union with Christ has been that of *theopoesis*, or deification. In theological shorthand, *theopoesis* means that the Son of God became what we are that we might become what he is. The concept sounds incredible, perhaps even offensive, as well as electrifying at first hearing. A cascade of phrases from the theologians we have been hearing on the ascension may serve to establish the idea:

- Irenaeus writes of 'the Word of God, our Lord Jesus Christ, who did, through His transcendent love, become what we are, that He might bring us to be even what he is in himself' (*Against Heresies*, 5, preface).

- Athanasius asserts that Jesus 'prayed for us, taking on Him what is ours, and He was giving what He received ... For as He for our sake became man, so we for His sake are exalted' (*Against the Arians*, 4.7).

- Gregory Nazianzen urges us to 'become like Christ, since Christ became like us'. This imitation is based on how Jesus has exalted us in union with himself: 'He came down that we might be exalted ... He ascended that He might draw to Himself us, who were lying low in the Fall of sin' (*Oration 1*, 5).

- The great synthesizer of preceding thought, Leo, declares that Jesus in his union with us is saying, 'For I have united you with Myself, and am become Son of Man that you might have power to be sons of God' (*Sermons*, 5)

- Calvin follows Athanasius in declaring, 'This is the wonderful exchange which, out of his measureless benevolence, he has made with us; that, becoming Son of man with us, he has made us sons of God with him; that, by his descent to earth, he has prepared an ascent to heaven for us' (*Institutes*, 4.17.2).

- Closer to our day, William Milligan has written: 'While the Redeemer comes to us, made in all things like unto His brethren, He comes chiefly as the embodiment of a higher sphere, as One who, uniting us to Himself in a real, not a fictitious union, makes us members of a heavenly family gathered together in that House which is His own, and citizens of a heavenly City of which He is at once the Foundation and the Light ... our whole human life is brought in Him within the scope of His consecrating power, and every part of it is presented to God as a trophy of His victory' (*Ascension of Our Lord*, 102, 149).

- Andrew Murray declares that 'the knowledge of Jesus as having entered heaven for us, and taken us in union with Himself into a heavenly life, is what will deliver the Christian from all that is low and feeble, and lift him into a life of joy and strength. To gaze upon the beauty of the heavenly Christ in the Father's presence, to whom all things are subject, will transform us into heavenly Christians, dwelling all the day in God's presence and overcoming every enemy' (*Holiest of All*, 65).

All this we have in Jesus Christ, who, in taking our humanity with him to heaven in his ascension, has taken us with him spiritually as well! This is a present reality. When Paul writes in the Ephesians passage of our being seated together with Christ in the heavenlies, he employs the aorist verb tense, which means completed action. It is done and we are there. When we consider what the ascension means in the personal spiritual lives of believers today, this wonderful exchange is at the heart. The exaltation of Jesus in the ascension has established our exaltation in union with him.

Yet, two sets of disturbing questions immediately arise when we consider such news. First, can this really be so? Are we really supposed to take this 'deification' as anything more than a metaphorical way of speaking? Second, if all this is indeed true, then why are Christians – no, why am I – so anaemic in faith and practice? Why is there such a gap between the truth of my life described in scripture and theology and the reality of the life I live in the world? To these questions we turn.

Deification or Humanization?

From the passage cited above, Irenaeus is credited with the famous line, paraphrased through the patristic writings and both used and misused throughout theology, 'God became man that man might become God.' In his treatment of Irenaeus' doctrine of the ascension, Douglas Farrow explores the proper way to understand this theological shorthand:

> Here, while we are still talking about recapitulation in terms of the gift of the Spirit, is the place to treat this famous quotation, which is a formula for 'deification' only as authentic humanization. ... the love of which Irenaeus speaks is twofold. It is first of all love by which the divine Son becomes human, so that humanity might be given a filial character and definition. But that filial character can only be stamped upon us by the Holy Spirit, and we are those who live as if the Spirit were not. Hence the love ... is also and especially the love by which the Son pursues us into the place of our fallenness, engaging himself with us as we actually are, in our decline rather than our advance. He who by nature *is* the man of the Spirit posits himself for our sake as

the man in need of the Spirit. Invading 'the land of the sepulture,' he passes through every phase of human life and through every stage of our own backwards career, placing all within the redemptive remit of the Spirit ... [so that] the Spirit in turn might create a living and fruitful man ... That is how he brings us to be even what he is himself: not God, for in being God he is unique; yet certainly those who are able in their very flesh 'to receive and bear God,' that is to become partakers of the Spirit.[1]

The deification is actually a radical *humanization*. It is based on the life of Jesus lived as a man in the power of the Holy Spirit. The Son of God 'pursues us into the place of our falleness', taking the position of a man in need of the Spirit. As we saw in Chapter 6, Jesus did not act out of his divine nature and power, but emptying himself, he was baptized, anointed to preach and teach, empowered for works of healing, and even raised from the dead – *by the Spirit*. We do not become the divine Son – he is unique. Rather, we, too, are fitted by the Spirit for communion with the Father and empowered for service as the Spirit unites us continually to Jesus the new Adam. In Christ, we become men and women of the Spirit; our exaltation is the re-creation of humanity lived in joyful dependence on God, out of his very life, as we were meant to be.[2]

Athanasius, another great patristic writer who dared to speak so highly of our exaltation, was also careful to set the boundaries of how we understand our partaking of the Son. He writes:

And He said this too, not that we might become such as the Father; for to become as the Father, is impossible for us creatures, who have been brought to be out of nothing ... For as, although there be one Son by nature, True and Only-begotten, we too become sons, not as He in nature and truth, but according to the grace of Him that calleth, and though we are men from the earth, are yet called gods, not as the True God or His Word, but as has pleased God who has given us that grace.[3]

Our sonship is by grace. We do not become children of God in 'nature and truth', but in continual dependence on grace and the union of God and humanity forged for us in Christ. Spiritual ascension, then, is the work of the Holy Spirit, with which we may cooperate. Athanasius continues:

> Therefore because of the grace of the Spirit which has been given to
> us, in Him we come to be, and He in us ... the Son is in the Father, as
> His own Word and Radiance; but we, apart from the Spirit, are
> strange and distant from God, and by the participation of the Spirit
> we are knit into the Godhead; so that our being in the Father is not
> ours, but is the Spirit's which is in us and abides in us ... For what the
> Word has by nature, as I said, in the Father, that He wishes to be
> given to us through the Spirit irrevocably ... It is the Spirit then
> which is in God, and not we viewed in our own selves; and as we are
> sons and gods because of the Word in us, so we shall be in the Son
> and in the Father, and we shall be accounted to have become one in
> Son and in Father, because that that Spirit is in us, which is in the
> Word which is in the Father.[4]

In the mutual indwelling of perichoresis, the Father, the Son, and
the Spirit are all in one another by a communion of essence and an
eternal exchange of love. So it is the Spirit 'which is in God, and
not we viewed in our own selves'. When the Spirit of Christ is in
us, we are said to be in him, participating by the Spirit in the Son's
relationship with the Father. But our communion is ever derived
from his and eternally dependent on the operation of the Holy
Spirit. Athanasius declares that we are 'accounted' to 'have
become one in Son and in Father', precisely and only because the
Spirit who is properly in the Father and in the Son has
condescended to be in us. Our participation is always derivative.

The answer to our first set of questions, then, is a resounding
'Yes! We really are supposed to take this deification seriously.'
God means us to participate in his triune life. But we take the
place given to us always remembering that Jesus said 'Apart
from me you can do nothing' (John 15:5). T. F. Torrance warns
us against developing spiritual vertigo, the dizziness that may
come from contemplating the heights to which we have been
raised in Christ. For we always run the risk of taking Christ's
exaltation of our humanity in the ascension to be our own
possession. We are in Christ only through the continuing
uniting work of the Holy Spirit. As Jesus lived as the man of the
Spirit, so we too share in his exaltation only by this constant
dependence on the Spirit's work. Torrance, echoing Calvin,
summarizes this for us as follows:

It is through the Spirit that things infinitely disconnected – disconnected by the 'distance' of the ascension – are nevertheless infinitely closely related. Through the Spirit Christ is nearer to us than we are to ourselves, and we who live and dwell on earth are yet made to sit with Christ 'in heavenly places', partaking of the divine nature in him.[5]

In this way, and this way only, are we truly exalted in Christ.

What Prevents Us?

While we recognize that such a mighty work is entirely of God, we also know that we have a part to play. We did not forge our union with Christ; he came to us. Yet, we are not merely inert lumps, which are only acted upon. We have a will to exercise, a role to play and a response to make. While we are 'God's workmanship', we have nevertheless been 'created in Christ Jesus to do good works which God prepared in advance for us to do' (Ephesians 2:10). There is a plan for us in which we are, to render Paul's language more literally, 'to walk about', participating in the life and works uniquely prepared for each of us. Such a response may be considered under the discipline of spiritual ascension.

But here, the second set of questions comes in to humble us. With all these rich truths in our possession, why are we still so poor in our daily response of gratitude and service? The answer is devastatingly simple, and twofold. First, we generally live in ignorance of all we have in Christ and so it remains inert in our experience. Secondly, this ignorance contributes to our natural sinful tendency to fail to renounce ourselves and wholeheartedly obey Christ in whom is all our life. We therefore need to recover the spiritual disciplines that will enable us to keep the glory of the ascension and continuing incarnation before us and to serve in joyful response.

Calvin's sermon on Acts 1:6–8 insightfully places the issue of ignorance in the context of the ascension narrative. This third sermon on the ascension examines the disciples' question to the resurrected Jesus just before his departure: 'Lord, are you at this time going to restore the kingdom to Israel?' (Acts 1:6). They wanted to know if their Lord who had proven victorious over death was now going to finish the job, according to their ideas, and re-establish the earthly kingdom of Israel. Rome would thus be overturned and their nation restored to its rightful place. Jesus replied to them, 'It is not for you to know the times or dates the Father has set by his own authority. But you will receive power when the Holy Spirit comes on you; and you will be my witnesses in Jerusalem, and in all Judea and Samaria, and to the ends of the earth' (Acts 1:7–8). There was a fact about the Father's eternal plan which was hidden from them. Jesus gave them no answers along the lines of their questions. Rather, he directed them to the mission of bearing witness to what had been revealed to them – Jesus himself – when the Holy Spirit came upon them in power.

Calvin teases out two kinds of error in the disciples' question and makes direct application to our own attempt at spiritual ascension. First, the disciples were overly curious about things they did not need to know, yet deeply ignorant about matters given to them of the utmost importance. Calvin realizes that we are all prone to curiosity except in the areas where it is most necessary for us to make enquiry. He remarks that we get a headache if we hear the truth twice, and do not want more than two words about difficult spiritual matters that are crucial to our salvation. 'But when someone tells us fables, lies, and things of no profit, oh, we shall never be tired of listening to them, we spend the whole day that way.'⁶ Long before people spent hours watching television or surfing the Internet while becoming indignant at a worship service that lasts a minute past noon, it seems they had the same difficulty focusing on what matters when trivia can fill the mind just as well.

To resist the natural tendency for our minds to wander, Calvin urges: 'As far as your mind can extend, employ yourself in knowing more and more the love that God has shown by giving us Jesus Christ His Well-Beloved Son. This is where we ought to employ all our life.'⁷ It takes tremendous discipline to hold onto the truth that has been revealed to us. Without constant attention, our minds and hearts follow the worldview of the culture around us. We go with its flow automatically unless we are consciously swimming against the stream. The gospel, the story of Jesus come among us, is not native to us. It is a story foreign to our sinful hearts. Without the discipline of a rigorous submission to the truth revealed to us, we will quickly distort the narrative and shape its meaning to be more amenable to our inclinations. Thus, we absolutely require the community of the church, the means of grace, and a consecrated leadership exercising biblical discipline to draw our attention to matters of necessity.

The rule of truth, the faith of the church through the ages, is never easy. On the contrary, beholding, contemplating and embracing the truth of the gospel is always daring to the ingrown will, always a stretch for the clouded mind, always a prod to the lazy heart. The further from the mainstream of contemporary thought a piece of the gospel narrative is, the more difficult it is to maintain in our minds as a coherent part of our worldview. Thus, the ascension of Jesus in the flesh is always slipping away from sight, and requires a constant retelling as part of the whole story if we are not to lose it altogether. For there is no outside incentive for the church to recover this crucial piece of our story when it can so easily be spiritualized in a postmodern culture.

Moreover, we do not merely neglect gospel priorities but insist on occupying our attention with questions that cannot be solved in this life. Calvin observes that 'everyone wishes to go poking into things that God wished to be hidden from us. We wish to control our Lord, and it seems to us He would have done better to do otherwise.'[8] The discussions in our churches and denominations reveal that we are constantly trying to figure out how God could have 'done better to do otherwise'. We want to rewrite the story to suit us, and to exempt us from the death to our egos and sinful wills that is the life of the gospel.

The charge so often levelled against those who confess the truth revealed in the Word is that of arrogance. How can we claim to have all the truth? How can we dare to say we know what God is like? Calvin's comments sweep away such criticisms as ludicrous. *We* do not know anything about God on our own; in fact what can be known about God we naturally tend to ignore or distort. All we can do is point to who has been revealed: Jesus Christ. As Paul writes, 'For we do not preach ourselves, but Jesus Christ as Lord, and ourselves as your servants for Jesus' sake'; we only see the light of God shining in his face because 'the God who said "Let light shine out of darkness" in creation shines the light of his Spirit into our hearts so we may see what he has done' (2 Corinthians 4:5, 6). The real struggle is to turn our wandering, warped minds towards the truth, to behold the ascended Lord in his Word and pray that such a vision will shape us to his image.

The Quest to Ascend Spiritually

Our work of response to the gospel is that of attuning our minds and wills to the reality that has been revealed. This is a means of transformation recognized through the centuries. John Chrysostom urged his congregation to 'ascend in thy thought' toward our Christ in heaven since 'we have as yet no means of seeing this with our bodily eyes'.[9] Elsewhere he exhorts us to 'Stretch forth the will, stretch forth as far as thou wilt, yea even to heaven itself.'[10] Fifteen centuries later, Andrew Murray explains:

> The knowledge of Jesus as having entered heaven for us, and taken us in union with Himself into a heavenly life, is what will deliver the Christian from all that is low and feeble, and lift him into a life of joy and strength. To gaze upon the beauty of the heavenly Christ in the Father's presence, to whom all things are subject, will transform us into heavenly Christians, dwelling all the day in God's presence and overcoming every enemy ... Blessed the man who knows to look away from all that he finds in himself of imperfection and failure, to look up and behold all the perfection and glory he finds in Jesus![11]

The study of the theology of the ascension is not an end in itself; its purpose is to lead us to 'gaze upon the beauty of the heavenly Christ in the Father's presence' so that we might be conformed more and more to be like him. Getting out of ourselves, we find the blessed life. Knowledge of what God has made known to us through the Spirit in the Word transforms our worship and prayer so that we experience reaching farther, getting closer, and more fully taking our place with Christ in the heavenly realms.

As a man who had lived many years as a pagan, indulging the desires of the flesh and the 'wisdom' of the age, Augustine knew from experience what truly satisfies the soul. He could therefore, at midlife, dare with confidence to send his readers in pursuit of life, wherever they supposed it to be, knowing they would return to him hungry for truth:

> Him let us love, Him let us love; He created these, nor is He far off . . . He is within the very heart, but yet hath the heart wandered from Him. Return to your heart . . . and cleave fast unto Him that made you. Stand with Him, and you shall stand fast. Rest in Him, and you shall be at rest. Whither go ye in rugged paths? Whither go ye? The good that you love is from Him; and as it has respect unto Him it is both good and pleasant, and justly shall it be embittered, because whatsoever cometh from Him is unjustly loved if He be forsaken for it. Why, then, will ye wander farther and farther in these difficult and toilsome ways? There is no rest where ye seek it. Seek what ye seek; but it is not there where ye seek? Ye seek a blessed life in the land of death; it is not there. For could a blessed life be what life itself is not?[12]

Augustine wisely, boldly challenges his audience to go on and seek with gusto all they believe they are seeking which will satisfy the soul's hunger. Pursue all the world has to offer. Do it with diligence. But he warns them that what they seek will not be there when they get to the end of the quest. Looking for life in the land of death will never work, though we may have to walk through that valley to believe it. When we return to our hearts, we will find that God is near and has been waiting for us.

In the next section, Augustine links the quest to the story of Jesus, and, in particular, to his ascension:

> But our very Life descended hither, and bore our death, and slew it, out of the abundance of His own life; and thundering He called loudly to us to return hence to Him . . . For He tarried not, but ran crying out by words, deeds, death, life, descent, ascension, crying aloud to us to return to Him. And He departed, and behold, He is here. He would not be long with us, yet left us not; for He departed thither, whence He never departed, because 'the world was made by Him.' And in this world He was, and into this world He came to save sinners, unto whom my soul doth confess, that He may heal it, for it hath sinned against Him. O ye sons of men, how long so slow of heart? Even now, after the Life is descended to you, will ye not

ascend and live? ... Descend that ye may ascend, and ascend to God
... Tell them this, that they may weep in the valley of tears, and so
draw them with thee to God.[13]

'Our very life' came down to us. And he was not silent or shy. He
ran to us, and 'thundering He called loudly to us to return'. All his
acts, whether in word or deed, dying or rising, were meant to call
us back to himself. He even ascended, departing from our grasp
that we might 'return to our heart, and there find Him'. He left our
sight so that he might come to our heart, to our innermost being.
Paradoxically, we ascend to where he is by descending. That
means leaving off pride, refusing to attempt to be our own gods
and make our own life, and instead humbling ourselves even as
we open our hearts. We look within our hearts, not to see more of
ourselves, but to find Christ and have our attention drawn away
to him, lifting us by the Spirit into the invigorating life for which
our weary souls have pined. Spiritual ascension is for Augustine a
necessary act on our part, based utterly on Christ's acts on our
behalf. What George Herbert said of scripture is true of Christ as
well: 'heav'n lies flat in thee, / Subject to ev'ry mounter's bended
knee'.[14] When we bend the knee of the heart *to* Christ, we ascend
to heaven *with* and *in* Christ.

Renunciation

Augustine understood that the quest for God, often pursued
amidst ignorance and wilfulness, ultimately leads us to the need
to submit to the truth of God as he has been revealed in Jesus
Christ. This brings us to the second error Calvin finds in the
disciples' question to the departing Jesus. They desire to 'triumph
at once and then to live wishfully without any pain'. This
weakness we all have in common with the apostles. For 'there is
no one who does not desire to reign with Jesus Christ in that
eternal salvation which He has promised us'. We are happy to
share Christ's seat in heaven, but we prefer to skip the part about
the cross. Calvin urges his congregation to 'now put our hand to
the work. Do we wish to be victorious with him? Let us fight,
since we are in time of war. If we wish to be sharers in all his

benefits, we must endure the hardship which He will permit to come to us in this world.' We have a role to play, and we must get on with it no matter what the cost. For, obvious as it seems, we are nevertheless continually undone in spiritual ascension by our unwillingness to renounce our love for this world and our own interests.[15]

Andrew Murray sees a crucial link between the two errors of ignorance and the failure to give over our lives:

> They wonder that they have so little of the peace and joy, of the purity and power which the Saviour gives, and which faith in Him ought to bring. The reason is simple, because Christ is only their Aaron, not their Melchizedek. They do indeed believe that He is ascended to heaven, and sits upon the throne of God; but they have not seen the direct connection of this with their daily spiritual life. They do not count upon Jesus working in them in the power of the heavenly life, and imparting it to them. They do not know their heavenly calling, with the all-sufficient provision for its fulfilment in them secured in the heavenly life of their Priest-King. And as a consequence of this, they do not see the need for giving up the world, to have their life and walk in heaven.[16]

For Murray, a deficiency in understanding all that the priesthood of the ascended Christ means to us blinds us to the need to give over control of our lives. Not knowing how available to us is the life of Christ in heaven, we fear to let go of this world we can see and know. Spiritual ascension through knowledge is vital for influencing our wills.

Knowledge and renunciation are really like the two pedals on a bicycle: one directly influences the other. Murray continues:

> Our great High Priest has His sanctuary in the heavens; there He dwells, there we find Him ... there He proves that He is a Priest who abides continually, and who gives those who come to God through Him the power to do it, too – to abide continually in His presence. ... [But] to enter in demands a very entire renunciation of the world and of self, a very real and true participation in Christ's humbling of Himself and becoming obedient unto death, even the death of the cross – in His death to sin. And it demands no less a very real experience of the mighty operation of God, which raised Him from the dead and set Him at His right hand ... The work done by Jesus in the heavenly sanctuary must have its counterpart in the heart that is to enter that sanctuary ... The new covenant does no violence to

man's will. It is only where the heart sees and believes what God has promised, and is ready at any cost to claim and possess it, that any blessing can be realised ... Our place is deep dependence, patient waiting, and implicit reliance on His mighty power ... There is no way but utterly ceasing from ourselves, dying to self, and waiting in absolute dependence and deep humility upon God ... Let us sink into the death of emptiness and nothingness and helplessness; let us, as dead, wait for the mighty operation of God.[17]

To take our place with the ascended Christ requires not only knowing all we have in him, but also recognizing how we have died with him, too, and then agreeing paradoxically to live out of that death.

Paul provides for us the paradigm which encompasses both of the concerns of Calvin and Murray:

Since, then, you have been raised with Christ, set your hearts on things above, where Christ is seated at the right hand of God. Set your minds on things above, not on earthly things. For you died, and your life is now hidden with Christ in God. When Christ, who is your life, appears, then you also will appear with him in glory. Put to death, therefore, whatever belongs to your earthly nature: sexual immorality, impurity, lust, evil desires and greed, which is idolatry. (Colossians 3:1–4)

The fact of our being raised with Christ directs us to respond by setting our minds and hearts on this reality. We 'lift up our hearts' toward a greater reality. This knowledge leads us to recognize the hard side of our new life — the old life has been crucified with Christ. We, on our own, are hidden in Christ. We bear this humiliation in hope of the glory to come when the ascended Lord returns for us. We are kept securely in the story of Jesus which has not yet been completed. He has swept us up in his coming and so our future is determined not by the world nor by our variable moods but by the certainty that the Triune God who began the world's redemption will complete it. Out of this knowledge, we dare to add our wills in agreement with God's purposes for us. We who have died with Christ now consciously put to death the impulses and activities of the sinful nature which, though slain in Christ, yet resides as a dead snake still moving for a while longer within us. Renunciation, or descent, is an essential aspect of spiritual ascent and the embracing of Christ's work on our behalf.

Clothing According to Our Station

There is a positive side to our response beyond expanding our minds and wills to know how Christ is towards us. Paul goes on to exhort his readers to the obverse of renunciation:

> Therefore, as God's chosen people, holy and dearly loved, clothe yourselves with compassion, kindness, humility, gentleness and patience. Bear with each other and forgive whatever grievances you may have against one another. Forgive as the Lord forgave you. And over all these virtues put on love, which binds them all together in perfect unity. (Colossians 3:12–14)

Following Christ into our place with him in heaven involves ascending in the way of love. Paul's metaphor is that of getting dressed according to our station. This is not pretending to be something we are not, but adorning our lives according to our identity in Christ. A pauper may have only one rag to put on, but children of the Most High have a splendid set of clothes they may choose to wear. The shining garment of Christ's righteousness upon us shimmers in all we do. Our choices for love and kindness, service and forgiveness adorn our appearance as those clearly belonging to him.

Once again we turn to Augustine for a sparkling illustration to link our acts of compassion to spiritual ascension. Because Christ is not only in heaven with his Father in splendour, but is here 'in His poor', we are called to make a connection with Christ in heaven by ministering to Jesus in his poor on earth:

> He then who could do so great things, was hungry, and athirst, was wearied, slept, was apprehended, beaten, crucified, slain. This is the way; walk by humility, that you may come to eternity. Christ-God is the Country whither we go; Christ-Man is the Way whereby we go. To Him we go, by Him we go; why fear we lest we go astray? He departed not from the Father; and came to us ... He has now risen again, and ascended into heaven, there He is, and sits at the right Hand of the Father: and here He is needy in His poor ... He is at once above, and below; above in Himself, below in His; above with the Father, below in us ...

> Fear Christ above; recognise Him below. Have Christ above
> bestowing His bounty, recognise Him here in need. Here He is poor,
> there He is rich. That Christ is poor here, He tells us Himself for me,
> 'I was an hungered, I was thirsty, I was naked, I was a stranger, I was
> in prison.' And to some He said, 'Ye have ministered unto Me,' and
> to some He said, 'Ye have not ministered unto Me.' . . . So then Christ
> is rich and poor; as God, rich; as Man, poor. Yea rich too now as
> Very Man He has ascended into heaven, sits at the right Hand of the
> Father; yet still He is poor and hungry here, thirsty, and naked.[18]

'Christ-God is the country whither we go.' Our goal is the
realization of the wonderful communion with his Father which he
has opened to us. We get to that far country through his descent
to us as man. Our union with Christ-man is strengthened when
we love him by loving his poor. Because the Son of God walked
among us in flesh that he yet retains, he has established the worth
of all flesh. Declaring himself to be fed and clothed when his
disciples feed and clothe even the 'least of these' (Matthew 25:40),
Jesus founded the Christian ethic of love for the needy.
Moreover, he articulated the link between loving action and
spiritual ascent. They are to be inseparable.

The most daring and engaged ministries of compassion and
evangelism will mark churches living in vivid awareness of the
continuing incarnation of Jesus. Our Lord is in heaven, but he is
also here among the least of the least. Remaining incarnate, he
directs us to cherish all those with whom he is a brother after the
flesh. Thus, no one is to be left out of the sphere of the church
living in the power of the Spirit of the ascended Jesus. As William
Milligan has said:

> The glorified Lord is human as well as Divine. Even at the right hand
> of God He is still the man Christ Jesus. The feelings, the emotions,
> the sympathies of His heart are exactly what they were when He
> welcomed the first symptoms of contrition in the woman who came
> to Him in Simon's house, or when He wept over the unbelief of
> Jerusalem. Even now He would leave no penitent uncheered, no
> mourner uncomforted, no friend unloved, no little child unblessed;
> and in all this He is the truly human as well as the Divine Priest of
> men . . . When the Church keeps this in view there is no human want
> or weakness strange to her. It is her part to heal every wound and to
> wipe away every tear.[19]

The heavenly life of Christ directs us away from pursuing the world, with its goods, its corridors of power and arenas of entertainment, as an end in itself, but at the same time sends us right into the world with all the sympathies of our Lord to the least and the lost.

Means of Grace: The Lord's Supper

Spiritual ascension requires full employment of the traditional means of grace. Committed to regular worship on the Lord's Day with his people, we will thus routinely witness baptisms. Each time, we recall our participation in the one baptism of Jesus Christ, who joined himself so closely to us that he went under the waters of consecration and obedience unto death for our sake. The sacrament is a sign of our incorporation into his one body, the church, whose head is in heaven. We study the scriptures and labour to imprint them on our minds and hearts so that the tracks are laid down along which the Holy Spirit may bring the knowledge of Jesus ascended which is so foreign to our usual thought. To the scriptures we add the great writings that have consistently nourished Christ's people, drinking from the well of ancient wisdom. We engage our daily activities with increasing consciousness that all we do and say is for the Lord's sake, no matter how menial or seemingly irrelevant. But knowing how great is the need beyond our usual sphere of activity, we intentionally join with those doing significant ministry to those who are poor in either body or soul. All of these activities are wrapped in prayer, both as regular time apart from the world to be with the Father and as a constant connection to the Triune God through the paces of daily life.

One of the means of grace in particular, however, relates to Jesus ascended: regular participation in the Lord's Supper. As we saw in Chapter 2, Calvin's bold insights into the nature of Christ at the Father's right hand arose in tandem with his understanding of Communion. At the table of grace, Jesus who is absent from us draws near by the work of the Holy Spirit. The elements do not literally become the body and blood of Jesus. But Jesus, who is still actually embodied, feeds us with the power, the energy and the virtue of his glorified life through the sacrament. He gives us the substance of his flesh, but that 'substance' arrives spiritually, not carnally, as the Spirit unites us with Jesus.[20] When we partake of the sacrament with faith that fixes on the reality of who Jesus is, we are lifted up into his presence and nourished by his very life.

Calvin explains:

> We teach that Christ is to be sought by faith, that he may manifest his presence; and the mode of eating which we hold is, that by the gift of his Spirit he transfuses into us the vivifying influence of his flesh ...
>
> The flesh of Christ is spiritually eaten by us, because he vivifies our souls in the very manner in which our bodies are invigorated by food: only we exclude a transfusion of substance ...
>
> By the virtue of his Spirit and his own divine essence, he not only fills heaven and earth, but also miraculously unites us with himself in one body, so that that flesh, although it remain in heaven, is our food. Thus I teach that Christ, though absent in body ... makes his flesh give life to us. For seeing he penetrates to us by the secret influence of his Spirit, it is not necessary, as we have elsewhere said, that he should descend bodily.
>
> For I do not simply teach that Christ dwells in us by his Spirit, but that he so raises us to himself as to transfuse the vivifying rigor of his flesh into us.[21]

Participation in the Supper is a profound Yes to the work the Spirit desires to do. We lift up our hearts in faith and believe that the Spirit is lifting us up to the ascended Christ to be fed with his very life. This is the visible enacting and strengthening of the work of the Spirit in joining us to Christ in salvation.[22] He quickens our faith to believe the gospel even as he unites us to Jesus, knitting us into the life of our saviour and all his benefits. The Lord's Supper confirms that work and tightens the bond of our union, in as much as partaking of the Supper in faith makes us more and more conscious of who we are in Christ, seated now with him in the heavenlies. Though we are already in Christ, the sacrament reveals that our union is not static, but dynamic. It can grow and deepen as the wonderful exchange is freely entered again and again. The Lord's Supper, then, is crucial if we seek to maintain a living vision of Jesus ascended.

Whatever? No, What of It!

Lastly, we must note one difficult reality facing those on the quest for spiritual ascension. Taking our place with Christ in heaven through the means of grace does not save us from conflict or suffering. Indeed, our sorrow will exceed that of those who are ignorant of how deeply the thorn of death has sunk into humanity. We will feel the futility of those who walk in the darkness, and be stung by the deprivation of those who have debased themselves or been diminished by others. The more conscious we are of being united to the man of sorrows who bears the marks of his piercing even now, the more our hearts will ache not only for our lot but for the sinking, desperate situation of the world about us. There is simply no way around this. But adjusting our expectations can be an immense help. We do not expect this world to be our home, for our home is with Christ in heaven. We do not demand to win here, for the victory celebration awaits us there.

Nevertheless, we are not without joy even amidst the most heart-breaking pangs of compassion. Those who live in growing awareness of their union with the ascended, incarnate Jesus have access to the deepest wells of joy, joy which arises from the very depths of the mirth of God. In his fourth ascension sermon, Calvin emboldens his congregation with these words:

> Thus, since He has gone up there, and is in heaven for us, let us note that we need not fear to be in this world. It is true that we are subject to so much misery that our condition is pitiable, but at that we need neither be astonished nor confine our attention to ourselves. Thus, we look to our Head Who is already in heaven, and say, 'Although I am weak, there is Jesus Christ Who is powerful enough to make me stand upright. Although I am feeble, there is Jesus Christ who is my strength. Although I am full of miseries, Jesus Christ is in immortal glory and what He has will some time be given to me and I shall partake of all His benefits. Yes, the devil is called the prince of this world. But what of it? Jesus Christ holds him in check; for He is King of heaven and earth. There are devils above us in the air who make war against us. But what of it? Jesus Christ rules above, having entire control of the battle. Thus, we need not doubt that He gives us the victory. I am here subject to many changes, which may cause me to lose courage. But what of it? The Son of God is my Head, Who is

exempt from all change. I must, then, take confidence in Him.' This is how we must look at His Ascension, applying the benefit to ourselves.[23]

Popular expression today reacts to a change in circumstances or requirements with a shrug of indifference and a curt 'Whatever.' In this way we detach ourselves from that which might make a claim on us. Calvin urges a kind of detachment as well, but not one which arises from indifference. Rather, out of the most profound hope, the Christian church looks upon the worst setbacks and sufferings and declares, in the very teeth of death and loss, 'What of it? Christ Jesus reigns in heaven, and so, at the deepest level, all is well. What of my circumstance? I am in Christ and he has triumphed. In him, by the Holy Spirit, I am kept in heaven.' The ascension provides the very ground for our peace in every circumstance.

Summary

As we have considered the ascension throughout these pages, we realize that this obscure theological subject brings us to the very heart of the gospel. It is an inseparable piece of the narrative, and vital to the future completion of the story of Jesus. The value of the ascension for us, however, at the most personal level, is not merely to help us make sense of the Christian faith. Rather, the ascension of Jesus in the flesh provides the grounds for asserting Christ's continuing incarnation. This means that he remains united to us. That union, of the eternal Son to our humanity, is absolutely vital to the hope that we might be united to him through the Holy Spirit. When by faith we grasp the reality that we are in Christ, that the wonderful exchange has occurred, then, with Chrysostom, we may 'understand that it is possible for thee to inhabit earth as it were heaven'.[24]

Andrew Murray has said it best of all those I have read:

> He is a Priest for ever, a Priest in the power of an endless life, a Priest who opens to us the state of life to which He Himself has entered in, and brings us there to live here on earth with the life of eternity in our bosom. . . . Jesus is in heaven *for thee*, to secure thee a life on earth

in the power and joy of heaven, to maintain the kingdom of heaven within thee, by that Spirit, through whom God's will is done on earth as it is in heaven.[25]

Jesus our High Priest is in heaven, living the state of life – the communion with his Father in the Spirit – in our name and on our behalf. One day 'we shall see face to face' (1 Corinthians 13:8). Though now we see but in a glass darkly, and experience our communion but thinly, we yet have the promise that right now, on earth, we may live 'with the life of eternity in our bosom'. Spiritually Christ Jesus brings us *there* so that we may live *here*, in the power and joy of heaven. We have our head in heaven, so we may drink from his living waters, the water of that far country even in this dry and parched desert of earth.

Chapter 9

Models for Recovering the Ascension in the Life of the Church

The doctrine of the ascension is not readily in the hearts and minds of church members. Taken by itself, the doctrine does not particularly appeal to their attention. It seems a dusty clause of the creed, dear perhaps to the odd theologian, but disconnected from normal everyday living. Introducing the ascension for the transformation of the church, then, requires some creativity in presentation and an appeal to the *results* of its reality. At the same time, employing the doctrine freshly requires taking it into the heart of ministry and the presentation of the gospel. Sermons, teaching, prayer disciplines, and even mission planning must all reflect a renewed emphasis on this event of our salvation history.

In an attempt to see the doctrine all the way through, from its biblical source to the daily life of the church, I use five models:

1. Preparation and use of core research for teaching and preaching in both the local and wider church.

2. A five-week teaching series entitled Rejoicing in Our Union with Christ, with consideration of the ascension as the foundation.

3. A thirty-day prayer guide for use by individuals.

4. An evening seminar series called Christ in the Marketplace for various vocations. The following details are offered as springboards for your own efforts to adapt this doctrine for recovery in your church situation.

5. A retreat programme with the ascension at its core, used in our local church for mission planning and subsequent ministry projects.

Model One: Use of Core Research

My sense of calling to explore the ascension led to several years of research on the subject. Most of that effort is contained in previous pages. The large number of quotations from theologians of the ascension is intended to be a resource for those pursuing the subject, pulling together what I consider to be the best of what has been written. From their work, we each create our own sermons, prayers, lectures and lessons.

It may, however, be helpful to see a few illustrations and trajectories from my sermons on the ascension here in North Carolina. Adapt them as you wish.

From 'With Christ on High (John 20:17)'
I am returning to my Father and your Father, to my God and your God. Without Christ, we are cut off from the Father and can hardly fathom, let alone embrace, the intimacy of such a name for God. But in Christ, we participate in the relationship he has with the Father. We are taken into that fellowship. Jesus' Father is our Father. His God, his relationship with God as a man, is ours. The God who comes to us in every hour invites us to participate in all he has. We partake *vicariously*, in his life, death, and resurrection, as if what happened to him has happened to us.

Such intimacy, though, occurs in the context of Jesus' saying that he is returning to his Father and our Father. Jesus' ascension into heaven is the completing step that makes all the benefits of his life among us available now. In fact, the doctrine of the ascension, so seldom discussed in the church, actually provides the gateway through which we may understand how we participate in the triune life of God through the work of Jesus Christ. The ascension provides the key to understanding how we may partake most fully of the Christ we have met in these stories from the gospels. Perhaps an example from daily life may provide insight into this mystery.

I once went to a concert without actually being there. For years I have had a great love for the Irish singer Van Morrison. His music nourishes my soul, and when I am running on empty, under stress, or just full of the passion of life, I often put on one of my two dozen Van Morrison CDs. His version of 'Be Thou My Vision' is so hearty it would please St Patrick himself. Strangely, two of my best friends in the world also find a soulmate in Morrison.

Several summers ago, one of these men, Cary, came to visit us while we were vacationing in the mountains. That first evening, after dinner, he said he had a story he wanted to tell me. He couldn't have told it over the phone; it had to wait to be told in person. Then he handed me a T-shirt − it was from the Van Morrison tour. 'You were there,' Cary said. And then he told me how it happened.

Van doesn't play a lot of concerts, and he rarely visits more than a handful of cities when he does tour. Sometimes we speculate about where he might be after a new album is released. Cary, who lives in Cincinnati, Ohio, had called a ticket company in New York City, just on a whim. 'Yes,' the voice said, 'Van's playing next Sunday night on the New Jersey shore.'

My friend thought instantly of getting tickets and then challenging us to find a way to get there. 'But it's sold out,' the operator said.

'Are you sure?' he asked. 'Could you check again?'

The agent punched her computer. 'I've got one seat.'

Van was playing more than four hundred miles away. The concert was on a Sunday night and Cary is a minister. So at noon, right after services, he bolted from the church door in his robes, changing as he drove. Stopping only for fuel, he arrived at the 8 p.m. concert an hour late. But Van had been delayed, and the music had just begun. Cary's ticket was in the twelfth row. The concert was incredible. And as he talked, I knew that in a very real sense I'd been there too.

Cary went without telling either friend. He went, though, in our name and on our behalf. He wasn't alone. And I felt as if I had been there. I wanted every detail. It was my trip, vicariously, as much as his. And I had the T-shirt to prove it. My man, my friend had gone up for me.

I don't know if you've ever had such a vicarious experience before. You may not even believe me when I tell you there was a mystical quality about hearing his story. I lived through him. If you've known such a feeling in even a modest way, though, then you are on the way to the meaning of the ascension. . . .

For Jesus, who took our humanity into himself, takes our humanity, literally, up into the presence of God. . . .

To return to our example, my friend Cary sat in the twelfth row of a Van Morrison concert, and in some sense, he took me with him. He went as my friend and representative. But my vicarious attendance was only a shadow of reality. Jesus Christ, as the head of humanity, ascended to his Father, in reality, in the flesh. Joined to Christ by the Holy Spirit through faith, you and I are there with him. Spiritually, we participate now in what Christ has accomplished in his resurrection body. This union is a foretaste of all that will come to us in the future. Paul tells us, 'God raised us up in Christ and seated us with him in the heavenly realms in Christ Jesus' (Ephesians 2:6). Not only did God come to where we are in Christ, but he has taken us up to be where he is! Christ wants us with him always and he has made it possible. . . .

Our man, Christ Jesus, has ascended the heights of heaven for us. He still bears his humanity fully, and that means he still bears us with him. You are there, in him. Our friend and brother Jesus, flesh of our flesh and bone of our bones, the new Adam, has ascended, and we went with him. Spiritually for now, yes, but nonetheless in reality.

From 'Whatever? No, What of It? (Acts 1:1–12)'
A few months ago, ESPN celebrated episode 25,000 of Sports Center. In the promo, a man asks, 'How did you ever keep track

of what episode it was? How do you know?' The camera cuts to someone in a giant bird mascot suit, sifting haphazardly through video tapes which are in total disarray around the room. The other man replies, 'Oh, we got a guy.'

Beneath the humour, there's a profound truth there. How do you know that when you die, you don't just rot in the grave for ever? We got a guy. A guy in heaven, in our name and on our behalf. He lives in a glorified body. He promises he will give one to us. How do you know, in a world such as this, that evil won't triumph? We got a guy. He got killed, and he rose. He is in heaven, preparing a place for us, preparing to restore all things. We got a guy. How do you know God will accept you at the judgement day? How can you be sure that you're really OK with God? We got a guy. In our name and on our behalf, he appears before the Father. He prays for us, he speaks our names. He is there, still in skin, as the pledge of our acceptance, as the pledge of what is to come. We got a guy.

After quoting from the Calvin sermon discussed at the close of Chapter 8, the sermon continued:

We have been dealing with one of the most difficult parts of Jesus-history to understand. It seems to have no connection to our lives. Yet, as we reflect, we realize that having a man in heaven on our behalf means everything.

Jesus has not forgotten us. He has taken our humanity with him. That is the guarantee of his return. Jesus has not dropped us. He holds in himself our very nature. By staying in skin, he as the one who is still man offers his perfect obedience *as a man* in our name and on our behalf. Jesus has not discarded this flesh which we love, this world which we love. The eternal Son of God has woven the stuff of creation for ever into his being. He cares about this world. He cares about the sparrows and about you and me. He cares enough to cleave to us for all time. There is no other religious conception like this on the face of the earth. Flesh is in heaven. Spirit and flesh are united. The ancient breach is healed. In Christ, we can be connected to God the Father.

Yes, this body of mine is failing, and people I love are fading.

But what of it? We got a guy in heaven who has secured eternal life. The church fails in its witness. We seem indistinguishable from the world and truth is everywhere muted and blunted. But what of it? We got a guy. The man Jesus is the Lord Christ, who reigns over all the kings of earth. His truth will triumph. Terror threatens, coarseness worsens, the world is a harder place to be every day. But what of it? We got a guy. This same Jesus who reigns will return. He will set all things right. So we are free to spend our lives in his service. Praise be to our exalted Lord!

From 'The New and Living Way (Hebrews 10:19–25)'

It has come to be known as the Ice Bowl. We actually have a member of this congregation who was there, on the famous frozen tundra of Lambeau Field in Green Bay one frigid day in January of 1967. Vince Lombardi, in his long coat and winter hat, strode the sidelines demanding more, and still more, from his players. The year before he had led his Packers to an NFL championship victory. Now he wanted the right to play in the first edition of what would come to be known as the Super Bowl. In his way were the Dallas Cowboys, an expansion team from the southlands which had never before had a winning season. The upstart Cowboys had taken the subzero temperatures in their stride and forged a 27–27 tie. Would the old order change on this hostile afternoon in Wisconsin?

Time was running out, as were the plays remaining. The Packers drove to within inches of the goal line. It was fourth down. What play would Lombardi call? Eleven men lined up against eleven men at the goal, all of them freezing cold and aching; all of them exhausted; every one of them determined. I was only eight years old when it occurred, but I remember watching, in warm and comfortable Miami, as the play seemed to unfold in slow motion. The Packers quarterback, and my hero, Bart Starr, got the hike. His line surged forward. The Cowboys pushed back. But one man, Jerry Kramer, the right guard, made a way. A tiny opening. Starr rode in over Kramer's back, the ball just crossing the line. Packers win. And the Super Bowl was just an exhibition in comparison. Thousands of miles away, a young boy could feel the moment – the struggle of men against men, labouring with all their might until one made a path for another.

Why do I tell you this story? Because after eight months this football fan is starved for the return of the game? Maybe. But I've also been searching for ways to illustrate the central idea of our text today: Jesus Christ, the new and living way. Jerry Kramer, against a staggering, hostile will opposing him, moved the pile. Bart Starr rode in on his back to glory. One man made a way for another.

Jesus Christ passed through the heavens. Against the surge of darkness, he drank the cup of obedience and went to the cross. Amidst the cackling jeers of the evil ones at his bloody defeat, he rose from the grave. The earth cracked, the tomb opened and Christ came forth triumphant. Then he returned to his Father. Still wearing our flesh, he passed through the heavens. The principalities and powers were disarmed. He led captivity captive – humanity, long captive to sin and death, rode in his train of glory as he made his way. Then, Jesus entered within the veil, into the Holy of Holies, the direct presence of God the Father. He entered, Hebrews tells us, as a forerunner for us. He appears there now, wearing our humanity, on our behalf. He is the new and living way to God.

Model Two: Teaching Series

During research on this project, I invited our Wednesday study group to join me for a series entitled Rejoicing in Our Union with Christ. The five-week programme was indeed a study of Jesus' ascension. But pastors are also programme directors and marketers. I knew we would fail to gather, much less keep an audience, by baldly calling the series A Study of the Ascension and then failing in the teaching to make connections to the lives of the people. So the core research had to be probed with a question: why does the ascension matter to ordinary people? The teaching strategy for the first class reveals the model for the whole series.

First, we began the class by considering the following:

The relationship between God and humanity is of utmost interest to us. It touches the most fundamental human longings, arising from a series of primal questions. Am I alone? Is there a Creator, a God? Is this God personal; can God in any way be known? And if so, can I be connected, related to this God? What has kept me from God before now and what is God's disposition towards me at this moment? Finally, will this relationship be of benefit and aid to me in the face of suffering, death and understanding my purpose?

The strategy, then, was to begin with the most basic existential questions and then lead the class to consider how they are answered in the triune being of God.

So, second, we turned to the essence of Christianity:

Christianity offers the most profound depths of relatedness to God ever uttered by human lips.

We profess that human beings may live in relationship with God so close, so intimate that the union of husband and wife in marriage is but a shadow of the communion offered between God and his people.

How have we come to know of this possibility of communion?

It has been revealed to us. God made himself known in Jesus Christ. From the appearing of Jesus Christ, when by the Holy Spirit's light we grasp that Jesus is God come to us as man, we learn the profound truth: God is love. The very being of God is composed of relatedness. . . .

God has shone his face in a particular way. And so he has revealed a way of relating to himself that involves a thorough and complete loss of ourselves, yet in such a way that we are not lost but rather found, restored and promoted to be more than we ever could be apart from God. It is a way of union that calls for the relinquishment of a quest to establish ourselves in independence from God and one another. Yet, we find that in the very relinquishing of our wills in this union, our identity as persons is not disintegrated but established. Our unique purpose is fulfilled through being connected to God and one another in a way best described as being members of one body.

The class was urged to see that our deepest, most pressing needs are met through the incarnation and work of the eternal Son of God.

Third, however, we require a union with Christ in order to share those benefits. So I distributed a quotation from Calvin:

Therefore, that joining together of Head and members, that indwelling of Christ in our hearts – in short, that mystical union are accorded by us the highest degree of importance, so that Christ, having been made ours, makes us sharers with him in the gifts with which he has been endowed. We do not, therefore, contemplate him outside ourselves from afar in order that his righteousness may be imputed to us but because we put on Christ and are engrafted into his body – in short, because he deigns to make us one with him. For this reason, we glory that we have fellowship of righteousness with him.[1]

So we considered that union with Christ has every implication for our identity, our hope, our behaviour, our relationships, and our mission. But how do we get united to Jesus?

The fourth step was to explore how the foundation for our union with Christ is his continuing union with us. That meant acknowledging our separation from God and the need for a mediator. Again, Calvin proved an invaluable help:

> It deeply concerned us, that he who was to be our Mediator should be very God and very man. ... Our iniquities, like a cloud intervening between Him and us, having utterly alienated us from the kingdom of heaven, none but a person reaching to him could be the medium of restoring peace.
>
> But who could thus reach to him? Could any of the sons of Adam? All of them, with their parents, shuddered at the sight of God. Could any of the angels? They had need of a head, by connection with which they might adhere to their God entirely and inseparably. What then? The case was certainly desperate, if the Godhead itself did not descend to us, it being impossible for us to ascend.
>
> Thus the Son of God behooved to become our Emmanuel, the God with us; and in such a way, that by mutual union his divinity and our nature might be combined; otherwise, neither was the proximity near enough, nor the affinity strong enough, to give us hope that God would dwell with us; so great was the repugnance between our pollution and the spotless purity of God.[2]

The person of Jesus, in being united with our human nature in all his works, is the basis for our saving, fulfilling union with him.

Fifth, the continuing union of Jesus with us, so vital to our salvation and life, is grounded in the event of his ascension in the flesh. Since he went up in his resurrected body, we have the hope that he remains united to our humanity and will return to us in that same form. This is why we must consider the nature and implications of Jesus' ascension.

The strategy, then, was to begin with the burning questions of the human soul and relate them to more familiar and foundational Christian teaching. When those basics are looked at in terms of union with Christ, however, the necessity for the continuing union is made clear. And that leads to the importance of the ascension. Thus, the ascension was made interesting, hopefully, by leading to its connection to the essence of human need and God's work of salvation in Christ.

Every week, we began by going over the sequence which follows from our need for union with Christ to the foundational importance of his ascension in the flesh. The study followed, in rudimentary form, the sequence of this book. We considered the nature of the event, as well as the ascension as the triumph of Jesus over the powers of evil and the pledge of our future glory. Special emphasis was given to a sixth movement in the sequence: our response of faith as described in terms of spiritual ascension. Though all our salvation is comprehended in Christ alone, nevertheless, in the Spirit's power, we undertake daily to put off the old nature and put on the new, seeking the things which are above, where Christ is in our name and on our behalf.

Each session we sang together great ascension hymns such as Matthew Bridges' 'Crown Him with Many Crowns', with its magnificent lines, 'Behold His hands and side, / Rich wounds yet visible above / in beauty glorified'.[3] We celebrated with Dix's 'Alleluia, Sing to Jesus', affirming that 'Thou within the veil hast entered, / Robed in flesh, our great High Priest; / Thou on earth both Priest and Victim / In the eucharistic feast.'[4] On the last night, everyone came dressed in Hawaiian shirts for a festive evening the night before the day traditionally marked as the Feast of the Ascension. In the course of our worship, we used a litany adapted from various lines from the patristic writers. I include it here as a summary of our time together:

Leader: God wished to become incarnate, to renew his image,
People: So he came looking for the lost sheep.

Leader: He searched the remote regions until the lost was found.
People: Now he takes it upon his shoulders and brings it to his Father.

Leader: The sheep is human nature, all we who have gone astray.
People: Today, he brings us home in his ascension,
Laying us on his heart, carrying us in his great arms.

Leader: See now how we have gained more than we lost in the Fall!
People: Having lost paradise, we have gained heaven.

Leader: Wounded within paradise, when we fell in Eden,
People: We have found healing east of Eden.

Leader: Having been killed by the tree of life,
People: We have been made whole by the Christ-killing tree.

Leader: Having been sunk in the port, the calm waters of paradise,
People: We have returned to life in the waves of the sea,
In the turmoil of the wild world.

Leader: Where is your mischief, then, pirate of humanity?
The cross on which our captain was fastened as to a mast,
People: Has become the rudder of our shipwrecked nature.

Leader: The cross steers us to the heavenly harbour.
People: For our captain has triumphed, he has guided us home.

Leader: Therefore rejoice. Look today to the second Adam.
People: He has been received into the highest heaven.

Leader: Christ's ascension is our uplifting.
People: We gained more in the new Adam than we lost in the first.

Leader: In Christ, we have penetrated the heights of heaven,
People: In his ascending, we are received into the Father's house.

Model Three: Thirty-Day Prayer Guides

At the beginning of the five-week ascension course, I distributed guides for daily prayer. The full text is in the Appendix, but the programme may be briefly described here. Participants were encouraged to use the guide daily, morning and evening, for a month. They were given two liturgies for both morning and evening to provide variety and to expand on the material available.

The first Morning Prayer followed a similar sequence of thought as the course. Participants hear the call of God to 'come up' to relationship with him and then pray through the block of our sin. A cry for salvation is answered with the affirmation of the descent of God in Christ and then to his ascent in exaltation. The prayer concludes with scriptures related to our taking our place with Christ in the heavenlies. Thus, people move in prayer, using scripture, through our salvation story, but in terms of the ascension motif.

The first Evening Prayer takes the worshippers through the ascension story and its implications, as related in Acts 1–3. The salvation events are repeated as we pray through Ephesians 2:4–10, claiming, as we do so, our seat with Christ in the heavenlies. Then, we stay with Ephesians, turning even as Paul does from doctrine to practical response, praying through passages in Ephesians 4–5 to put on the new self in accord with Christ.

The second Morning Prayer focuses on our citizenship in heaven. From Ephesians 2 and Philippians 3, we claim our place as God's people in Christ, members of his household and citizens of his realm. This leads to the wonderful declaration of Christian identity in 1 Peter 2 of our being a chosen people and royal priesthood. We then allow Peter to remind us how we are aliens and strangers in the world, even as a passage from Hebrews 11 also does. From rejoicing before God in our identity in Christ, we move to the call to respond, returning to Colossians 3 and Paul's reminder to set our hearts on things above. We follow that chapter in its extended description of laying aside aspects of the old life and taking up the qualities of the new. The session ends with praying through the vision of the heavenly city in Revelation 22.

The second Evening Prayer entirely follows the book of Hebrews and quotations from the Psalms employed therein. The prayers lift up Jesus as our brother who shares in our flesh and blood. Then they celebrate him as our great and effective High Priest and also our forerunner behind the veil into God's presence on our behalf. We rejoice in his present ministry as our priest. In response to this, we follow Hebrews' exhortation to enter boldly into the divine throne room, fixing our eyes on Jesus throughout our earthly sojourn. We make the sacrifice of praise from our lips and receive the benediction that God will equip us even now for every good work.

The Prayer Guides included a response form with five questions, which people were asked to return after the thirty days. The responses were telling. Here is a sample:

Praying each day about my relationship with the ascended Jesus has:

- made me feel closer to Christ [echoed by five others] and made it clearer that Christ is still human.
- made me focus more on the role of Christ who sits at the right hand of God and intercedes not only for me but for all people.
- given me renewed confidence that the intent of my prayers is conveyed to God even when I struggle to get the words right.
- made me feel more confident that I am *heard*.

What it means to me that Jesus is still incarnate in heaven and acting as a priest on my behalf:

- He thinks that no person is beneath him.
- He has prepared a place for me and is waiting for me – like a light in the window of heaven.
- My feeble attempts at prayer are being interpreted by Christ and carried to the Father.
- He is a *person* and not something spirit-like and he is my advocate before God.
- He understands my needs and will always help me.

What it means in daily life to consider that I am even now seated with Christ in the heavenlies:

- I have a responsibility to keep Christ at the *absolute center* of everything I say and do.
- Christ continues to hold me in his grasp even when I make choices which are not in his best interest nor mine.
- It gives me courage to do what I know is right.
- I am even now a citizen of heaven and an alien in this temporary interlude on earth.
- It reminds me to keep my heart and mind where they ought to be – on Christ.

What perspective a focus on the ascended Christ gives to the pressures, goals, affairs and duties of this life:

- Christ becomes the centrality of earthly existence. ... We trust his redeeming love, kept by the promise that he will never forsake us and allow us to be plucked out of His keeping.

- It has reminded me that while important battles remain to be fought, the victory has been won, thus the outcome doesn't depend on my efforts.
- Gives me confidence that he understands and gives help in every situation, also gives me his power to do his work.
- Everything in daily life takes its place as unimportant in comparison with the ascended Christ. Things on earth seem much less stressful or problematic.

What difference it makes in terms of how I relate to other people and the needs of the world after concentrating on my heavenly citizenship:

- My view of the needs of other people and the world is enhanced by being close to Christ and considering how he viewed them.
- Helps me to be more forgiving in my relationships with others.
- I try to let forgiveness be my watchword in every action I take.
- I am here to praise God in all that I say and do; I need to be less self-centered, and work harder to help those in need.
- I live in the world but am not of the world. I am no longer satisfied with worldly existence. I feel a kinship with all people and wish to serve Christ and his Church by making him known to others. I desire to grow in His likeness to be of service to those I meet – knowing all the time that life on this earth is just a glimpse of what God has prepared for those who love Him and those who try to seek his will daily.

The responses indicate the truth that focusing on Christ changes us more towards his image, from glory to glory. They also suggest that the concepts of the continuing union, the nature of the ascension and the priesthood of Christ are not beyond the grasp of laypeople willing to study. In particular, the sense of heavenly citizenship seems to have been internalized by the respondents. In that sense, our goal is being realized. The ascension can be a curing story for those afflicted by the disease of the world being too much with us.

Model Four: Christ in the Marketplace

A growing emphasis in our church focuses upon each person's primary mission field as his or her sphere of influence in daily life. One strategy for curing an over-identification with the world is the elimination of compartmentalization. If church members consider their brief times at church as the only time they labour in God's kingdom, then the world claims them nearly all the time. But if we can understand all of life as falling under Christ's dominion and redemption, then their heavenly citizenship can have a much wider, deeper expression. So I have been interested in helping people think through how their particular vocation is a mission field. To date, seminars have been offered for educators, medical personnel and people in business and industry. Within each specific vocation the ascended Jesus has been shown to be the key.

After praising the group for the unique and important contributions of their vocation, I asked participants to discuss in groups these five questions, adapted to the specific mission field:

1. How do you see your task as a Christian on the mission field of [education, medicine, business]?

2. What are some of the roles you play for [students, patients, clients]?

3. What joys are there in this ministry?

4. What burdens do you feel, or difficulties do you encounter, in being a Christian on the mission field of [education, medicine, business]?

5. What theology, or words about God, do you wish for to help you do your work?

After discussing answers in the large group, we spent a brief time looking at scripture passages related to the respective fields. When possible, I tried to help them identify their work with the ministry of Jesus. This was not difficult in relation to teaching children or healing the sick. For the businesspeople, we had to look at the story of Lydia (Acts 16), who used the wealth created by her business in purple goods to supply a house in which the church could meet. We considered how the ethical standards of the Decalogue and the teachings of Jesus apply in daily business situations. And we noted the difficulty of speaking to people who do not share the culture or the language of our faith. In every case, the Son of God who draws us up to heaven while yet retaining his humanity is the model for being in the world though not of the world, for handling the goods of the world while touching them but lightly.

The last section of the evening focused on enhancing one's mission field wherever possible. We considered how to bring the values of heaven into play in the arena of the world. Some activities are as overt as a doctor offering to pray with a patient. Others are as subtle, yet crucial, as a teacher creating an environment safe from teasing and ridicule so that students catch a scent of the kingdom though it is never mentioned by name. In business, such enhancements range from direct expressions of faith to honesty in transactions and Christian love in dealing with co-workers even if they are not playing by the same rules.

The participants, some thirty-five educators, fifteen medical personnel and three businesspeople (poor scheduling for that event), enjoyed being shown the positive aspects of the arenas in which they spend so much of their time and energy. There was a thirst to hear praise for their work from the church, and a genuine delight in gleaning that God is delighted in what they are doing even if it is not specifically religious. Surprisingly, most had never considered how their work can actually be mission that is pleasing to God. As simple as this concept is, people were yearning to hear it from the pastor. These seminars taught me that increasing the heavenly aspects of one's life can be a far better motivator in ceasing to over-identify with the world than any number of sermons exposing worldliness. This model, grounded in the continuing incarnation of Christ through the ascension, has proved very popular among our people. They drank in theology painlessly and returned to their work energized.

Model Five: Retreat for Mission Planning

A retreat for our church officers and staff addressed a pressing issue: how to discern in what ways God was calling us to distribute the tithe on our recent capital campaign. This opportunity brought to the fore the need to understand the purpose of our church's mission work. Jesus ascended would be at the core of these discussions.

We began after worship by dividing into small groups for scripture study. Each examined different passages so that in the end five groups considered seventeen different passages. One group considered key texts related to our citizenship in heaven and our sojourn as strangers on earth. Another looked at verses concerned with simple, godly living to set an example for those who do not know Christ. A third group examined the call to care for the poor issued in the Old Testament and from Jesus. The fourth considered Jesus' words about his mission and the ways he passed it on to us. The last considered the Great Commission as it is given in various ways leading to the vision of the new heaven and new earth.

Then we returned to put all the perspectives together. As the groups reported, we made note of how we are both called out *from* the world and sent *to* the world. We live for heaven but labour on the earth with heaven's energy and values. The group had thus come through their own study to a consideration of the postures the church has had towards the world through the centuries (discussed in this book in Chapter 7). We discussed what happens when the church acts in the world doing good deeds yet fails to bear witness to the history and future of Jesus. We pondered aloud what happens when the church speaks the story of Jesus but fails to address the world at the point of its most urgent and pressing need. We noted the danger of giving away the uniqueness of our story so as not to offend the world and the obverse danger of condemning the world by wielding the gospel as a spiritual bludgeon.

Working from our pressing decision about mission funding through the scripture passages and these potential errors for the church, the group was then ready to consider how the ascension and the church's place in the world intersect. Farrow's analysis proved helpful here, though if introduced without a context it would have been way too dense. I felt a full sense of 'buy-in' from the group as we concluded that Christians remain distinct from the world in order to present ourselves to the world in the name of Christ. This follows the example of our Lord who, as we noted earlier, is absent in his glorified humanity precisely so that he may keep on presenting that humanity to the world through the Spirit. The church bears witness in its actions and words that the ascended and returning Jesus is the goal and end of every life. It is this world Jesus loves. He has gone to prepare a place for us, but it is we flesh-and-blood humans for whom he will return. The church now urges the world, by words and works of love inseparably offered together, to join the preparation of the bride for the bridegroom.

With these theological reflections in place, we were able quickly and harmoniously to consider the various mission proposals before us. The group embraced most vigorously those projects which combine both the sharing of the gospel and the enacting of Christ's love for the least. There was, as well, an interest in making all our mission activity more hands-on and personally engaged in by our members. The continually incarnate Christ set the pace for us.

Since that fresh beginning, new ministries have been decidedly more engaging. We have begun a partnership with an elementary school near our church. The vast majority of students there may be described as 'at risk' of future difficulties. The first year, we offered more than twenty-five tutor-mentors. These volunteers provide an hour a week in which the primary goal is showing love and consistency to children whose home lives are often chaotic. A tide of enthusiasm for this partnership has arisen as church members are finding many other practical ways of showing that we have adopted this needy school, from making hygiene kits to giving Christmas presents to establishing a fund for emergency family needs. Then, in the second year, we began an after-school programme at a home owned by the church across the street from the school. Twice monthly, more than thirty students come for an hour of games, snacks, crafts and Bible study. Because the programme is voluntary, we are able to teach the gospel freely. Because the families trusted us after the first year, they send their children enthusiastically. Financially, the project costs us very little. Our members, however, are more engaged with hearts, hands and time than ever before. Of all the mission work we have done, seldom have we proclaimed the gospel so directly in work *and* word.

Secondly, a ministry to men struggling with homosexuality has begun. While our denomination wrestles and fights over the issue, our local church is now providing safe space and leadership to support men who recognize the conflict between the biblical vision of human sexuality and their own desires. They gather for prayer, Bible study and support. As noted previously, our church has avoided getting involved in controversial areas such as homosexuality. The decision to begin this ministry did not come without dire warnings from medical professionals that we might do considerable damage to people in even suggesting their sexual orientation could change. Yet the testimony of the two young men asking the session for help moved our elders to take the risk. Could it be that the person of the ascended God-man has inspired us?

As we noted, there has been a tendency in the past for our church to shy away from the sharp edges of ministry and theology. But in the last few years these areas have been engaged. The assessment of our church described in Chapter 1 must be updated. Our congregation is discussing the person of Jesus more, even risking conflict to do so, yet loving one another and the community more than before. Assessing how recovering Jesus ascended directly affects a church is surely nearly impossible. Yet, it seems to this pastor that the invigoration over the long term is real.

Chapter 10

Three Concluding Images

And Ruth said, 'Entreat me not to leave thee, or to return from following after thee: for whither thou goest, I will go; and where thou lodgest, I will lodge: thy people shall be my people, and thy God my God: Where thou diest, will I die, and there will I be buried: the LORD do so to me, and more also, if aught but death part thee and me.' (Ruth 1:16–17, AV)

These words from Ruth indicate a love beyond expectation, a devotion that transcends pragmatic concerns. The young widow of Moab would not leave her Hebrew mother-in-law, also a widow. She resolved to live as a stranger in a strange land rather than part from one she loved. Though Naomi had renamed herself Bitter because of her circumstances, Ruth clung to her with a tenacious compassion that would one day burst forth with the fruit of new life. This story offers a type for the coming of Jesus, whose lineage included Ruth.

Perhaps we could be so bold as to consider that, in his descent, the Son of God said tenderly to humanity, 'Entreat me not to leave thee, or to return from following after thee'. He came down to us, among our fractured relationships, our pierced hearts, our hungry bellies and wandering souls, and he promised, 'for whither thou goest, I will go; and where thou lodgest, I will lodge'. Jesus, the only begotten Son of the Father, donned our flesh. He tabernacled among us, pitching his tent in the midst of the dust and dailiness of life.

Ruth would not leave Naomi though apparently there was no

gain in following her, and no reason to continue except love. In her words of faithfulness we hear the words of Jesus the Son of God to us. He would not leave off pursuing us despite our lack of promise, but instead left his country for ours. Even as Ruth pledged to love Naomi to the end, so Jesus in his faithfulness determined that where we die – in disgrace, as a result of the sin which plunged the creation into bondage to decay, in frailty, and in the hands of powers beyond our control – he also would die, on the cross in utter forsakenness.

Perhaps, too, we could imagine that, in his rising and ascending, Jesus speaks the words of Ruth again, now reversing the pronouns to make an invitation to us: 'I entreat you not to leave me, or to return from following after me. For whither I go, you will go.' Then, suddenly we may hear so many of his sayings reverberating with a fullness of meaning beyond even that of the moment at which they were spoken: Yes, follow me now. I go to prepare a place for you. And where I lodge, you may lodge. And if I go and prepare a place for you, I will come again, and receive you unto myself; that where I am, there you may be also. You are my people, and my God is your God. Go to my brothers and tell them, I am returning to my Father and your Father, to my God and your God. Not even death can part us now. Where I live now you will live also. So ascend by me to our Father's house.

After all our reflections, the story of Ruth and Naomi brings the ascension to us in loving clarity. The Son of God became what we are and would not give it up. Rather than forsake us, he took that humanity to heaven. United to him by the power of the Holy Spirit we share in his incarnate life at the right hand of the Father. One day we shall be there face to face. The ascension is the news, and the basis for that news, of Christ's continuing incarnation. So this event, as a fundamental doctrine of the faith, transforms the vision of the church in its relationship to the world. First, it raises our sight beyond the vanity of this world when it persists in its myth of self-sufficiency and independence from God. Second, even as we stand staring after our departed Lord longing to follow him, he redirects us to look again at this world. We view it now from heaven's vantage point, with the heart-reaching compassion of the saviour who remains fully united, eternally pledged, to our humanity. With one eye cocked towards Christ in heaven, the church is sent with the other eye focused on the little ones whom Jesus loves, the lambs he longs to gather home.

Staying in the Ship and Staying the Course

So the church must live in a lover's tension with the world and often faces the same conflict within itself. We would naturally shrink from such a constant sense of being unsettled. But there is no place to go. To make the world our home would be to perish with it. To leave the world and hide would be a dereliction of our calling. A church committed to the truth of Jesus that his ascension in the flesh demands is a church that offers safety to a dying world. In a sermon based on the story in Matthew 14 of Jesus crossing a stormy sea to meet his disciples out on their boat, buffeted by the waves, Augustine writes:

> Yet in all this that the Lord did, He instructs us as to the nature of our life here. In this world there is not a man who is not a stranger; though all do not desire to return to their own country. Now by this very journey we are exposed to waves and tempests; but we must needs be at least in the ship. For if there be perils in the ship, without the ship there is certain destruction. For whatever strength of arm he may have who swims in the open sea, yet in time he is carried away and sunk, mastered by the greatness of its waves ...
>
> Meanwhile the ship which carries the disciples, that is, the Church, is tossed and shaken by the tempests of temptation; and the contrary wind, that is, the devil her adversary, rests not, and strives to hinder her from arriving at rest. But greater is 'He who maketh intercession for us.' For in this our tossing to and fro in which we toil, He gives us confidence in coming to us, and strengthening us; only let us not in our trouble throw ourselves out of the ship, and cast ourselves into the sea. For though the ship be in trouble, still it is the ship. She alone carries the disciples, and receives Christ. There is danger, it is true, in the sea; but without her there is instant perishing. Keep yourself therefore in the ship, and pray to God. For when all counsels fail, when even the rudder is unserviceable, and the very spreading of the sails is rather dangerous than useful, when all human help and strength is gone, there remains only for the sailors the earnest cry of entreaty, and pouring out of prayer to God. He then who grants to

sailors to reach the haven, shall He so forsake His own Church, as not to bring it on to rest?[1]

We must be at least in the ship, the church. For though there are storms while on board, outside of her in the sea there is but 'instant perishing'. And 'though the ship be in trouble, still it is the ship'. The boat on wind-tossed Galilee yet bore the disciples on their mission to the other side. The church yet carries the followers of Jesus across the waves towards the haven of our home in heaven. There is no other conveyance. From the beginning, the church has been in peril on its mission to, and through, the world. Strength fades, sails sag and even the rudder seems 'unserviceable'. We have never been without challenge and conflict. But Jesus came to the disciples in the fourth watch when they were past exhaustion and brought peace. He comes to us still through the Holy Spirit with a promise of a final return when all sojourning will cease and we will arrive at a safe harbour on the shores of the fair, far country.

With such a vision before him, Augustine urges his congregation to 'Keep yourself therefore in the ship, and pray to God.' So we engage the challenges in the church and the world that our mission and evangelism might increase. We recognize that in either venue we might lose status, or worse, in our proclamation of the sharp, shining truth of Jesus ascended. Yet we flee neither the ship of the church nor the seas of the world. We struggle the whole of the night long. The sailors cry out to God to save them through the storm and direct their course. As we do so in turn, we cling to the hope that the ship is making for its harbour. Wondrously, we find that, with the vision of the ascended Christ before us, it is given to us to catch on the wind the scent of that country for which we sail.

Once Jesus ascended the mountain to pray while the disciples fared forward on their own. In their hour of need they cried out for him and he came to them as the Master of the sea, walking on the waves with peace in his voice. He has ascended now to say his prayers on our behalf in heaven. But he has not forgotten where we are. We still cry out in the storm, and he still comes in the gift of the Holy Spirit. The Spirit runs between the church and her Lord, on a road made of prayer. Prompting, then carrying, the prayers of the church to the Son, the same Spirit returns to the church on earth bearing the answers of the Father to the prayers of his Son. So we are able to carry on in our mission to the world and our journey out of the world. The ascended incarnate one who reigns in heaven in our name and on our behalf undergirds it all.

Investing Against All Odds

In Jeremiah 32, we read that the Lord instructed Jeremiah to purchase an ancestral property in his home town of Anathoth, just outside Jerusalem. The timing could not have been worse for a real estate transaction. The King of Babylon was even then besieging Jerusalem and no one had any doubt about his future success. Nevertheless, Jeremiah obeyed and redeemed the land from his cousin. As God instructed him, he had the documents of purchase placed in a clay jar so that they would be preserved through the years. The reason for preserving the deed was God's promise that 'Houses, fields and vineyards will again be bought in this land' (Jeremiah 32:15).

Jeremiah bought the field on the eve of destruction and plunder. He redeemed his family land to hold the title in hope against the years of exile. Sealed in a vessel of clay, the title to a piece of the promised land would endure until the age of forsakenness ended and a glorious restoration ensued. A foolish investment in the short term, Jeremiah made a pledge for the future in trust that God would be as good as his word.

In the incarnation, Jesus bought the field of our flesh. He purchased the redemption of humanity and bore the surety of that redemption in a vessel of clay. In his ascension in the flesh, Jesus holds now for us in heaven the hope of a glorified humanity against the ravages of mortality we endure in the world. Surely to the powers and principalities that strut their authority in this present age, this retention of humanity appears as foolish as a field bought before all land is swept up by a mighty king. We suffer here the pressure of foreign occupation, often staring stunned as all we hold dear is plundered, and wandering confused in a strange land whose very language sounds alien to our ears. Worse yet, we may begin to believe that Babylon is all there is, with the memory and hope of Jerusalem far receded. Yet, the ascension rightly, boldly taught and preached calls us to a magnificent hope. Jesus holds title to our humanity as a pledge of future restoration. He maintains our flesh through his continuing incarnation. While we are pilgrims through a barren world, we sojourn with the knowledge that the Promised Land is held in trust in the very nerves and sinews of the still incarnate Christ.

These images rescue the church from mortal despair and an over-identification with the world. The sight of the ascended Jesus dawning in our hearts through the Holy Spirit transforms the church. When we live and serve in this hope, the desert valley of the world turns to a place of springs as we pass.

Notes

Abbreviations

ANF   *The Ante-Nicene Fathers*. Ed. Alexander Robers and James Donaldson, American ed., A. Cleveland Coxe. 10 vols. Edinburgh: T & T Clark and Grand Rapids: William B. Eerdman's Publishing Company, 1993.

NPNF *A Select Library of Nicene and Post Nicene Fathers of the Christian Church*. Ed. Phillip Schaff. 1st series: 14 vols; 2nd series: 13 vols. Edinburgh: T & T Clark and Grand Rapids: William B. Eerdman's Publishing Company, 1989.

Introduction

1. C. S. Lewis, *Miracles* (Glasgow: Fontana Books, 1960), 151.
2. Frederic W. Farrar, *The Life of Christ as Represented in Art* (New York: Macmillan and Company, 1895), 455.
3. Unless otherwise noted, all scripture quotations are taken from the New International Version (Grand Rapids: Zondervan, 1984).
4. John Knox, *The Works of John Knox*, vol. 2, collected and ed. David Laing (Edinburgh: Bannatyne Club, 1854), 102.
5. Karl Barth, *Church Dogmatics. Vol. IV: The Doctrine of Reconciliation, Part 2*, ed. G. W. Bromiley and T. F. Torrance (Edinburgh: T & T Clark, 1958), 100–1.
6. John Calvin, *Institutes of the Christian Religion*, ed. John T. McNeil, trans. Ford Lewis Battles (Philadelphia: Westminster Press, 1960), 2.16.5. Unless otherwise noted, all quotations from the *Institutes* are from the Battles translation.

Chapter 1
The World is Too Much With Us

1. William Wordsworth, 'The World Is Too Much With Us', in *Major British*

Poets of the Romantic Period, ed. William Heath (New York: Macmillan Publishing Co., Inc., 1973), 245.

2. Lesslie Newbigin, *A Word in Season: Perspectives on Christian World Missions* (Grand Rapids: William B. Eerdmans Publishing Company, 1994), 52.

3. See Walter Wink, *Naming the Powers: The Invisible Forces that Determine Human Existence* (Philadelphia: Fortress Press, 1987), 69–86.

4. Walter Wink, *Transforming Bible Study*, 2nd edn. (Nashville: Abingdon Press, 1989), 145–7.

5. Newbigin, *A Word in Season*, 54.

6. Douglas Farrow, *Ascension and Ecclesia: On the Significance of the Doctrine of the Ascension for Ecclesiology and Christian Cosmology* (Grand Rapids: William B. Eerdmans Publishing Company, 1999), 80.

7. William Milligan, *The Ascension and Heavenly Priesthood of Our Lord* (London: Macmillan and Co., 1894), 199.

8. Ibid., 334–5.

9. Andrew Murray, *The Holiest of All* (Springdale, Pa.: Whitaker House, 1996), 26, 459. The available reprints of Murray's work seldom give original publication dates. Murray lived from 1828 to 1917, and we can safely surmise that this work was written during Murray's most productive years, after 1881.

10. Henry Barclay Swete, *The Ascended Christ: A Study in the Earliest Christian Teaching* (London: Macmillan and Co., Limited, 1910), 163.

11. George Barna, *The Second Coming of the Church* (Nashville: Word Publishing, 1998), 7.

12. Ibid., 23, 61.

13. Ibid., 6.

14. Ibid., 123.

15. Ibid., 121.

16. D. A. Carson, *The Gagging of God* (Grand Rapids: Zondervan Publishing House, 1996), 434–5.

17. Swete, *The Ascended Christ*, 155, 160.

18. Murray, *The Holiest of All*, 46.

Chapter 2
The Ascension as Public Truth

1. Cf. 'We do not doubt but that the selfsame body which was born of the virgin, was crucified, dead, and buried, and which did rise again, did ascend into the heavens': The *Scots Confession*, in *The Constitution of the Presbyterian Church (USA), Part 1: The Book of Confessions* (Louisville, Ky.: The Office of the General Assembly, 1999), 3.11 and 'having the very same body in which he suffered, with the essential properties thereof (but without mortality and other common infirmities belonging to this life), really united to his soul, he rose again from the dead ... forty days after his resurrection, he, in our nature, and as our head ... visibly went up into the highest heavens': Westminster Larger Catechism, ibid., 7.162–3.

2. Justin Martyr, *Fragments on the Resurrection, ANF*, vol. 1, 9; Tertullian, *On the Resurrection of the Flesh, ANF*, vol. 3, 51.
3. *The Anathemas Against Origen, NPNF*, 2nd series, vol. 14, 10.
4. Origen, *De Principiis, ANF*, vol. 4, 2.11.6.
5. See Farrow, *Ascension and Ecclesia*, 101, in which he exposes Origen's transfer of Christological issues 'from the public arena of human history to the private arena of the soul ... the fatal transition from history to philosophy is accomplished just here, in the decapitation of Jesus-history which naturally follows any such reinterpretation of the ascension as Origen attempts'.
6. Augustine, *The City of God, NPNF*, 1st series, vol. 2, 22.8.
7. John Chrysostom, *Homilies on the Acts of the Apostles*, 1st series, vol. 11, Homily 2.
8. George Gilpin the Elder, *The Bee Hive of the Romish Church* (London: 1579), in Hans Rudi Weber, *Die Umsetzung der Himmelfahrt Christi in die Zeichenhafte Liturgie* [The Role of the Ascension of Christ in the Symbolic Liturgy] (Bern: Peter Lang, 1987), 124; I have modernized the spelling.
9. John Shelby Spong, 'A Call for a New Reformation', *The Fourth R*, 11:6 (July/Aug. 1998), 26. See also his *A New Christianity for a New World: Why Traditional Faith is Dying and How a New Faith is Being Born* (San Francisco: HarperSanFrancisco, 2001), 120.
10. Richard Holloway, *The Scotsman* (Edinburgh), 3 Jan. 2000.
11. Theologians as fine as William Milligan and J. G. Davies are tempted toward this compromise. Milligan seems of two minds on this issue, probably due to the science available in his day. On the one hand we may follow him when he writes, 'As certainly as Jesus rose in the body, *i.e.* in a glorified body, so certainly was He raised to heaven in that body which was destined for the heavenly life, and the Apostles thought of Him as continuing to inhabit that glorified body in heaven. (*Ascension of Our Lord*, 14). He clarifies this later: 'If our Lord in his superterrestrial state has a body ... this body must be in one way or another adapted to the sphere in which He is now living (19–20). But on the other hand, Milligan backs away from the orthodox view when he says, 'The words "which is heaven" point to no locality, but to the state or condition of being to which our Lord belonged ... When, therefore, we speak of our Lord's ascension into heaven, we have to think less of a transition from locality than of a transition from one condition to another' (23, 26). Finally, he concludes, 'when our Lord ascended into heaven, He did so in human as well as in His Divine nature; or that, in laying aside the garment of "flesh" in which he had been clothed, He did not lay aside the humanity which He had assumed' (27). It appears that he desires to be orthodox in his insistence on the full humanity of the ascended Christ, and his theology bears those marks. Perhaps, though, the pull of the contemporary science caused him to back off from asserting ascension in the flesh. Similarly, J. G. Davies, in an otherwise brilliant book, asserts, 'Ascension involved no

physical movement to a localized heaven': *He Ascended into Heaven: A Study in the History of the Doctrine* (London: Lutterworth Press, 1958), 178. Yet, the 'hypostatic union was ... an abiding reality' (180). He attempts to solve his dilemma by affirming, 'It is the manhood of Christ, which has entered heaven through the Ascension' (180–1). Davies' position could have been strengthened by insisting on the glorified flesh of Christ.

12. Lesslie Newbigin, *Truth to Tell: The Gospel as Public Truth* (Grand Rapids: William B. Eerdmans Publishing Company and Geneva: WCC Publications, 1991), 2.

13. Ibid., 11.

14. See Bruce M. Metzger, 'The Meaning of Christ's Ascension', in *Search the Scriptures: New Testament Studies in Honor of Raymond T. Stamm*, ed. J. M. Myers, O. Reimherr, and H. N. Bream (Leiden: E. J. Brill, 1969), 119, in which he discusses the removal of the ascension reference in some manuscripts of Luke (a western non-interpolation) as an attempt at harmonization of Luke and Acts, which, he contends, still does not satisfy the implication of the narrative that a significant parting occurred.

15. See Peter Toon, *The Ascension of Our Lord* (Nashville: Thomas Nelson Publishers, 1984), 12.

16. See K. C. Thompson, *Received Up Into Glory: A Study of the Ascension* (London: Faith Press, 1964), 48.

17. Toon, *The Ascension of Our Lord*, 12. See also Davies, *He Ascended into Heaven*, 47.

18. Farrow, *Ascension and Ecclesia*, 39–40.

19. Thomas F. Torrance, *Space, Time and Resurrection* (Grand Rapids: William B. Eerdmans Publishing Company, 1976), 109.

20. Swete, *The Ascended Christ*, 6–8, 10.

21. Torrance, *Space, Time and Resurrection*, 109.

22. Bruce M. Metzger, 'The Meaning of Christ's Ascension', 124–5 observes that even a schoolchild promoted to the next higher class realizes that this language means more than simply moving from a room on the ground floor to the second floor. He asserts, 'the ascension should not be regarded as a journey from earth to heaven, which required a certain number of minutes, days, months, or years to be accomplished. In other words, the ascension, properly understood, has no more to do with Ptolemaic astronomy than does the incarnation ... the New Testament writers use ordinary language of physical elevation to suggest a metaphorical or analogical meaning.'

23. Farrow, *Ascension and Ecclesia*, 39.

24. Thompson, *Received Up Into Glory*, 65. See also John Calvin, *Acts of the Apostles, Vol. 1*, ed. David W. Torrance and Thomas F. Torrance, trans. T. H. L. Parker (Grand Rapids: William B. Eerdmans Publishing Company, 1965), 34.

25. Barth, *Church Dogmatics*, IV/ii, 97.

26. James Benjamin Wagner, *Ascendit ad Coelos: The Doctrine of the Ascension in*

the *Reformed and Lutheran Theology of the Period of Orthodoxy* (Winterthur: Verlag P. G. Keller, 1964), 30.

27. John Calvin, *Second Defense of the Pious and Orthodox Faith Concerning the Sacraments*, in *Selected Works of John Calvin*, *vol. 2*, eds Henry Beveridge and Jules Bonnet, trans. Henry Beveridge, (Albany, Ore: Books for the Ages, 1998), 270.

28. Jürgen Moltmann, *The Way of Jesus Christ: Christology in Messianic Dimensions* (San Francisco: HarperSanFrancisco, 1998), 332.

29. Swete, *The Ascended Christ*, p. xiv.

30. Lewis, *Miracles*, 161–2.

31. See Calvin, *Institutes*, 2.16.15.

32. Augustine, *A Treatise on Faith and the Creed*, NPNF, 1st series, vol. 3, 6. See also Calvin, *Institutes*, 4.17.26.

33. Gregory Nazianzen, *To Cleodonius the Priest Against Apollinarius*, NPNF, 2nd series, vol. 7.

34. Lewis, *Miracles*, 153.

35. Wagner, *Ascendit ad Coelos*, 28–9.

36. Ibid., 33.

37. Ibid., 42, 49.

38. John Walvoord, 'The Present Work of Christ. Part I: The Ascension of Christ,' *Bibliotheca Sacra*, 481 (Jan. 1964), 4.

39. See Farrow, *Ascension and Ecclesia*, 172–80, and Torrance, *Space, Time and Resurrection*, 123–35, as well as the discussion in the next section of the text.

40. Luther himself seemed to be searching for a more 'relational' view of how a physical body can be present to many people in many places simultaneously. He developed an understanding of three 'modes' of physical presence: 1. the usual, local, circumscribed manner; 2. a spiritual, uncircumscribed mode in which, for example, Christ was present yet able to pass through locked doors; and 3. the divine mode whereby all things are present to God at once. Luther asserted that the glorified manhood of Jesus participated in this third mode through the divine–human union, thus making Jesus able to come to his people directly in the Lord's Supper. So, Luther asserts this omni-relational way of being present as a characteristic of the exalted Christ (though denying that the humanity of Christ in and of itself is ever universally extended). It is just here that we may wish he and Calvin could have spoken to each other! Luther goes to great lengths to maintain the integrity of Christ's continuing incarnation while explaining his omnipresence. He stays anchored by returning to simple scriptural affirmations ('This is my body, Christ is at the Right Hand of the Father'). Yet, his discussions lack any development of the place of the Holy Spirit. One can feel the strain this places on maintaining a clear picture of the continuing humanity. See in particular his *Confession Concerning Christ's Supper*, ed. 2nd trans. Robert H. Fischer, in *Luther's Works*, vol. 37 (Philadelphia: Muhlenberg Press, 1961), 207–26. As we will see later,

discerning the Spirit as the link between Jesus ascended and his followers still on earth is Calvin's dynamic, relational solution that keeps both the body of Jesus and his real presence with us intact.

41. Calvin, *Institutes*, 4.17.29.
42. Ibid., 4.17.18.
43. Ibid., 4.17.10.
44. Farrow, *Ascension and Ecclesia*, 178.
45. Calvin, *Institutes*, 4.17.28.
46. Ibid., 4.17.29.
47. John Calvin, *The First Epistle of Paul the Apostle to the Corinthians*, ed. David W. Torrance and Thomas F. Torrance, trans. John W. Fraser (Grand Rapids: William B. Eerdmans Publishing Company, 1960), 246–7. See also Calvin's *The Gospel According to St. John*, vol. 2, ed. David W. Torrance and Thomas F. Torrance, trans. John W. Fraser (Grand Rapids: William B. Eerdmans Publishing Company, 1960), 159, *Second Defense of the Orthodox Faith*, 269–70, *Clear Explanation of Sound Doctrine Concerning the True Partaking of the Flesh and Blood of Christ in the Holy Supper*, in *Selected Works*, vol. 2, 509, and Ronald Wallace, *Calvin's Doctrine of the Word and Sacrament* (Eugene, Ore: Wipf and Stock Publishers, 1982), 197–233.
48. John Calvin, *The Second Epistle of Paul the Apostle to the Corinthians*, ed. David W. Torrance and Thomas F. Torrance, trans. T. A. Smail (Grand Rapids: William B. Eerdmans Publishing Company, 1964), 75.
49. Torrance, *Space, Time and Resurrection*, 123–32.
50. Milligan, *Ascension of Our Lord*, 133–4.
51. For the genesis of this thought see Thomas F. Torrance, *Royal Priesthood: A Theology of Ordained Ministry*, 2nd edn (Edinburgh: T&T Clark, 1993; 1st edn 1955), 58–9.
52. Milligan, *Ascension of Our Lord*, 45–6.
53. Swete, *The Ascended Christ*, 13.

Chapter 3
The Triumph of Jesus

1. Christopher Wordsworth, 'See the Conqueror Mounts in Triumph', in *The Hymnal*, ed. Clarence Dickinson, (Philadelphia: Presbyterian Board of Christian Education, 1933), 173.
2. Swete, *The Ascended Christ*, 18.
3. Douglas Farrow, 'Confessing Christ Coming', unpublished lecture given at the Scholarly Engagement with Anglican Doctrine 2001 International Ecumenical Conference, Charleston, SC, 12–14 Jan. 2001, now revised and published in Christopher R. Seitz (ed.), *Nicene Christianity: The Future for a New Ecumenism* (Grand Rapids: Brazo Press, 2001). my notes.
4. This is surely what Luther was after in juxtaposing two prints on the same page: one of Jesus ascending (leaving his footprints on the mount lest there be any doubt that it was a physical ascension) and the other of the pope being cast down into hell. Jesus' ascension in the first century had a direct

bearing on the religious and political powers in the sixteenth century: Martin Luther, *Passional Christi und Antichristi*, available at Pitts Theology Library Digital Image Archive, < www.pitts.emory.edu/woodcuts/ 1521LuthWW/0000915.jpg > .

5. Farrow, 'Confessing Christ Coming'.

6. Ibid.

7. For example, see John 12: 23, in which Jesus, predicting his death, says, 'The hour has come for the Son of Man to be glorified' or 17:1, 'in which Jesus begins his high priestly prayer, 'Father, the time has come. Glorify your Son, that your Son may glorify you.'

8. Torrance, *Space, Time and Resurrection*, 110.

9. Matthew Bridges, 'Crown Him with Many Crowns', *The Hymnal*, 190.

10. Davies, *He Ascended into Heaven*, 19–24.

11. Swete, *The Ascended Christ*, 23.

12. Justin Martyr, *Dialogue of Justin, Philosopher and Martyr with Trypho, a Jew*, ANF, vol. 1, 36.

13. Barbara Brown Taylor, 'The Day we were Left Behind,' *Christianity Today*, 42:6 cp. Bibliog. (18 May 1998), 46.

14. From the usual funeral prayers of Dr Jon Walton, Westminster Presbyterian Church, Wilmington, Del., during the years 1985–91, who got the phrase from an unremembered source.

15. Henri J. M. Nouwen, *The Return of the Prodigal Son: A Story of Homecoming* (New York: Doubleday, 1992), 55–8.

16. George Herbert, 'Affliction (3)', in Gerrit Scott Dawson, *Love Bade Me Welcome: Daily Readings with George Herbert* (Lenoir, NC: Glen Lorien Books, 1997), 141.

17. Irenaeus, *Against Heresies*, ANF, vol. 1, 5.21.1.

18. Irenaeus, *Against Heresies*, 5.21.3.

19. Tertullian, *Five Books Against Marcion*, ANF, vol. 3, 5.8.

20. Tertullian, *Scorpiace*, ANF, vol. 3, 10 (emphasis mine).

21. Athanasius, *Four Discourses Against the Arians*, NPNF, 2nd series, vol. 4, 1.11.41 (emphases mine).

22. See Gregory Nazianzen, *Oration 45*, 25, NPNF, 2nd series, vol. 5, and Cyril of Jerusalem, *Catechetical Lectures*, 14.18, 23–5, ibid., vol. 5.

23. Ambrose of Milan, *Exposition of the Christian Faith*, NPNF, 2nd series, vol. 10, 4.1.5–7.

24. Ibid., 4.2.15.

25. For a Reformation comparison, we may note a similar tension in Heinrich Bullinger's 'Second Helvetic Confession'. In Chap. 11, he declares that 'Jesus Christ our Lord is the unique and eternal Savior of the human race, and thus of the whole world'. Then, after establishing that faith alone is necessary to receive this grace, he declares in Chap. 16 that 'this faith is a pure gift of God which God alone of his grace gives to his elect according to his measure, when, to whom, and to the degree he wills'. A universal and a particular redemption are thus held in tension. Heinrich Bullinger,

'The Second Helvetic Confession' in *The Book of Confessions* (Louisville, Ky.: Office of the General Assembly, Presbyterian Church (USA), 2001), 5.077, 5.113.

26. Quoted in Davies, *He Ascended into Heaven*, 127.
27. Henry W. Baker, 'The King of Love', ed. Clarence Dickinson, *The Hymnal* (Philadelphia: Presbyterian Board of Christian Education, 1933), 99.
28. Ambrose, *Three Books on the Holy Spirit*, NPNF, 2nd series, vol. 10, 1.5.66.
29. Augustine, *Sermons on Selected Lessons of the New Testament*, NPNF, 1st series, vol. 6, 78.4.
30. John Chrysostom, *Homilies on the Epistle to the Ephesians*, NPNF, 1st series, vol. 13, 11.
31. Davies, *He Ascended into Heaven*, 142.
32. More recently, Barth expressed it beautifully: 'As the Son of God, He goes into the far country. As the Son of Man He returns home. And what He brings with Him – we might almost say as the spoils of the divine mercy – from that far country, what He places in closest proximity to God from the greatest distance, is the human essence assumed by Him': *Church Dogmatics*, IV/ii, 100.
33. Quoted ibid., 123–4.
34. Quoted ibid., 143.
35. Leo the Great, *Sermons*, NPNF, 2nd series, vol. 12, 73.4 (italics mine).
36. Caroline Maria Noel, 'At the Name of Jesus', *The Presbyterian Hymnal: Hymns, Psalms and Spiritual Songs* (Louisville, Ky.: Westminster/John Knox Press, 1990), 148.
37. Swete, *The Ascended Christ*, 33.

Chapter 4
The Ascension and the Person of Christ

1. As this study turns to the person of Christ, it is time to note that I am not unaware of the discussion concerning the titles *Son of Man* and *Son of God*. Indeed, it can be argued that in their Biblical context, *Son of Man* was more of a divine title than *Son of God*, which could refer simply to a person. These debates notwithstanding, contemporary ears hear in harmony with patristic theology. So, in this study, *Son of Man* usually refers to Jesus' humanity, while *Son of God* usually refers to his divinity. It is understood that both phrases have further, deeper layers of meaning as well.

2. We touch here upon the doctrines of the *anhypostasia* and the *enhypostasia*, illuminated by T. F. Torrance in his Christological lectures. The *anhypostasia*, understood as *without independent existence*, 'repudiates any form of adoptionism, that is the adoption of a pre-existing man to become Son of God. The *enhypostasia* directs us to see Christ *in a particular being*, and so preserves the acknowledgement of the full humanity of Jesus, and indeed of his historical Person as a Man among other men: Thomas F. Torrance, 'The Reformed Doctrine of Christ', unpub. lecture, New College, Edinburgh, 1964.' As we will see, the doctrine of the ascension safeguards

both the particular humanity and the eternal divinity of Christ. See also T. F. Torrance, *Theology in Reconstruction*, (London: SCM Press, 1965), 131.

3. Andrew Purves, 'Jesus Christ: Lord in History', *Theology Matters*, 7:2 (Mar./Apr. 2001), 12.
4. Ronald C. Rhodes, 'The New Age Christology of David Spangler', *Bibliotheca Sacra*, 576 (Oct. 1987), 412.
5. Richard Ostling, 'Book Depicts America's Two-Party System on Scripture', *Telegraph* (Macon, Ga.), 21 Apr. 2001, 8C.
6. Farrow, *Ascension and Ecclesia*, 6.
7. Anna Case-Winters, 'Who Do You Say That I Am? Believing in Jesus Christ in the 21st Century', < http://www.covenantnetwork.org/casewinters.html >, visited 12 Nov. 2002.
8. Ibid.
9. Paul Capetz, 'Response to Anna Case-Winters' "Who Do You Say That I Am?"' < http://www.covenantnetwork.org/capetz.html >, visited 12 Nov. 2002.
10. I have quoted it in the Authorized Version because that translation preserves the final phrase 'which is in heaven'. This crucial passage deserves some textual consideration. Such reliable ancient sources as Codex Vaticanus (*c.* 350) and Codex Sinaiticus (*c.* 340) do not contain this phrase. Yet, Codex Alexandrinus (*c.* 450) in a corrected form does contain it, as well as several manuscripts from the ninth century (Codices Theta, Delta, Psi and Omega), which are in or resemble the Byzantine tradition. Commentators such as Barrett, Brown and Beasley-Murray argue that, though the manuscript evidence is not conclusive, the very difficulty of the reading speaks for the phrase. Most notably, numerous church fathers view the phrase as part of the inspired text. Hippolytus, Novatian, Origen, Hilary, Basil, Chrysostom, Cyril, Theodoret and Augustine all employ the phrase in their use of John 3:13. Furthermore, even if the phrase is ultimately excised from the canon, the thought is still preserved by the use of the perfect tense of *anabaino* in 3:13, indicating that in some sense the Word has already ascended. Moreover, John 1:18 indicates that the Only Begotten is presently, continuously, in the bosom of the Father, and that could well apply to his time among us on earth. For the present purposes, then, I will take the phrase as authentic as we consider its use in the patristic writers.
11. Hippolytus, *Against the Heresy of One Noetus*, ANF, vol. 5, 4.
12. Novatian, *A Treatise of Novatian Concerning the Trinity*, ANF, vol. 5, 13 (emphasis mine).
13. Ibid., 14.
14. Ibid., 17.
15. John Chrysostom, *Homilies on the Gospel According to St. John*, NPNF, 1st series, vol. 14, 27.
16. The ascensions of Enoch (Genesis 5:24) and Elijah (2 Kings 2:11) represent being spared from the experience of death (Hebrews 11:5), but not

personal triumph over death or triumphant ascension. Their ascensions are derivative in 'earnest' of the resurrection and ascension of Christ. See Ambrose, *Exposition of the Faith*, 4.1.8: 'We do nowhere read as of one abiding in celestial glory, unless it was after that the Lord, by earnest of His own Resurrection, burst the bonds of hell and exalted the souls of the godly. Enoch, then, was translated, and Elias caught up; both as servants, both in the body, but not after resurrection from the dead, nor with the spoils of death and triumphal train of the Cross, had they been seen of angels.'

17. Augustine, *Sermons on Selected Lessons*, 73.3.
18. In addition to the preceding quotation from Augustine, see also Jerome, *Letter 59. To Marcella*, NPNF, 2nd series, vol. 6: 'The Divine Nature exists everywhere in its entirety. Christ, therefore, was at one and the same time with the apostles and with the angels; in the Father and in the uttermost parts of the sea.' And see Gregory Nazianzen, *Oration 29*: 'What He was He continued to be; what He was not He took to Himself ... He dwelt in the womb – but He was recognized by the Prophet, himself still in the womb, leaping before the Word, for Whose sake He came into being. He was wrapped in swaddling clothes – but He took off the swathing bands of the grave by His rising again. He was laid in a manger – but He was glorified by Angels, and proclaimed by a star, and worshipped by the Magi.'
19. Ephraim the Syrian, *Nineteen Hymns on the Nativity of Christ in the Flesh*, NPNF, 2nd series, vol. 13, 3.
20. Augustine, *Tractates on John*, NPNF, 1st series, vol. 7, 12.8.
21. Ibid.
22. Ibid., 27.4.
23. Hilary of Poitiers, *On the Trinity*, NPNF, 2nd series, vol. 9, 10.54 (emphasis mine).
24. There are numerous other references relating John 3 and John 6 to the person of Christ. See, for example, John Cassian (d. *c.* 430), *The Seven Books on the Incarnation of the Lord, Against Nestorius*, NPNF, 2nd series, vol. 11, 7.22. He makes the connection that the ascension reveals valuable information on the person of Christ. See also Hermias Sozomen, *Ecclesiastical History of Sozomen*, NPNF, 2nd series, vol. 2, 6.27, in which the Palestinian historian quotes Gregory Nazianzen using John 3 to combat Apollinarian heresies. And see Leo, 'On the Feast of the Nativity', in which he stands fully in the stream of Augustine and Chrysostom.
25. Tertullian, *On the Resurrection*, 51 (emphasis mine).
26. Quoted in Davies, *He Ascended into Heaven*, 119.
27. Irenaeus, *Against Heresies*, 3.17.1: 'For God promised, that in the last times He would pour Him [the Spirit] upon [His] servants and handmaids, that they might prophesy; wherefore He did also descend upon the Son of God, made the Son of man, becoming accustomed in fellowship with Him to dwell in the human race, to rest with human beings, and to dwell in the

workmanship of God, working the will of the Father in them, and renewing them from their old habits into the newness of Christ.'

28. Ibid., 5.8.1.
29. Hilary, *On the Trinity*, 3.16.
30. Murray, *The Holiest of All*, 72–4.
31. H. R. Mackintosh, *The Person of Christ*, ed. T. F. Torrance (Edinburgh: T&T Clark, 2000), 77.
32. Ibid., 50.

Chapter 5
Union with Christ: The Head and First Fruits

1. Athanasius, *Against the Arians*, 1.11.41.
2. Ibid., 1.11.43 (emphasis mine).
3. Of course, the concept that the humanity the Son of God took to himself was sinful human flesh which he bore sinlessly is not universally accepted, yet it has good support in the patristic writers. See first Nazianzen's famous formula, 'For that which He has not assumed He has not healed; but that which is united to His Godhead is also saved. If only half Adam fell, then that which Christ assumes and saves may be half also; but if the whole of his nature fell, it must be united to the whole nature of Him that was begotten, and so be saved as a whole': *To Cledonius*, 101. See also Basil: 'Our Lord assumed the natural affections to establish His real incarnation, and not by way of semblance of incarnation, and that all the affections derived from evil that besmirch the purity of our life, He rejected as unworthy of His unsullied Godhead. It is on this account that He is said to have been "made in the likeness of flesh of sin"; ... not, as these men hold, in likeness of flesh, but of flesh of sin. It follows that He took our flesh with its natural afflictions, but "did no sin"': Basil, *Letters*, NPNF, 2nd series, vol. 8, 261.3. Compare also Augustine, *The Enchiridion*, 108 and Leo, *Sermons*, 46.2.
4. Quoted in Davies, *He Ascended into Heaven*, 132.
5. Calvin, *Institutes*, 4.17.2.
6. Gregory Nazianzen, *Oration 40*, 45 (emphasis mine).
7. Interestingly, Gregory makes a distinction (hinting at the contemporary Greek bias against matter) between the 'flesh' and the 'body', in order to preserve the continuing nature of the incarnation without implying that mortal frailty or human corruption entered heaven. Christ's body is 'a more godlike body', but the hypostatic union in him between God and man remains intact.
8. Gregory of Nyssa, *Against Eunomius*, NPNF, 2nd series, vol. 5, 5.3 (emphasis mine).
9. Ibid., 12.1 (emphasis mine).
10. C. Baxter Kruger, *Home* (Jackson, Miss.: Perichoresis Press, 1996), 10.
11. Gregory of Nyssa, *Against Eunomius*, 12.1.
12. George Hendry, *The Gospel of the Incarnation* (Philadelphia: Westminster Press, 1958), 45, 62.

13. Compare, for example, T. F. Torrance, *Trinitarian Faith* (Edinburgh: T&T Clark, 1988), Chap. 2 with Duncan Rankin's dissertation 'Carnal Union with Christ in the Theology of T. F. Torrance' (New College, Edinburgh, 1999), and with *The Westminster Confession of Faith*, Chaps 7–11.

14. Calvin, *Institutes*, 3.1.1.

15. Swete, *The Ascended Christ*, 74, 77.

16. Irenaeus, *Against Heresies*, 3.19.3.

17. Ambrose, *Exposition of the Christian Faith*, 4.3.30–2.

18. Augustine, *Sermons on Selected Lessons*, 41.7–8 (spelling of translation modernized).

19. Compare Calvin, *Institutes*, 3.2.24, in which he declares that through faith 'we must, with both hands, keep firm hold of that alliance by which he has riveted us to himself'.

20. Augustine, *On the Merits and Forgiveness of Sins, and on the Baptism of Infants*, NPNF, 1st series, vol. 5, 1.60.

21. Ibid.

22. Swete, *The Ascended Christ*, 71.

23. William H. Marrevee, *The Ascension of Christ in the Works of St. Augustine* (Ottawa: University of Ottawa Press, 1967), 136–41.

24. Augustine, *Sermons on Selected Lessons*, 94.

25. Gregory of Nyssa, *Against Eunomius*, 2.8.

26. Ibid.

27. Quoted in Davies, *He Ascended into Heaven*, 116, (emphasis mine).

28. Ibid., 116–17.

29. Ibid., 150.

30. John Chrysostom, *Homilies on the First Epistle of Paul to Timothy*, NPNF, 1st series, vol. 13, 15 (spelling of translation modernized).

31. Quoted in Davies, *He Ascended into Heaven*, 120.

32. Iibid., 124.

33. Murray, *The Holiest of All*, 366–7.

Chapter 6
The Priesthood of Christ in the Power of the Holy Spirit

1. John Calvin, *The Epistle of Paul the Apostle to the Hebrews*, trans. T. H. L. Parker, ed. David W. Torrance and Thomas F. Torrance, *Calvin's New Testament Commentaries*, vol. 8 (Grand Rapids: William B. Eerdmans Publishing Company, 1965), 87.

2. James B. Torrance, *Worship, Community and the Triune God of Grace* (Downer's Grove, Ill.: Inter-Varsity Christian Press, 1996), 38–9. Professor Torrance's exposition underlies my thought here.

3. 'The significant fact is that, while in Word Jesus exercises his prophetic ministry, in His action He exercises His priestly ministry. It is as Suffering Servant of the Lord that he combines both': Torrance, *Royal Priesthood*, 9.

4. Cf. Tertullian, *An Answer to the Jews*, ANF, vol. 3, 14, in which he says that

Jesus 'after His resurrection was "clad with a garment down to the foot," and named Priest of God the Father unto eternity.'

5. On the question of when and whether Jesus actually took his blood into heaven, and when the offering was complete, see later in this chapter.
6. John Calvin, *Institutes of the Christian Religion*, trans. Henry Beveridge (Albany, Or: Books for the Ages, 1996), 3.20.18.
7. Calvin, *Epistle to the Hebrews*, 133.
8. Ibid., 140.
9. Ibid., 139.
10. My research, while far from exhaustive, has yielded precious little in the fathers beyond the bare acknowledgement of Jesus as priest. James Torrance suggests this is due to the Arian controversy, during which naming Christ as priest might have been exploited by the Arians as evidence that Christ was a creature: *A Passion for Christ*, 66.
11. Walvoord, 'Present Work of Christ', 11.
12. Toon, *Ascension of Our Lord*, 59, 64, 66. See also Theodore Turnau III, 'The Life of Jesus, after the Ascension', *Westminster Theological Journal*, 56:2 (Fall 1994), 393, in which he uncritically adopts Toon's position regarding Milligan.
13. Milligan, *Ascension of Our Lord*, 142.
14. Swete, *The Ascended Christ*, 47.
15. Torrance, *Royal Priesthood*, 13.
16. Milligan, *Ascension of Our Lord*, 97, 100.
17. Irenaeus, *Against Heresies*, 3.18.7.
18. See also Augustine, *Enchiridion*, Chap. 108 and *Tractates on John*, 41.5: 'To take then away the separating wall, which is sin, the Mediator has come, and the priest has Himself become the sacrifice.' Also Calvin, *Institutes*, 2.12.1: 'The case was certainly desperate, if the Godhead itself did not descend to us, it being impossible for us to ascend ... Had man remained free from all taint, he was of too humble a condition to penetrate to God without a Mediator. What, then, must it have been, when by fatal ruin he was plunged into death and hell, defiled by so many stains, made loathsome by corruption; in fine, overwhelmed with every curse? It is not without cause, therefore, that Paul, when he would set forth Christ as the Mediator, distinctly declares him to be man.'
19. Murray, *The Holiest of All*, 180–1.
20. Milligan, *Ascension of Our Lord*, 128.
21. Ibid., 117.
22. Murray, *The Holiest of All*, 241.
23. Swete, *The Ascended Christ*, 51.
24. Compare Derek Thomas, *Taken Up Into Heaven: The Ascension of Christ* (Durham: Evangelical Press, 1996), 70–1.
25. On this there is broad agreement, from Gregory Nazianzen, *Oration 30*, 5, to Calvin, *Institutes*, 3.11.1, 3.14.21, 3.20.36–8, to Toon, *Ascension of Our Lord*, 64–6.

26. Gregory Nazianzen, *Oration 30*, 14.
27. Torrance, *Royal Priesthood*, 14–15, 17.
28. Calvin, *Epistle to the Hebrews*, 140–1, 215.
29. Calvin, *Institutes*, 2.15.6, Beveridge trans.
30. J. Torrance, 'Prayer and the Priesthood of Christ', in *Passion for Christ*, 60, 62, 58.
31. Augustine, *On the Psalms*, 86.1.
32. Calvin, *Institutes*, 3.20.19, Beveridge trans.
33. John Calvin, *The Deity of Christ and Other Sermons*, trans. Leroy Nixon, (Audubon, NJ: Old Paths Publications, 1997), 236–7.
34. Torrance, *A Passion for Christ*, 63–4.

Chapter 7
Citizens of a Far Country

1. Torrance, *Royal Priesthood*, 59–60.
2. Farrow, *Ascension and Ecclesia*, 46–9.
3. Ibid., 97, 99.
4. Ibid., 102, 72.
5. Ibid., 114, 128, 130.
6. Ibid., 72.
7. Ibid., 73.
8. Idid., 80.
9. See Gerald F. Hawthorne, *Philippians* (Dallas: Word Publishing, 1983), 170.
10. Swete, *The Ascended Christ*, 155.
11. Ibid., 156.
12. *The Epistle of Mathetes to Diognetus*, ANF, vol. 1, 5.
13. Peter Brown, *Augustine of Hippo* (Berkeley: University of California Press, 1967) masterfully summarizes, analyses and explains *The City of God*. He weaves together many Augustine quotations from a variety of sources, many of them obscure, and in his own translation. To do justice to the richness of Brown's exposition, I will in this section be quoting his translations of Augustine.
14. Augustine, in Brown, *Augustine of Hippo*, 315, 323.
15. Ibid., 324.
16. Ibid., 325.
17. Ibid., 326.
18. Ibid.
19. Milligan, *Ascension of Our Lord*, 229, 232–3, 290.
20. Ibid., 288.

Chapter 8
Spiritual Ascension

1. Farrow, *Ascension and Ecclesia*, 62.
2. Barth's clarification is helpful here. We do not become divine, because the

humanity of Jesus is not made divine but rather exalted for communion with the Father in the Spirit: 'The human essence of the Son of God will always be human essence, although united with his divine essence, and therefore exalted in and by Him, set at the side of the Father, brought into perfect fellowship with Him ... But it will still be humanity and not deity – human and not divine essence.' Thus, 'God becomes man in order that man may – not become God, but come to God': *Church Dogmatics*, IV/ii, 106, 72.

3. Athanasius, *Against the Arians*, 3.25.19.
4. Athanasius, *Against the Arians*, 3.25.24–5.
5. Torrance, *Space, Time and Resurrection*, 135.
6. Calvin, *Deity of Christ*, 224.
7. Ibid.
8. Ibid., 227.
9. John Chrysostom, *Homilies on the Epistle of St. Paul to the Romans*, NPNF, 1st series, vol. 11, 14.
10. Chrysostom, *Homilies on John*, 22.
11. Murray, *Holiest of All*, 65, 76.
12. Augustine, *The Confessions of St. Augustine*, NPNF, 1st series, vol. 1, 4.12. (paraphrase mine).
13. Ibid., 4.12.19.
14. George Herbert, 'Holy Scripture (1)', in *Love Bade Me Welcome*, 109.
15. Calvin, *Deity of Christ*, 228.
16. Murray, *Holiest of All*, 237.
17. Murray, *Holiest of All*, 265–6, 270, 272, 274, 278, 282.
18. Augustine, *Sermons on Selected Texts*, 73.3–4.
19. Milligan, *Ascension of Our Lord*, 258, 288.
20. Cf. Wallace, *Calvin's Doctrine of the Word and Sacrament*, 199–203.
21. Calvin, *Second Defense of the Orthodox Faith*, 263–7.
22. Cf. John Calvin, *Clear Explanation of Sound Doctrine*, 507: 'As the divine majesty and essence of Christ fills heaven and earth, and this is extended to the flesh; therefore, independently of the use of the Supper, the flesh of Christ dwells essentially in believers, because they possess the presence of his deity.'
23. Calvin, *Deity of Christ*, 238–9.
24. John Chrysostom, *Homilies on Matthew*, NPNF, 1st series, vol. 10, 12.4.
25. Murray, *Holiest of All*, 225.

Chapter 9
Models for Recovering the Ascension

1. Calvin, *Institutes*, 3.11.10.
2. Ibid., 2.12.1, Beveridge translation.
3. Bridges, 'Crown Him with Many Crowns'.
4. William Chatterton Dix, 'Alleluia, Sing to Jesus', *The Presbyterian Hymnal: Hymns, Psalms and Spiritual Songs* (Louisville, Ky.: Westminster/John Knox Press, 1990), 144.

Chapter 10
Three Concluding Images

1. Augustine, *Sermons on Selected Lessons*, 25.2.4 (modernized translation).

Appendix

Prayer Guides

Morning Prayer I

Ascending into Heaven

The Call to Come Up

The earth is the LORD's, and everything in it,
the world, and all who live in it;
for he founded it upon the seas
and established it upon the waters. (Psalm 24:1–2)

In the last days
the mountain of the LORD's temple will be established
as chief among the mountains;
it will be raised above the hills,
and all nations will stream to it.
Many peoples will come and say,
'Come, let us go up to the mountain of the LORD,
to the house of the God of Jacob.
He will teach us his ways,
so that we may walk in his paths.
Come, O house of Jacob,
let us walk in the light of the LORD.' (Isaiah 2:2–3, 5)

The Block

Who may ascend the hill of the LORD?
Who may stand in his holy place?
He who has clean hands and a pure heart,
who does not lift up his soul to an idol
or swear by what is false. (Psalm 24:3–4)

[But] All of us have become like one who is unclean,
and all our righteous acts are like filthy rags;

we all shrivel up like a leaf,
and like the wind our sins sweep us away.
No one calls on your name
or strives to lay hold of you;
for you have hidden your face from us
and made us waste away because of our sins. (Isaiah 64: 6–7)

The Cry for Salvation

Oh, that you would rend the heavens and come down,
that the mountains would tremble before you!
For when you did awesome things that we did not expect,
you came down, and the mountains trembled before you.
Since ancient times no one has heard,
no ear has perceived,
no eye has seen any God besides you,
who acts on behalf of those who wait for him. (Isaiah 64:1, 3–4)

The Descent

For us and for our salvation, he came down from heaven. (Nicene Creed)

Christ Jesus, being in very nature God,
did not consider equality with God something to be grasped,
but made himself nothing,
taking the very nature of a servant,
being made in human likeness.
And being found in appearance as a man,
he humbled himself
and became obedient to death –
even death on a cross! (Philippians 2:6–8)

The Ascent

Therefore God exalted him to the highest place
and gave him the name that is above every name,
that at the name of Jesus every knee should bow,
in heaven and on earth and under the earth,
and every tongue confess that Jesus Christ is Lord,
to the glory of God the Father. (Philippians 2:9–11)

Give Thanks

What, then, shall we say in response to this? If God is for us, who can be against us? He who did not spare his own Son, but gave him up for us all – how will he not also, along with him, graciously give us all things? Who will bring any charge against those whom God has chosen? It is God who justifies. Who is he that condemns? Christ Jesus, who died – more than that, who was raised to life – is at the right hand of God and is also interceding for us. (Romans 8:31–4)

Taking Our Place with Him

[So,] Lift up your heads, O you gates;
be lifted up, you ancient doors,
that the King of glory may come in.
Who is this King of glory?
The LORD strong and mighty,
the LORD mighty in battle.
Lift up your heads, O you gates;
lift them up, you ancient doors,
that the King of glory may come in.
Who is he, this King of glory?
The LORD Almighty –
he is the King of glory. (Psalm 24:7–10)

Since, then, you have been raised with Christ, set your hearts on things above, where Christ is seated at the right hand of God.

Set your minds on things above, not on earthly things.

For you died, and your life is now hidden with Christ in God.

When Christ, who is your life, appears, then you also will appear with him in glory.

And so, whatever you do, whether in word or deed, do it all in the name of the Lord Jesus, giving thanks to God the Father through him. (Colossians 3:1–4, 17)

Evening Prayer I

Ascending into Heaven

Praying through the Story

When he had said this, as they were watching, [Jesus] was lifted up, and a cloud took him out of their sight. While he was going and they were gazing up toward heaven, suddenly two men in white robes stood by them. They said, 'Men of Galilee, why do you stand looking up toward heaven? This Jesus, who has been taken up from you into heaven, will come in the same way as you saw him go into heaven.' (Acts 1:9–11)

[Peter said,] 'Jesus of Nazareth, a man attested to you by God with deeds of power, wonders, and signs that God did through him among you, as you yourselves know – this man, handed over to you according to the definite plan and foreknowledge of God, you crucified and killed by the hands of those outside the law. But God raised him up, having freed him from death, because it was impossible for him to be held in its power. This Jesus God raised up, and of that all of us are witnesses.

Being therefore exalted at the right hand of God, and having received from the Father the promise of the Holy Spirit, he has poured out this that you both see and hear. Therefore let the entire house of Israel know with certainty that God has made him both Lord and Messiah, this Jesus whom you crucified.' (Acts 2:22–4, 32–3, 36)

Repent therefore, and turn to God so that your sins may be wiped out, so that times of refreshing may come from the presence of the Lord, and that he may send the Messiah appointed for you, that is, Jesus, who must remain in heaven until the time of universal restoration that God announced long ago through his holy prophets. (Acts 3:17–21)

What God Has Done

God, who is rich in mercy, out of the great love with which he loved us, even when we were dead through our trespasses, made us alive together with Christ

– by grace you have been saved –

and raised us up with him and seated us with him in the heavenly places in Christ Jesus,

so that in the ages to come he might show the immeasurable riches of his grace in kindness toward us in Christ Jesus.

For by grace you have been saved through faith, and this is not your own doing; it is the gift of God – not the result of works, so that no one may boast.

For we are what he has made us, created in Christ Jesus for good works, which God prepared beforehand to be our way of life. (Ephesians 2:4–10)

Our Response

So I tell you this, and insist on it in the Lord, that you must no longer live as the Gentiles do, in the futility of their thinking. They are darkened in their understanding and separated from the life of God because of the ignorance that is in them due to the hardening of their hearts. Having lost all sensitivity, they have given themselves over to sensuality so as to indulge in every kind of impurity, with a continual lust for more.

You, however, did not come to know Christ that way. Surely you heard of him and were taught in him in accordance with the truth that is in Jesus. You were taught, with regard to your former way of life, to put off your old self, which is being corrupted by its deceitful desires; to be made new in the attitude of your minds; and to put on the new self, created to be like God in true righteousness and holiness.

Be imitators of God, therefore, as dearly loved children and live a life of love, just as Christ loved us and gave himself up for us as a fragrant offering and sacrifice to God. (Ephesians 4:17–24; 5:1–2)

Morning Prayer II

Citizenship

For through [Christ] we both have access to the Father by one Spirit.

Consequently, you are no longer foreigners and aliens, but **fellow citizens with God's people and members of God's household,** built on the foundation of the apostles and prophets, with Christ Jesus himself as the chief cornerstone. In him the whole building is joined together and rises to become a holy temple in the Lord. And in him you too are being built together to become a dwelling in which God lives by his Spirit. (Ephesians 2:18–22)

But our citizenship is in heaven. And we eagerly await a Saviour from there, the Lord Jesus Christ, who, by the power that enables him to bring everything under his control, will transform our lowly bodies so that they will be like his glorious body. (Philippians 3:20–1)

But you are a chosen people, a royal priesthood, a holy nation, a people belonging to God, that you may declare the praises of him who called you out of darkness into his wonderful light. Once you were not a people, but now you are the people of God; once you had not received mercy, but now you have received mercy.

Dear friends, I urge you, as **aliens and strangers in the world,** to abstain from sinful desires, which war against your soul. Live such good lives among the pagans that, though they accuse you of doing wrong, they may see your good deeds and glorify God on the day he visits us. (1 Peter 2:9–12)

All these people were still living by faith when they died. They did not receive the things promised; they only saw them and welcomed them from a distance. And they admitted that they were **aliens and strangers on earth.** People who say such things show that they are looking for a country of their own. If they had been thinking of the country they had left, they would have had opportunity to return. Instead, they were longing for **a better country** – **a heavenly one.** Therefore God is not ashamed to be called their God, for he has prepared a city for them. (Hebrews 11:13–16)

The Code of the City

Since, then, you have been raised with Christ, **set your hearts on things above**, where Christ is seated at the right hand of God. Set your minds on things above, not on earthly things. For you died, and your life is now hidden with Christ in God. When Christ, who is your life, appears, then you also will appear with him in glory.

Put to death, therefore, whatever belongs to your earthly nature: sexual immorality, impurity, lust, evil desires and greed, which is idolatry. Because of these, the wrath of God is coming. You used to walk in these ways, in the life you once lived. But now you must rid yourselves of all such things as these: anger, rage, malice, slander, and filthy language from your lips. Do not lie to each other, since you have taken off your old self with its practices and have put on the new self, which is being renewed in knowledge in the image of its Creator. Here there is no Greek or Jew, circumcised or uncircumcised, barbarian, Scythian, slave or free, but Christ is all, and is in all.

Therefore, as God's chosen people, holy and dearly loved, **clothe yourselves** with compassion, kindness, humility, gentleness and patience. Bear with each other and forgive whatever grievances you may have against one another. Forgive as the Lord forgave you. And over all these virtues **put on love**, which binds them all together in perfect unity.

Let the peace of Christ rule in your hearts, since as members of one body you were called to peace. And be thankful. Let the word of Christ dwell in you richly as you teach and admonish one another with all wisdom, and as you sing psalms, hymns and spiritual songs with gratitude in your hearts to God. And whatever you do, whether in word or deed, do it all in the name of the Lord Jesus, giving thanks to God the Father through him. (Colossians 3:1–17)

The Final Vision

Then the angel showed me the river of the water of life, as clear as crystal, flowing from the throne of God and of the Lamb down the middle of the great street of the city. On each side of the river stood the tree of life, bearing twelve crops of fruit, yielding its fruit every month. And the leaves of the tree are for the healing of the nations. No longer will there be any curse. The throne of God and of the Lamb will be in the city, and his servants will serve him. They will see his face, and his name will be on their foreheads. There will be no more night. They will not need the light of a lamp or the light of the sun, for the Lord God will give them light. And they will reign for ever and ever.

'Behold, I am coming soon! My reward is with me, and I will give to everyone according to what he has done. I am the Alpha and the Omega, the First and the Last, the Beginning and the End.

'Blessed are those who wash their robes, that they may have the right to the tree of life and may go through the gates into the city.' (Revelation 22:1–5,12–14)

Evening Prayer II

The Living Way of Hebrews

The LORD says to my Lord:
'Sit at my right hand
until I make your enemies
a footstool for your feet.'
The LORD has sworn
and will not change his mind:
'You are a priest forever,
in the order of Melchizedek.' (Psalm 110:1, 4)

Jesus Our Brother

Yet at present we do not see everything subject to him.

But we see Jesus, who was made a little lower than the angels,
now crowned with glory and honour because he suffered death,
so that by the grace of God he might taste death for everyone.

In bringing many sons to glory, it was fitting that God,
for whom and through whom everything exists,
should make the author of their salvation perfect through suffering.

Both the one who makes men holy and those who are made holy are
of the same family. [They are 'all of one'.]

So Jesus is not ashamed to call them brothers. He says,
'I will declare your name to my brothers;
in the presence of the congregation I will sing your praises.'
And again,

'I will put my trust in him.'

And again he says, 'Here am I, and the children God has given me.'

Since the children have flesh and blood, he too shared in their humanity so that by his death he might destroy him who holds the power of death – that is, the devil – and free those who all their lives were held in slavery by their fear of death. (Hebrews 2:9–15)

Jesus Our Priest

Therefore, since we have a great high priest who has gone through the heavens, Jesus the Son of God, let us hold firmly to the faith we profess.

For we do not have a high priest who is unable to sympathize with our weaknesses, but we have one who has been tempted in every way, just as we are – yet was without sin.

Let us then approach the throne of grace with confidence, so that we may receive mercy and find grace to help us in our time of need. (Hebrews 4:14–16)

Jesus Our Forerunner

We have this hope as an anchor for the soul, firm and secure. It enters the inner sanctuary behind the curtain, where Jesus, who went before us, has entered on our behalf. He has become a High Priest forever, in the order of Melchizedek. (Hebrews 6:19–20)

Jesus At Work For Us Now

Because Jesus lives for ever, he has a permanent priesthood. Therefore he is able to save completely those who come to God through him, because he always lives to intercede for them. (Hebrews 7:24–25)

The point of what we are saying is this: We do have such a high priest, who sat down at the right hand of the throne of the Majesty in heaven, and who serves in the sanctuary, the true tabernacle set up by the Lord, not by man. (Hebrews 8:1–2)

For Christ did not enter a man-made sanctuary that was only a copy of the true one; he entered heaven itself, now to appear for us in God's presence. (Hebrews 9:24)

Our Response: To Enter the Holy Place in Him

Therefore, brothers, since we have confidence to enter the Most Holy Place by the blood of Jesus, by a new and living way opened for us through the curtain, that is, his body, and since we have a great priest over the house of God, let us draw near to God with a sincere heart in full assurance of faith, having our hearts sprinkled to cleanse us from a guilty conscience and having our bodies washed with pure water. Let us hold unswervingly to the hope we profess, for he who promised is faithful. And let us consider how we may spur one another on toward love and good deeds. (Hebrews 10:19–24)

Let us fix our eyes on Jesus, the author and perfecter of our faith, who for the joy set before him endured the cross, scorning its shame, and sat down at the right hand of the throne of God. (Hebrews 12:2)

Let us, then, go to him outside the camp, bearing the disgrace he bore. For here we do not have an enduring city, but we are looking for the city that is to come.

Through Jesus, therefore, let us continually offer to God a sacrifice of praise – the fruit of lips that confess his name.

And do not forget to do good and to share with others, for with such sacrifices God is pleased. (Hebrews 13:13–16)

Benediction

May the God of peace, who through the blood of the eternal covenant brought back from the dead our Lord Jesus, that great Shepherd of the sheep, equip you with everything good for doing his will, and may he work in us what is pleasing to him, through Jesus Christ, to whom be glory for ever and ever. Amen. (Hebrews 13:20–1)

Select Bibliography

Allen, Diogenes. *Spiritual Theology: The Theology of Yesterday for Spiritual Help Today*. Cambridge: Cowley Publications, 1997.

Ambrose of Milan. *Exposition of the Christian Faith*. Ed. Philip Schaff and Henry Wace. *A Select Library of Nicene and Post-Nicene Fathers of the Christian Church*, 2nd series, vol. 10. Edinburgh: T&T Clark and Grand Rapids: William B. Eerdmans Publishing Company, 1993.

The Anathemas Against Origen. Ed. Philip Schaff and Henry Wace, *A Select Library of Nicene and Post-Nicene Fathers of the Christian Church*, 2nd series, vol. 14. Edinburgh: T&T Clark and Grand Rapids: William B. Eerdmans Publishing Company, 1993.

Athanasius. *Four Discourses Against the Arians*. Ed. Philip Schaff and Henry Wace, *A Select Library of Nicene and Post-Nicene Fathers of the Christian Church*, 2nd series, vol. 4. Edinburgh: T&T Clark and Grand Rapids: William B. Eerdmans Publishing Company, 1989.

Atkinson, Peter. *Ascension Now: Implications of Christ's Ascension for Today's Church*. Collegeville, Minn.: Liturgical Press, 2001.

Augustine. *The City of God*. Ed. Philip Schaff, *A Select Library of Nicene and Post-Nicene Fathers of the Christian Church*, 1st series, vol. 2. Edinburgh: T&T Clark and Grand Rapids: William B. Eerdmans Publishing Company, 1993.

_____. *The Confessions of St. Augustine*. Ed. Philip Schaff, *A Select Library of Nicene and Post-Nicene Fathers of the Christian Church*, 1st series, vol. 1. Edinburgh: T&T Clark and Grand Rapids: William B. Eerdmans Publishing Company, 1993.

_____. *The Enchiridion*. Ed. Philip Schaff, *A Select Library of Nicene and Post-Nicene Fathers of the Christian Church*, 1st series, vol. 3. Edinburgh: T&T Clark and Grand Rapids: William B. Eerdmans Publishing Company, 1993.

_____. *On the Merits and Forgiveness of Sins, and on the Baptism of Infants*. Ed. Philip Schaff, *A Select Library of Nicene and Post-Nicene Fathers of the Christian Church*, 1st series, vol. 5. Edinburgh: T&T Clark and Grand Rapids: William B. Eerdmans Publishing Company, 1993.

_____. *On the Psalms*. Ed. Philip Schaff, *A Select Library of Nicene and Post-Nicene Fathers of the Christian Church*, 1st series, vol. 8. Edinburgh: T&T Clark and Grand Rapids: William B. Eerdmans Publishing Company, 1993.

_____. *Sermons on Selected Lessons of the New Testament*. Ed. Philip Schaff, *A Select Library of Nicene and Post-Nicene Fathers of the Christian Church*, 1st series, vol. 6. Edinburgh: T&T Clark and Grand Rapids: William B. Eerdmans Publishing Company, 1993.

_____. *Tractates on John*. Ed. Philip Schaff, *A Select Library of Nicene and Post-Nicene Fathers of the Christian Church*, 1st series, vol. 7. Edinburgh: T&T Clark and Grand Rapids: William B. Eerdmans Publishing Company, 1993.

_____. *A Treatise on Faith and the Creed*. Ed. Philip Schaff, *A Select Library of Nicene and Post-Nicene Fathers of the Christian Church*, 1st series, vol. 3. Edinburgh: T&T Clark and Grand Rapids: William B. Eerdmans Publishing Company, 1993.

Balthasar, Hans Urs von. *Credo: Meditations on the Apostle's Creed*. New York: Crossroad, 1990.

Barna, George. *The Second Coming of the Church*. Nashville: Word Publishing, 1998.

Barth, Karl. *Church Dogmatics. Vol. IV: The Doctrine of Reconciliation, Part 2*. Ed. G. W. Bromiley and T. F. Torrance. Edinburgh: T&T Clark, 1958.

_____. *Dogmatics in Outline*. New York: Harper and Row Publishers, 1958.

Basil. *Letters*. Ed. Philip Schaff and Henry Wace, *A Select Library of Nicene and Post-Nicene Fathers of the Christian Church*, 2nd series, vol. 8. Edinburgh: T&T Clark and Grand Rapids: William B. Eerdmans Publishing Company, 1989.

Berkhoff, Louis. *Systematic Theology*. Edinburgh: Banner of Truth, 1938.

Bonhoeffer, Dietrich. *Life Together*. New York: Harper and Brothers Publishers, 1954.

The Book of Concord: The Confessions of the Evangelical Lutheran Church. Trans. and ed. Theodore G. Tappert. Philadelphia: Fortress Press, 1959.

Brown, Peter. *Augustine of Hippo*. Berkeley: University of California Press, 1967.

Calvin, John. *The Acts of the Apostles, Vol. 1*. Ed. David W. Torrance and Thomas F. Torrance. Trans. W. J. G. McDonald. Grand Rapids: William B. Eerdmans Publishing Company, 1965.

_____. *The Deity of Christ and Other Sermons*. Trans. Leroy Nixon. Audubon, NJ: Old Paths Publications, 1997.

_____. *The Epistle of Paul the Apostle to the Hebrews*. Ed. David W. Torrance and Thomas F. Torrance. Trans. T. H. L. Parker. Grand Rapids: William B. Eerdmans Publishing Company, 1965.

_____. *The First Epistle of Paul to the Corinthians*. Ed. David W. Torrance and Thomas F. Torrance. Trans. John W. Fraser. Grand Rapids: William B. Eerdmans Publishing Company, 1960.

_____. *The Gospel According to St. John, Vols. 1 and 2*. Ed. David W. Torrance and Thomas F. Torrance. Trans. T. H. L. Parker. Grand Rapids: William B. Eerdmans Publishing Company, 1961.

_____. *Institutes of the Christian Religion*. Ed. John T. McNeill. Trans. Ford Lewis Battles. Philadelphia: Westminster Press, 1960.

_____. *Institutes of the Christian Religion*. Trans. Henry Beveridge. Grand Rapids: William B. Eerdmans Publishing Company, 1979.

_____. *The Second Epistle of Paul to the Corinthians*. Ed. David W. Torrance and Thomas F. Torrance. Trans. T. A. Smail. Grand Rapids: William B. Eerdmans Publishing Company, 1964.

_____. *Selected Works of John Calvin: Tracts and Letters, Vol. 2*. Ed. Henry Beveridge and Jules Bonnet. Trans. Henry Beveridge. Albany, Ore.: Books for the Ages, 1998.

Carson, D. A. *The Gagging of God*. Grand Rapids: Zondervan Publishing House, 1996.

Cassian, John. *The Seven Books on the Incarnation of the Lord, Against Nestorius*. Ed. Philip Schaff and Henry Wace, *A Select Library of Nicene and Post-Nicene Fathers of the Christian Church*, 2nd series, vol. 11. Edinburgh: T&T Clark and Grand Rapids: William B. Eerdmans Publishing Company, 1989.

Chan, Simon. *Spiritual Theology: A Systematic Study of the Christian Life*. Downers Grove, Ill.: Inter-Varsity Press, 1998.

Chrysostom, John. *Homilies on the Acts of the Apostles*. Ed. Philip Schaff, *A Select Library of Nicene and Post-Nicene Fathers of the Christian Church*, 1st series, vol. 11. Edinburgh: T&T Clark and Grand Rapids: William B. Eerdmans Publishing Company, 1993.

_____. *Homilies on the Epistle of St. Paul to the Romans*. Ed. Philip Schaff, *A Select Library of Nicene and Post-Nicene Fathers of the Christian Church*, 1st series, vol. 11. Edinburgh: T&T Clark and Grand Rapids: William B. Eerdmans Publishing Company, 1993.

_____. *Homilies on the Epistle to the Ephesians*. Ed. Philip Schaff, *A Select Library of Nicene and Post-Nicene Fathers of the Christian Church*, 1st series, vol. 13. Edinburgh: T&T Clark and Grand Rapids: William B. Eerdmans Publishing Company, 1993.

_____. *Homilies on the First Epistle of St. Paul to Timothy*. Ed. Philip Schaff, *A Select Library of Nicene and Post-Nicene Fathers of the Christian Church*, 1st series, vol. 13. Edinburgh: T&T Clark and Grand Rapids: William B. Eerdmans Publishing Company, 1993.

_____. *Homilies on the Gospel According to St. John*. Ed. Philip Schaff, *A Select Library of Nicene and Post-Nicene Fathers of the Christian Church*, 1st series, vol. 14. Edinburgh: T&T Clark and Grand Rapids: William B. Eerdmans Publishing Company, 1993.

_____. *Homilies on Matthew*. Ed. Philip Schaff, *A Select Library of Nicene and Post-Nicene Fathers of the Christian Church*, 1st series, vol. 10. Edinburgh: T&T Clark and Grand Rapids: William B. Eerdmans Publishing Company, 1993.

Clement of Alexandria. *The Stromata*. Ed. Alexander Roberts and James Donaldson, American ed. A. Cleveland Coxe, *The Ante-Nicene Fathers*, vol. 2. Edinburgh: T&T Clark and Grand Rapids: William B. Eerdmans, 1993.

Colson, Charles, with Pearcy, Nancy. *How Now Shall We Live?* Wheaton, Ill.: Tyndale House, 1999.

The Constitution of the Presbyterian Church (USA), Part 1: The Book of Confessions. Louisville, Ky.: The Office of the General Assembly, 1999.

Cyril of Jerusalem. *Catechetical Lectures.* Ed. Philip Schaff and Henry Wace, *A Select Library of Nicene and Post-Nicene Fathers of the Christian Church,* 2nd series, vol. 7. Edinburgh: T&T Clark and Grand Rapids: William B. Eerdmans Publishing Company, 1989.

Daughters, Kenneth Alan. 'The Theological Significance of the Ascension'. *The Emmaus Journal,* 3:2 (Winter 1994).

Davies, J. G. *He Ascended into Heaven: A Study in the History of the Doctrine.* London: Lutterworth Press, 1958.

Dawson, Gerrit Scott. *Love Bade Me Welcome.* Lenoir, NC: Glen Lorien Books, 1997.

Donne, Brian K. *Christ Ascended: A Study in the Significance of the Ascension of Jesus Christ in the New Testament.* Exeter: Paternoster Press, 1983.

Ephraim the Syrian. *Nineteen Hymns on the Nativity of Christ in the Flesh.* Ed. Phillip Schaff and Henry Wace, *A Select Library of Nicene and Post-Nicene Fathers of the Christian Church,* 2nd series, vol. 13. Edinburgh: T&T Clark and Grand Rapids: William B. Eerdmans Publishing Company, 1989.

Mathetes. *The Epistle of Mathetes to Diognetus.* Ed. Alexander Roberts and James Donaldson, American ed. A. Cleveland Coxe, *The Ante-Nicene Fathers,* vol. 1. Edinburgh: T&T Clark and Grand Rapids: William B. Eerdmans Publishing Company, 1993.

Farrar, Frederick. *The Life of Christ as Represented in Art.* New York: Macmillan and Company, 1895.

Farrow, Douglas. *Ascension and Ecclesia: On the Significance of the Doctrine of the Ascension for Ecclesiology and Christian Cosmology.* Grand Rapids: William B. Eerdmans and Sons, 1999.

_____. 'Confessing Christ Coming'. In *Nicene Christianity: The Future for a New Ecumenism.* Ed. Christopher R. Seitz. Grand Rapids: Brazo Press, 2001.

_____. 'Karl Barth on the Ascension: An Appreciation and Critique'. *International Journal of Systematic Theology,* 2:2 (July 2000).

Geisler, Norman L. 'The Significance of Christ's Physical Resurrection'. *Bibliotheca Sacra,* 582 (Apr. 1989).

Gilpin, George, the Elder. *The Bee Hive of the Romish Church.* London, 1579. Reprinted in Hans Rudi Weber (ed.), *Die Umsetzung der Himmelfahrt Christi in die Zeichenhafte Liturgie.* Bern: Peter Lang, 1987.

Glodo, Michael. 'Singing with the Savior'. *RTS Quarterly,* 17:1 (Spring 1998).

Gooding, David. *An Unshakable Kingdom: The Letter to the Hebrews for Today.* Leicester: Inter-Varsity Press, 1989.

Gregory Nazianzen. *Orations.* Ed. Philip Schaff and Henry Wace, *A Select Library of Nicene and Post-Nicene Fathers of the Christian Church,* 2nd series, vol. 5. Edinburgh: T&T Clark and Grand Rapids: William B. Eerdmans Publishing Company, 1989.

_____. *To Cleodonius the Priest Against Apollinarius.* Ed. Philip Schaff and Henry Wace, *A Select Library of Nicene and Post-Nicene Fathers of the Christian Church,* 2nd series, vol. 5. Edinburgh: T&T Clark and Grand Rapids: William B. Eerdmans Publishing Company, 1989.

Gregory of Nyssa. *Against Eunomius.* Ed. Philip Schaff and Henry Wace, *A Select Library of Nicene and Post-Nicene Fathers of the Christian Church,* 2nd series, vol. 5. Edinburgh: T&T Clark and Grand Rapids: William B. Eerdmans Publishing Company, 1989.

Hendry, George. *The Gospel of the Incarnation.* Philadelphia: Westminster Press, 1958.

Herbert, George. Selected poems reproduced in Gerrit Scott Dawson, *Love Bade Me Welcome.* Lenoir, NC: Glen Lorien Books, 1997.

Hilary of Poitiers. *On the Trinity.* Ed. Philip Schaff and Henry Wace, *A Select Library of Nicene and Post-Nicene Fathers of the Christian Church,* 2nd series, vol. 9. Edinburgh: T&T Clark and Grand Rapids: William B. Eerdmans Publishing Company, 1989.

Hippolytus. *Against the Heresy of One Noetus.* Ed. Alexander Roberts and James Donaldson, American ed. A. Cleveland Coxe, *The Ante-Nicene Fathers,* vol. 5. Edinburgh: T&T Clark and Grand Rapids: William B. Eerdmans Publishing Company, 1993.

The Incarnate Son of God: The Feasts of Jesus Christ and the Virgin Mary. Ed. Catherine Aslanoff. Trans. Paul Meyendorff. Crestwood, NY: St Vladimir's Seminary Press, 1995.

Irenaeus. *Against Heresies.* Ed. Alexander Roberts and James Donaldson, American ed. A. Cleveland Coxe, *The Ante-Nicene Fathers,* vol. 1. Edinburgh: T&T Clark and Grand Rapids: William B. Eerdmans Publishing Company, 1993.

Jerome. *Letter 5. To Marcella.* Ed. Philip Schaff and Henry Wace, *A Select Library of Nicene and Post-Nicene Fathers of the Christian Church,* 2nd series, vol. 6. Edinburgh: T&T Clark and Grand Rapids: William B. Eerdmans Publishing Company, 1989.

Justin Martyr. *Dialogue of Justin, Philosopher and Martyr with Trypho, a Jew.* Ed. Alexander Roberts and James Donaldson, American ed. A. Cleveland Coxe, *The Ante-Nicene Fathers,* vol. 1. Edinburgh: T&T Clark and Grand Rapids: William B. Eerdmans Publishing Company, 1993.

_____. *Fragments on the Resurrection.* Ed. Alexander Roberts and James Donaldson, American ed. A. Cleveland Coxe, *The Ante-Nicene Fathers,* vol. 1. Edinburgh: T&T Clark and Grand Rapids: William B. Eerdmans Publishing Company, 1993.

Knox, John. *The Works of John Knox.* 6 vols. Collected and ed. David Laing. Edinburgh: Bannatyne Club, 1846–64.

Kruger, C. Baxter. *God is For Us.* Jackson, Miss.: Perichoresis Press, 1995.

_____. *Home.* Jackson, Miss.: Perichoresis Press, 1996.

Leo the Great. *Sermons.* Ed. Philip Schaff and Henry Wace, *A Select Library of Nicene and Post-Nicene Fathers of the Christian Church,* 2nd series, vol. 10.

Edinburgh: T&T Clark and Grand Rapids: William B. Eerdmans Publishing Company, 1989.

Lewis, C. S. *Miracles: A Preliminary Study*. Glasgow: Fontana Books, 1960.

Lewis, Peter. *The Glory of Christ*. London: Hodder & Stoughton, 1992.

Luther, Martin. *Confession Concerning Christ's Supper*. Ed. and Trans. Robert H. Fischer, *Luther's Works*, vol. 37: *Word and Sacrament III*. Philadelphia: Muhlenberg Press, 1961.

_____. *The Sacrament of the Body and Blood of Christ – Against the Fanatics*. Ed. Abdel Ross Wentz, Trans. Frederick C. Ahrens, *Luther's Works*, vol. 36: *Word and Sacrament II*. Philadelphia: Muhlenberg Press, 1959.

_____. *That These Words of Christ, 'This Is My Body,' etc., Still Stand Firm Against the Fanatics*. Ed. and trans. Robert H. Fischer, *Luther's Works*, vol. 37: *Word and Sacrament III*. Philadelphia: Muhlenberg Press, 1961.

McKim, Donald K. 'The Grand Farewell'. *Christianity Today*, 36:36 (18 May 1992).

Mackintosh, H. R. *The Person of Christ*. Ed. T. F. Torrance. Edinburgh: T&T Clark, 2000.

McLain, Wayne. *A Resurrection Encounter: The Rufus Mosely Story*. Minneapolis: Macalester Park Publishing Company, 1997.

MacLeod, David J. 'The Present Work of Christ in Hebrews'. *Bibliotheca Sacra*, 590 (Apr. 1991).

Marrevee, W. H. *The Ascension of Christ in the Works of St. Augustine*. Ottawa: University of Ottawa Press, 1967.

Metzger, Bruce M. 'The Meaning of Christ's Ascension'. In *Search the Scriptures: New Testament Studies in Honor of Raymond T. Stamm*. Ed. J. M. Myers, O. Reimherr, and H. N. Bream. Leiden: E. J. Brill, 1969.

Milligan, William. *The Ascension and Heavenly Priesthood of Our Lord*. London: Macmillan and Co., Limited, 1894.

_____. *The Resurrection of Our Lord*. London: Macmillan and Co., Limited, 1905.

Moltmann, Jürgen. *The Way of Jesus Christ: Christology in Messianic Dimensions*. San Francisco: HarperSanFrancisco, 1998.

Murray, Andrew. *The Holiest of All*. Springdale, Pa.: Whitaker House, 1996.

Newbigin, Lesslie. *The Gospel in a Pluralist Society*. Grand Rapids: William B. Eerdmans Publishing Company, 1989.

_____. *The Light Has Come: An Exposition of the Fourth Gospel*. Grand Rapids: William B. Eerdmans Publishing Company, 1982.

_____. *The Open Secret: An Introduction to the Theology of Mission*. Grand Rapids: William B. Eerdmans Publishing Company, 1995.

_____. *Truth to Tell: The Gospel as Public Truth*. Grand Rapids: William B. Eerdmans Publishing Company, 1991.

_____. *A Word in Season: Perspectives on Christian World Mission*. Grand Rapids: William B. Eerdmans Publishing Company, 1997.

Niebuhr, H. Richard. *Christ and Culture*. New York: Harper and Row Publishers, 1951.

Nouwen, Henri J. M. *The Return of the Prodigal Son: A Story of Homecoming.* New York: Doubleday, 1992.

Novatian. *A Treatise of Novatian Concerning the Trinity.* Ed. Alexander Roberts and James Donaldson, American ed. A. Cleveland Coxe, *The Ante-Nicene Fathers*, vol. 5. Edinburgh: T&T Clark and Grand Rapids: William B. Eerdmans, 1993.

Old, Hughes Oliphant. *The Reading and Preaching of the Scriptures in the Worship of The Christian Church*, vols. 1 and 2. Grand Rapids: William B. Eerdmans Publishing Company, 1998.

Origen. *De Principiis.* Ed. Alexander Roberts and James Donaldson, American ed. A. Cleveland Coxe, *The Ante-Nicene Fathers*, vol. 1. Edinburgh: T&T Clark and Grand Rapids: William B. Eerdmans Publishing Company, 1993.

Ostling, Richard. 'Book Depicts America's Two-Party System on Scripture'. *Telegraph*, 21 Apr. 2001.

Ouspensky, Leonard, and Lossky, Vladmir. *The Meaning of Icons.* Trans. G. E. H. Palmer and E. Kadloubovsky. Crestwood, NY: St Vladimir's Seminary Press, 1983.

Pannenberg, Wolfhart. *Systematic Theology, Vol. 1.* Trans. by Geoffrey W. Bromiley. Grand Rapids: William B. Eerdmans Publishing Company, 1991.

Parsons, Mikeal C. *The Departure of Jesus in Luke-Acts: The Ascension Narratives in Context.* Sheffield: Sheffield Academic Press, 1987.

Pryor, John W. 'The Johannine Son of Man and the Descent-Ascent Motif.' *Journal of the Evangelical Theological Society*, 34:3 (Sept. 1991).

Purves, Andrew. ' Jesus Christ is the Same Yesterday, Today, and Forever'. In *A Cry of Need and of Joy: Confessing the Faith in a New Millennium*, vol. 1, ed. Richard E. Burnett. Lenoir, NC: Reformation Press, 2002.

_____. 'Jesus Christ: Lord in History'. *Theology Matters* 7:2 (Mar./Apr. 2001).

Rankin, Duncan. 'Carnal Union with Christ in the Theology of T. F. Torrance'. Ph.D. diss., New College, University of Edinburgh, 1999.

Ratzinger, Joseph., ed. *The Catechism of the Catholic Church.* Mahwah, NJ: Paulist Press, 1994.

Reardon, Patrick Henry. *Christ in the Psalms.* Ben Lomond, Calif.: Conciliar Press, 2000.

Rhodes, Ronald C. 'The New Age Christology of David Spangler'. *Bibliotheca Sacr*, 562 (Apr. 1984).

Robinson, Edward. 'The Resurrection and Ascension of Our Lord'. *Bibliotheca Sacra*, 597 (Jan. 1993).

Schaeffer, Francis. *How Should We Then Live?* Old Tappan, NJ: Fleming H. Revel Company, 1976.

_____. *True Spirituality.* Wheaton, Ill.: Tyndale House Publishers, 1971.

Smail, Tom. *The Giving Gift: The Holy Spirit in Person.* London: Darton, Longman & Todd, Ltd, 1994.

_____. *Once and for All: A Confession of the Cross.* London: Darton, Longman & Todd, Ltd, 1998.

Sozomen, Hermias. *Ecclesiastical History of Sozomen.* Ed. Philip Schaff and Henry

Wace, *A Select Library of Nicene and Post-Nicene Fathers of the Christian Church*, 2nd series, vol. 2. Edinburgh: T&T Clark and Grand Rapids: William B. Eerdmans Publishing Company, 1989.

Spinks, Bryan D. 'The Ascension and the Vicarious Humanity of Christ: The Christology and Soteriology behind the Church of Scotland's Anamnesis and Epiklesis'. In *Time and Community*, ed. J. N. Alexander. Washington, DC: Pastoral Press, 1990. Spong, John Shelby. 'A Call for a New Reformation'. *The Fourth R*, 11:4 (July/Aug. 1998).

_____. *A New Faith for a New World*. San Francisco: HarperSanFrancisco, 2001.

Swete, Henry Barclay. *The Appearances of Our Lord after the Passion: A Study in the Earliest Christian Tradition*. London: Macmillan and Co., Ltd, 1907.

_____. *The Ascended Christ: A Study in the Earliest Christian Teaching*. London: Macmillan and Co., Ltd, 1910.

Taylor, Barbara Brown. 'The Day we were Left Behind'. *Christianity Today*, 42:6 (18 May 1998).

Tertullian. *An Answer to the Jews*. Ed. Alexander Roberts and James Donaldson, American ed. A. Cleveland Coxe, *The Ante-Nicene Fathers*, vol. 3. Edinburgh: T&T Clark and Grand Rapids: William B. Eerdmans Publishing Company, 1993.

_____. *Five Books Against Marcion*. Ed. Alexander Roberts and James Donaldson, American ed. A. Cleveland Coxe, *The Ante-Nicene Fathers*, vol. 3. Edinburgh: T&T Clark and Grand Rapids: William B. Eerdmans Publishing Company, 1993.

_____. *On the Resurrection*. Ed. Alexander Roberts and James Donaldson, American ed. A. Cleveland Coxe, *The Ante-Nicene Fathers*, vol. 3. Edinburgh: T&T Clark and Grand Rapids: William B. Eerdmans Publishing Company, 1993.

_____. *Scorpiace*. Ed. Alexander Roberts and James Donaldson, American ed. A. Cleveland Coxe, *The Ante-Nicene Fathers*, vol. 1. Edinburgh: T&T Clark and Grand Rapids: William B. Eerdmans Publishing Company, 1993.

Thomas, Derek. *Taken Up Into Heaven: The Ascension of Christ*. Durham: Evangelical Press, 1996.

Thompson, K. C. *Received Up Into Glory: A Study of the Ascension*. London: Faith Press, 1964.

Toon, Peter. *The Ascension of Our Lord*. Nashville: Thomas Nelson Publishers, 1984.

Torrance, James B. *Worship, Community and the Triune God of Grace*. Downers Grove, Ill.: Inter-Varsity Christian Press, 1996.

Torrance, Thomas, Torrance, James B., and Torrance, David W. *A Passion for Christ: The Vision that Ignites Ministry*. Ed. Gerrit Dawson and Jock Stein. Edinburgh: Handsel Press and Lenoir, NC: PLC Publications, 1999.

Torrance, Thomas F. *The Christian Doctrine of God: One Being, Three Persons*. Edinburgh: T&T Clark, 1996.

_____. *The Mediation of Christ*. Edinburgh: T&T Clark, 1992.

_____. 'The Reformed Doctrine of Christ'. Unpublished lecture delivered at New College, Edinburgh University, 1964.

_____. *Royal Priesthood: A Theology of Ordained Ministry*. 2nd edn. Edinburgh: T&T Clark, 1993.

_____. *Scottish Theology. From John Knox to John McLeod Campbell*. Edinburgh: T&T Clark, 1996.

_____. *Space, Time and Incarnation*. Edinburgh: T&T Clark, 1969.

_____. *Space, Time and Resurrection*. Grand Rapids: William B. Eerdmans Publishing Company, 1976.

_____. *Theology in Reconstruction*. SCM Press Ltd, 1965.

_____. *Trinitarian Faith*. Edinburgh: T&T Clark, 1988.

Turnau, Theodore A. 'The Life of Jesus, after the Ascension'. *Westminster Theological Journal*, 56:2 (Fall 1994).

Wagner, James Benjamin. *Ascendit ad Coelos: The Doctrine of the Ascension in the Reformed and Lutheran Period of Orthodoxy*. Winterthur: Verlag P. G. Keller, 1964.

Wallace, Ronald. *Calvin's Doctrine of the Word and Sacrament*. Eugene, Ore.: Wipf & Stock Publishers, 1997.

Walvoord, John F. 'The Present Work of Christ. Part I: The Ascension of Christ'. *Bibliotheca Sacra*, 481 (Jan. 1964).

_____. 'The Present Work of Christ. Part V: The Present Work of Christ in Heaven'. *Bibliotheca Sacra*, 485 (Jan. 1965).

Westcott, Brooke Foss. *The Revelation of the Risen Lord*. London: Macmillan and Co., 1902.

Wink, Walter. *Naming the Powers: The Invisible Forces that Determine Human Existence*. Philadelphia: Fortress Press, 1987.

_____. *Transforming Bible Study*. 2nd edn. Nashville: Abingdon Press, 1989.

Wordsworth, William. 'The World Is Too Much with Us'. In *Major British Poets of the Romantic Period*, ed. William Heath. New York: Macmillan Publishing Co., Inc., 1973.

Zizioulas, John. *Being as Communion: Studies in Personhood and the Church*. Crestwood, NY: St Vladimir's Seminary Press, 1993.

Index

Titles of publications, and non-English words are shown in *italics*.

adoptionist Christology 75
Against the Arians 93–5
Against Eunomius 109
Against Heresies 63
Ambrose of Milan 66–8, 69, 103–4
anabaino 37–8
analambano 38–9
Apostle's Creed 4
Ascension Day celebrations 33, 70–2, 110–13
assumption, ascension as 38
Athanasius 65–6, 93–5, 164, 167–8
Augustine 32, 69
  and Christ's presence in earth and heaven 82, 84–6, 177–8
  and the church 207–8
  City of God, The 157–9
  and resurrection body 42
  and spiritual quest 173–4
  totus Christus 104–7, 139

Baker, Henry 68

Barna, George 23–4
Barth, Karl 8, 39, 226
Basil 95
Bee Hive of the Romish Church, The 33
benediction, priestly role 121–2
bodily ascension 31–5, 42–50
Borg, Marcus 75
Bridges, Matthew 57
busyness, effect on church 19

Calvin, John 101, 165, 181–2
  and Christ's priesthood 125, 133–4, 138, 140
  and confidence in Christ 81–2
  and heaven 39–40
  and Lord's Supper 46–9, 179–80
  and priesthood 120
  and spiritual discipline 169–71, 174–5
  and union with Christ 192–3
Calvinist beliefs on ascension 44–5

captives procession 69–70
Carson, D.A. 26
Christ *see* Jesus Christ
Christian behaviour 156, 177–9
Chrysostom, John 32–3, 69, 88,
    172–4
  and firstfruits 110–13
  and Jesus as divine and
    human 81–2
church
  challenges of the
    ascension 74–7
  mission 144–5, 151–3,
    159–61, 177–9, 200–3
  renewal through the
    ascension 185–203
  withdrawal from the
    world 147–8
  worldliness 13–25, 150–51
citizenship
  of earth 155–7
  of heaven 153–5
City of God, The 157–9
Colossians 59, 176, 177
1 Corinthians 103, 108
Cyril of Alexandria 55

Davies, J.G. 60, 70, 110, 112
Day of Atonement 120–2
deification 164–9
Deuteronomy 108
Dialogue with Trypho 61–2
divinity of Jesus 73–91

earthly citizenship 155–7
Easter Day ascension 36–7
enthronement psalms 60–1
Ephesians 59, 77, 80, 163
Ephraem 83–4
Epistle of Mathetes 155–6
Eucharist 46–8, 125–6, 179–80
evangelism, lack of 19

exaltation of humility 97–101
exaltation psalms 66–8
*Exposition of the Christian
    Faith* 66–8

Farrar, Frederick 6–7
Farrow, Douglas 37, 39, 47, 55,
    56, 147, 148, 149,
  deification as
    humanization 166–7
  mission of the church 151–2
firstfruits 108–113

Gagging of God, The 26
gates of heaven 67
Gregory of Nazianzen 43,
    132–3, 165
Gregory of Nyssa 97–101,
    109

heaven 39–42
  citizenship of 153–5
  gates 67
Hebrews 123–4, 154
Hendry, George 100
Herbert, George 63, 174
heresies, returning to modern
    church 75–6
High Priest
  ancient Israel 119–22
  Jesus as 122–38
Hilary of Poitiers 86, 89
Hippolytus 78–9
Holloway, Richard 34
Holy Spirit
  as gift from Jesus 54, 96
  Jesus living through 131–2
  uniting church with
    Christ 46–7
Hugo, Victor 118
humanity of Jesus 73–91
humanization 167

incarnation   83–4, 86–7
incarnational redemption   100
intercession of Jesus   132–3
Irenaus   63–4, 89, 102–3, 129,
    164, 166
Israel, High Priest   119–20

Jeremiah   209
Jesus Christ
    ascended body   31–5, 42–50
    as divine and human   73–91,
        178–9
    entrance into heaven   65–8
    glorified in scripture   56–9
    as head   101–4
    as king   8–9, 53–6
    as priest   8, 117–19, 122–41,
        182–3
    as prophet   8
    as the prodigal son   62
    as sacrifice   125–34
    simultaneous presence on earth
        and in heaven   82–7
    as the Word incarnate   78–9
1 John   17
John Crysostom see Chrysostom,
    John
John's Gospel   77, 85, 99, 106,
    112
joy from union with Christ   181
Justin Martyr   32, 61–2

kingdom on earth, error of the
    church   148–50
kingly role of Christ   8–9, 53–6
Knox, John   8
Kruger, C. Baxter   98–9

Leo the Great   71, 165
Leo Imperator   111
Les Miserables   118–19
letters to the Churches,

Revelation   14
Leviticus   120–1
Lewis, C.S.   5, 41, 43–4
litany on the ascension   194–5
Lord's Supper   46–8, 125–6,
    179–80
Luke   36, 58
Lutheran beliefs on
    ascension   44–5

Mackintosh, H.R.   91
Mark's Gospel   57–8
Marrevee, William   107
Mathetes, Epistle of   155–6
Matthew's Gospel   57
Maximus of Turin   69, 70–1
Metzger, Bruce M.   214
Milligan, William   22, 51, 127,
    130, 160, 178
    and priesthood of Jesus   128
    and union with Jesus   165
mission of the church   144–5,
    151–3, 159–61, 177–9
Moltmann, J.   40
multiple ascensions   36–7
Murray, Andrew   114, 165
    and ascension significance for
        church   26
    and priesthood of Jesus   130,
        182–3
    and spiritual growth   172,
        175–6
    and union with Jesus   90
    and worldliness   22–3

nativity   83–4, 86–7
New and Living Way, The
    (sermon)   190–1
Newbigin, Lesslie   14, 17–18,
    35–6
Novatian   79–81
Nouwen, Henri   62

offering of Jesus 125–34
once-for-all offering of
    Jesus 126–8
Origen 32, 43, 147

Paul 47, 56, 163
    and Christ as head 101
    and Christ's glory 58–9
    and Christ's victory over
        death 65
    and Christian behaviour 176,
        177
    and citizenship of heaven 7,
        153
    firstfruits imagery 108–9
perpetual offering of
    Christ 126–34
personal mission fields, impact of
    the ascension 198–200
Peter 58, 154
    Pentecost sermon 60
Philippians 7, 58, 153
physical ascension 31–5, 42–50
pledge of resurrection 87–9
prayer and Christ's
    priesthood 138–41
prayer guides 195–8
*Present Work of Christ in Heaven,
    The* 127
priesthood of Christ 8, 117–19,
    122–41
priests, Israel 122–41
private truth 35
prophetic role of Christ 8
Psalms 60–1, 64, 66–8, 79, 137,
    145–6
public truth 35–6
Purves, Andrew 74

redemption, and continuing
    incarnation 5–7
Reformation

ascension beliefs 33, 44–5
    and once-for-all offering of
        Christ 126
reign of Jesus 8–9, 53–6
Rembrandt, painting of the
    prodigal son 62
renunciation 174–7
resurrection body of Jesus
    42–50
*Resurrection of the Flesh, On
    the* 87–8
Return of the Prodigal Son, The 62
Revelation 58, 154
    letters to the churches 14
Ruth 205–6

sacrifice
    in Israel 121
    Jesus as 125–34
salvation, and continuing
    incarnation 5–7
Satan, triumph over 64
scapegoat 121
Scorpiace 65
Scot's Confession 8
*Second Coming of the Church,
    The* 23–4
Space, Time and Resurrection 49
Spangler, David 75
spiritual ascension 163–84
Spong, John 34
suffering 181
Swete, Henry Barclay 40, 54–5,
    61, 127, 131, 155
    and ascension significance for
        the church 26, 51
    and Jesus as head 101–2,
        107
    and manner of ascension 38
    and offering of Jesus 128
    and victory of Jesus 72
    and worldliness 23

Taylor, Barbara Brown   62
teaching on the ascension
    191–5
Tertullian   32, 64–5, 87–8
theopoesis   164–6
Thompson, K.C.   39
1 Timothy   97
Toon, Peter   37, 127–8
Torrance, James   121
    and Christ's priesthood
        138–9, 140
Torrance, Thomas   57, 74, 128,
    168–9
    and ascension significance for
        the church   144–5
    and Christ's priesthood   133
    and manner of ascension   37,
        39, 49
    and our relation to Jesus   50
    totus Christus   104–7, 139
Trinity, On the   86

union with Christ   93–114,
    163–9
uniqueness of Christ, church's
    difficulty with   19–20

victor's procession   61–2

Wagner, James   44
Walvoord, John   45, 127
Whatever? No, What of It?
    (sermon)   188–90
Wink, Walter   14–15
With Christ on High
    (sermon)   186–8
Word incarnate   78–9
Wordsworth, Christopher   53
Wordsworth, William   13
worldliness of the church   13–25,
    150–1
worship and the priesthood of
    Christ   134–8

CPSIA information can be obtained at www.ICGtesting.com
Printed in the USA
BVOW040022210212

283376BV00004B/39/P